The Heart, The Diamond and
The Lotus Sutra

Important teachings of the Buddha
on awakening and enlightenment

F. Lepine Publishing
2008 Edition
ISBN 978-0-9810613-3-7
www.FLEPINE.com

Table of Contents

The Prajna Paramita Heart Sutra

When the Bodhisattva Avalokitesvara
Was Coursing in the Deep Prajna Paramita,
He Perceived That All Five Skandhas Are Empty.
Thus He Overcame All Ills and Suffering.

Oh, Sariputra, Form Does Not Differ From the Void, and the Void Does Not Differ From Form.

Form is Void and Void is Form; the Same is True For Feelings, Perceptions, Volitions and Consciousness.

Sariputra, the Characteristics of the Voidness of All Dharmas Are Non-Arising, Non-Ceasing, Non-Defiled, Non-Pure, Non-Increasing, Non-Decreasing.

Therefore, in the Void There Are No Forms,

No Feelings, Perceptions, Volitions or Consciousness.
No Eye, Ear, Nose, Tongue, Body or Mind;
No Form, Sound, Smell, Taste, Touch or Mind Object,
No Realm of the Eye,
Until We Come to No Realm of Consciousness.

No Ignorance and Also No Ending of Ignorance, Until We Come to No Old Age and Death and No Ending of Old Age and Death.

Also, There is No Truth of Suffering, of the Cause of Suffering, of the Cessation of Suffering, Nor of the Path.

There is No Wisdom, and There is No Attainment Whatsoever.

Because There is Nothing To Be Attained, the Bodhisattva Relying On Prajna Paramita Has No Obstruction in His Mind.

Because There is No Obstruction, He Has No Fear,

And He Passes Far Beyond Confused Imagination,

And Reaches Ultimate Nirvana.

The Buddhas of the Past, Present and Future, By Relying on Prajna Paramita, Have Attained Supreme Enlightenment.

Therefore, the Prajna Paramita is the Great Magic Spell, the Spell of Illumination, the Supreme Spell, Which Can Truly Protect One From All Suffering Without Fail.

Therefore He Uttered the Spell of Prajnaparamita, Saying

Gate, Gate, Paragate, Parasamgate, Bodhi Svaha.

Vajracchedika Prajnaparamita Sutra

(The Diamond Sutra)

1

This is what I heard one time when the Buddha was staying in the monastery in Anathapindika's park in the Jeta Grove near Sravasti with a community of 1,250 bhiksus, fully ordained monks.

That day, when it was time to make the round for alms, the Buddha put on his sanghati robe and, holding his bowl, went into the city of Sravasti to seek alms food, going from house to house. When the alms round was completed, he returned to the monastery to eat the midday meal. Then he put away his sanghati robe and his bowl, washed his feet, arranged his cushion, and sat down.

2

At that time, the Venerable Subhuti stood up, bared his right shoulder, put his knee on the ground, and, folding his palms respectfully, said to the Buddha, "World-Honored One, it is rare to find someone like you. You always support and show special confidence in the bodhisattvas.

"World-Honored One, if sons and daughters of good families want to give rise to the highest, most fulfilled, awakened mind, what should they rely on and what should they do to master their thinking?"
The Buddha replied, "Well said, Subhuti! What you have said is absolutely correct. The Tathagata always supports and shows special confidence in the bodhisattvas. Please listen

with all of your attention and the Tathagata will respond to your question. If daughters and sons of good families want to give rise to the highest, most fulfilled, awakened mind, they should rely on the following way."

The Venerable Subhuti said, "Lord, we are so happy to hear your teachings."

3

The Buddha said to Subhuti, "This is how the bodhisattva mahasattvas master their thinking. 'However many species of living beings there are -- whether born from eggs, from the womb, from moisture, or spontaneously; whether they have form or do not have form; whether they have perceptions or do not have perceptions; or whether it cannot be said of them that they have perceptions or that they do not have perceptions, we must lead all these beings to the ultimate nirvana so that they can be liberated. And when this innumerable, immeasurable, infinite number of beings has become liberated, we do not, in truth, think that a single being has been liberated,'

"Why is this so? If, Subhuti, a bodhisattva holds on to the idea that a self, a person, a living being, or a life span exists, that person is not an authentic bodhisattva."

4

"Moreover, Subhuti, when a bodhisattva practices generosity, he does not rely on any object--that is to say he does not rely on any form, sound, smell, taste, tactile object, or dharma--to practice generosity. That, Subhuti, is the spirit in which a bodhisattva should practice generosity, not relying on signs. Why? If a bodhisattva practices generosity without relying on signs, the happiness that results cannot be conceived of or measured. Subhuti, do you think that the space in the Eastern Quarter can be measured?"

"No, World-Honored One."

"Subhuti, can space in the Western, Southern, and Northern Quarters, above and below be measured?"
"No, World-Honored One."

"Subhuti, if a bodhisattva does not rely on any concept when practicing generosity, then the happiness that results from that virtuous act is as great as space. It cannot be measured. Subhuti, the bodhisattvas should let their minds dwell in the teachings I have just given."

5

"What do you think, Subhuti? Is it possible to grasp the Tathagata by means of bodily signs?"

"No, World-Honored One. When the Tathagata speaks of bodily signs, there are no signs being talked about."

The Buddha said to Subhuti: "In a place where there is something that can be distinguished by signs, in that place there is deception. If you can see the signless nature of signs, then you can see the Tathagata."

6

The Venerable Subhuti said to the Buddha, "In times to come, will there be people who, when they hear these teachings, have real faith and confidence in them?"

The Buddha replied, "Do not speak that way, Subhuti. Five hundred years after the Tathagata has passed away, there will still be people who enjoy the happiness that comes from observing the precepts. When such people hear these words, they will have faith and confidence that here is the truth. We should know that such people have sown seeds not only during the lifetime of one Buddha, or even two, three, four, or five Buddhas, but have, in truth, planted wholesome seeds during the lifetimes of tens of thousands of Buddhas. Anyone who, for only a second, gives rise to a pure and clear confidence upon hearing these words of the Tathagata, the Tathagata sees and knows that person, and he or she will attain immeasurable happiness because of this understanding. Why?

"Because that kind of person is not caught up in the idea of a self, a person, a living being, or a life span. They are not caught up in the idea of a dharma or the idea of a non-dharma. They are not caught up in the notion that this is a sign and that is not a sign. Why? If you are caught up in the idea of a dharma, you are also caught up in the ideas of a self, a person, a living being, and a life span. If you are caught up in the idea that there is no dharma, you are still caught up in the ideas of a self, a person, a living being, and a life span. That is why we should not get caught up in dharmas or in the idea that dharmas do not exist. This is the hidden meaning when the Tathagata says,'Bhiksus, you should know that all of the teachings I give to you are a raft.[1] All teachings must be abandoned, not to mention non-teachings."

7

"What do you think, Subhuti, has the Tathagata arrived at the highest, most fulfilled, awakened mind? Does the Tathagata give any teaching?"

The Venerable Subhuti replied, "As far as I have understood the Lord Buddha's teachings, there is no independently existing object of mind called the highest, most fulfilled, awakened mind, nor is there any independently existing teaching that the Tathagata gives. Why? The teachings that the Tathagata has realized and spoken of cannot be conceived of as separate, independent existences and therefore cannot be described. The Tathagata's teaching is not self-existent nor is it non-self-existent. Why? Because the noble teachers are only distinguished from others in terms of the unconditioned."

8

"What do you think, Subhuti? If someone were to fill the 3,000 chiliocosms with the seven precious treasures as an act of generosity, would that person bring much happiness by this virtuous act?"

The Venerable Subhuti replied, "Yes, World-Honored One. It is because the very natures of virtue and happiness are not virtue and happiness that the Tathagata is able to speak about virtue and happiness."

The Buddha said, "On the other hand, if there is someone who accepts these teachings and puts them into practice, even if only a gatha of four lines, and explains them to someone else, the happiness brought about by this virtuous act far exceeds the happiness brought about by giving the seven precious treasures. Why? Because, Subhuti, all Buddhas and the dharma of the highest, most fulfilled, awakened mind of all Buddhas arise from these teachings. Subhuti, what is called Buddhadharma is everything that is not Buddhadharma."

9

"What do you think, Subhuti? Does a Stream-Enterer think, 'I have attained the fruit of stream-entry.'?"

Subhuti replied, "No, World-Honored One. Why? Stream-Enterer means to enter the stream, but in fact there is no stream to enter. One does not enter a stream that is form, nor a stream that is sound, smell, taste, touch, or object of mind. That is what we mean when we say entering a stream."

"What do you think, Subhuti? Does a Once-Returner think, 'I have attained the fruit of Once-Returning.'?"

Subhuti replied, "No, World-Honored One. Why? Once-Returner means to go and return once more, but in truth there is no going just as there is no returning. That is what we mean when we say Once-Returner."

"What do you think, Subhuti? Does a Non-Returner think like this,'I have attained the fruit of No-Return.'?"

Subhuti replied,"No, World-Honored One. Why? No-Return means not to return to this world, but in fact there cannot be any Non-Returning. That is what we mean when we say Non-Returner."

"What do you think, Subhuti? Does an Arhat think like this, 'I have attained the fruit of Arhatship'?"

Subhuti replied, "No, World-Honored One. Why? There is no separately existing thing that can be called Arhat. If an Arhat gives rise to the thought that he has attained the fruit of Arhatship, then he is still caught up in the idea of a self, a person, a living being, and a life span. World-Honored One, you have often said that I have attained the concentration of peaceful abiding and that in the community, I am the Arhat who has most transformed need and desire. World-Honored One, if I were to think that I had attained the fruit of Arhatship, you certainly would not have said that I love to dwell in the concentration of peaceful abiding."

10

The Buddha asked Subhuti, "In ancient times when the Tathagata practiced under Buddha Dipankara, did he attain anything?"

Subhuti answered, "No, World-Honored One. In ancient times when the Tathagata was practicing under Buddha Dipankara, he did not attain anything."
"What do you think, Subhuti? Does a bodhisattva create a serene and beautiful Buddha field?"

"No, World-Honored One. Why? To create a serene and beautiful Buddha field is not in fact creating a serene and beautiful Buddha field. That is why it is called creating a serene and beautiful Buddha field."

The Buddha said, "So, Subhuti, all the bodhisattva mahasattvas should give rise to a pure and clear intention in this spirit. When they give rise to this intention, they should not rely on forms, sounds, smells, tastes, tactile objects, or objects of mind. They should give rise to an intention with their minds not dwelling anywhere.'

"Subhuti, if there were someone with a body as big as Mount Sumeru, would you say that his was a large body?"

Subhuti answered, "Yes, World-Honored One, very large. Why? What the Tathagata says is not a large body, that is known as a large body."

11

"Subhuti, if there were as many Ganges Rivers as the number of grains of sand in the Ganges, would you say that the number of grains of sand in all those Ganges Rivers is very many"

Subhuti answered, "Very many indeed, World-Honored One. If the number of Ganges Rivers were huge, how much more so the number of grains of sand in all those Ganges Rivers."

"Subhuti, now I want to ask you this: if a daughter or son of good family were to fill the 3,000 chiliocosms with as many precious jewels as the number of grains of sand in all the Ganges Rivers as an act of generosity, would that person bring much happiness by her virtuous act?"

Subhuti replied, "Very much, World-Honored One."

The Buddha said to Subhuti, "If a daughter or son of a good family knows how to accept, practice, and explain this sutra to others, even if it is a gatha of four lines, the happiness that results from this virtuous act would be far greater."

12

"Furthermore, Subhuti, any plot of land on which this sutra is proclaimed, even if only one gatha of four lines, will be a land where gods, men, and asuras will come to make offerings just as they make offerings to a stupa of the Buddha. If the plot of land is regarded as that sacred, how much more so the person who practices and recites this sutra. Subhuti, you should know that that person attains something rare and profound. Wherever this sutra is kept is a sacred site enshrining the presence of the Buddha or one of the Buddha's great disciples."

13

After that, Subhuti asked the Buddha, "What should this sutra be called and how should we act regarding its teachings?"

The Buddha replied,"This sutra should be called *The Diamond that Cuts through Illusion* because it has the capacity to cut through illusions and afflictions and bring us to the shore of liberation. Please use this title and practice according to its deepest meaning. Why? What the Tathagata has called the highest, transcendent understanding is not, in fact, the highest, transcendent understanding. That is why it is truly the highest, transcendent understanding:"

The Buddha asked,"What do you think, Subhuti? Is there any dharma that the Tathagata teaches?"

Subhuti replied, "The Tathagata has nothing to teach, World-Honored One."

"What do you think, Subhuti? Are there many particles of dust in the 3,000 chiliocosms?"

"Very many, World-Honored One."

"Subhuti, the Tathagata says that these particles of dust are not particles of dust, That is why they are truly particles of dust. And what the Tathagata calls chiliocosms are not in fact chiliocosms. That is why they are called chiliocosms!"

"What do you think, Subhuti? Can the Tathagata be recognized by the possession of the thirty-two marks?"

The Venerable Subhuti replied, "No, World-Honored One. Why? Because what the Tathagata calls the thirty-two marks are not essentially marks and that is why the Tathagata calls them the thirty-two marks."

"Subhuti, if as many times as there are grains of sand in the Ganges a son or daughter of a good family gives up his or her life as an act of generosity and if another daughter or son of a good family knows how to accept, practice, and explain this sutra to others, even if only a gatha of four lines, the happiness resulting from explaining this sutra is far greater."

14

When he had heard this much and penetrated deeply into its significance, the Venerable Subhuti was moved to tears. He said, "World-Honored One, you are truly rare in this world. Since the day I attained the eyes of understanding, thanks to the guidance of the Buddha, I have never before heard teachings so deep and wonderful as these. World-Honored One, if someone hears this sutra, has pure and clear confidence in it, and arrives at insight into the truth, that person will realize the rarest kind of virtue. World-Honored One, that insight into the truth is essentially not insight. That is what the Tathagata calls insight into the truth.

"World-Honored One, today it is not difficult for me to hear this wonderful sutra, have confidence in it, understand it, accept it, and put it into practice. But in the future, in 500 years, if there is someone who can hear this sutra, have confidence in it, understand it, accept it, and put it into practice, then certainly the existence of someone like that will be great and rare. Why? That person will not be dominated by the idea of a self, a person, a living being, or a life span. Why? The idea of a self is not an idea, and the ideas of a person, a living being, and a life span are not ideas either. Why? Buddhas are called Buddhas because they are free of ideas."

"The Buddha said to Subhuti, "That is quite right. If someone hears this sutra and is not terrified or afraid, he or she is rare. Why? Subhuti, what the Tathagata calls parama-paramita, the highest transcendence, is not essentially the highest transcendence, and that is why it is called the highest transcendence.

"Subhuti, the Tathagata has said that what is called transcendent endurance is not transcendent endurance. That is why it is called transcendent endurance. Why? Subhuti, thousands of lifetimes ago when my body was cut into pieces by King Kalinga, I was not caught in the idea of a self, a person, a living being, or a life span. If, at that time, I had been caught up in any of those ideas, I would have felt anger and ill-will against the king.

"I also remember in ancient times, for 500 lifetimes, I practiced transcendent endurance by not being caught up in the idea of a self, a person, a living being, or a life span. So, Subhuti, when a bodhisattva gives rise to the unequalled mind of awakening, he has to give up all ideas. He cannot not rely on forms when he gives rise to that mind, nor on sounds, smells, tastes, tactile objects, or objects of mind. He can only give rise to that mind that is not caught up in anything.

"The Tathagata has said that all notions are not notions and that all living beings are not living beings. Subhuti, the Tathagata is one who speaks of things as they are, speaks what is true, and speaks in accord with reality. He does not speak deceptively or to please people. Subhuti, if we say that the Tagthagata has realized a teaching, that teaching is neither graspable nor deceptive.

"Subhuti, a bodhisattva who still depends on notions to practice generosity is like someone walking in the dark. He will not see anything. But when a bodhisattva does not depend on notions to practice generosity, he is like someone with good eyesight walking under the bright light of the sun. He can see all shapes and colors.

"Subhuti, if in the future there is any daughter or son of good family who has the capacity to accept, read, and put into practice this sutra, the Tathagata will see that person with his eyes of understanding. The Tathagata will know that person, and that person will realize the measureless, limitless fruit of her or his virtuous act."

15

"Subhuti, if on the one hand, a daughter or son of a good family gives up her or his life in the morning as many times as there are grains of sand in the Ganges as an act of generosity, and gives as many again in the afternoon and as many again in the evening, and continues doing so for countless ages; and if, on the other hand, another person listens to this sutra with complete confidence and without contention, that person's happiness will be far greater. But the happiness of one who writes this sutra down, receives, recites, and explains it to others cannot be compared.

"In summary, Subhuti, this sutra brings about boundless virtue and happiness that cannot be conceived or measured. If there is someone capable of receiving, practicing, reciting, and sharing this sutra with others, the Tathagata will see and know that person, and he or she will have inconceivable, indescribable, and incomparable virtue. Such a person will be able to shoulder the highest, most fulfilled, awakened career of the Tathagata. Why? Subhuti, if one is content with the small teachings, if he or she is still caught up in the idea of a self, a person, a living being, or a life span, he or she will not be able to listen, receive, recite, and explain this sutra to others. Subhuti, any place this sutra is found is a place where gods, men, and asuras will come to make offerings. Such a place is a shrine and should be venerated with formal ceremonies, circumambulations, and offerings of flowers and incense."

16

"Furthermore, Subhuti, if a son or daughter of good family, while reciting and practicing this sutra, is disdained or slandered, his or her misdeeds committed in past lives, including those that could bring about an evil destiny, will be eradicated, and he or she will attain the fruit of the most fulfilled, awakened mind. Subhuti, in ancient times before I met Buddha Dipankara, I had made offerings to and had been attendant of all 84,000 multi-millions of buddhas. If someone is able to receive, recite, study, and practice this sutra in the last epoch, the happiness brought about by this virtuous act is hundreds of thousands times greater than that which I brought about in ancient times. In fact, such happiness cannot be conceived or compared with anything, even mathematically. Such happiness is immeasurable.

"Subhuti, the happiness resulting from the virtuous act of a son or daughter of good family who receives, recites, studies, and practices this sutra in the last epoch will be so great that if I were to explain it now in detail, some people would become suspicious and disbelieving, and their minds might become disoriented. Subhuti, you should know that the meaning of this sutra is beyond conception and discussion. Likewise, the fruit resulting from receiving and practicing this sutra is beyond conception and discussion."

17

At that time, the Venerable Subhuti said to the Buddha, "World-Honored One, may I ask you again that if daughters or sons of good family want to give rise to the highest, most fulfilled, awakened mind, what should they rely on and what should they do to master their thinking?"

The Buddha replied, "Subhuti, a good son or daughter who wants to give rise to the highest, most fulfilled, awakened mind should do it in this way: 'We must lead all beings to the shore of awakening, but, after these beings have become liberated, we do not, in truth, think that a single being has been liberated.' Why is this so?

Subhuti, if a bodhisattva is still caught up in the idea of a self, a person, a living being or a life span, that person is not an authentic bodhisattva. Why is that?

"Subhuti, in fact, there is no independently existing object of mind called the highest, most fulfilled, awakened mind. What do you think, Subhuti? In ancient times, when the Tathagata was living with Buddha Dipankara, did he attain anything called the highest, most fulfilled, awakened mind?"

"No, World-Honored One. According to what I understand from the teachings of the Buddha, there is no attaining of anything called the highest, most fulfilled, awakened mind."

The Buddha said, "Right you are, Subhuti. In fact, there does not exist the so-called highest, most fulfilled, awakened mind that the Tathagata attains. Because if there had been any such thing, Buddha Dipankara would not have predicted of me, 'In the future, you will come to be a Buddha called Shakyamuni.' This prediction was made because there is, in fact, nothing that can be attained that is called the highest, most fulfilled, awakened mind. Why? Tathagata means the suchness of all things (dharmas). Someone would be mistaken to say that the Tathagata has attained the highest, most fulfilled, awakened mind since there is not any highest, most fulfilled, awakened mind to be attained. Subhuti, the highest, most fulfilled, awakened mind that the Tathagata has attained is neither graspable nor elusive. This is why the Tathagata has said, 'All dharmas are Buddhadharma.' What are called all dharmas are, in fact, not all dharmas. That is why they are called all dharmas.

"Subhuti, a comparison can be made with the idea of a great human body."

Subhuti said, "What the Tathagata calls a great human body is, in fact, not a great human body."

"Subhuti, it is the same concerning bodhisattvas. If a bodhisattva thinks that she has to liberate all living beings, then she is not yet a bodhisattva. Why? Subhuti, there is no independently existing object of mind called bodhisattva. Therefore, the Buddha has said that all dharmas are without a self, a person, a living being, or a life span. Subhuti, if a bodhisattva thinks, 'I have to create a serene and beautiful Buddha field[1], that person is not yet a bodhisattva. Why? What the Tathagata calls a serene and beautiful Buddha field is not in fact a serene and beautiful Buddha field. And that is why it is called a serene and beautiful Buddha field. Subhuti, any bodhisattva who thoroughly understands the principle of non-self and non-dharma is called by the Tathagata an authentic bodhisattva."

18

"Subhuti, what do you think? Does the Tathagata have the human eye?"
Subhuti replied,"Yes, World-Honored One, the Tathagata does have the human eye."
The Buddha asked, "Subhuti, what do you think? Does the Tathagata have the divine eye?"
Subhuti said, "Yes, World-Honored One, the Tathagata does have the divine eye."
"Subhuti, what do you think? Does the Tathagata have the eye of insight?"
Subhuti replied,"Yes, World-Honored One, the Tathagata does have the eye of insight."
"Subhuti, what do you think? Does the Tathagata have the eye of transcendent wisdom?"
"Yes, World-Honored One, the Tathagata does have the eye of transcendent wisdom."
The Buddha asked, "Does the Tathagata have the Buddha eye?"
"Yes, World-Honored One, the Tathagata does have the Buddha eye."
"Subhuti, what do you think? Does the Buddha see the sand in the Ganges as sand?"
Subhuti said, "World-Honored One, the Tathagata also calls it sand."

"Subhuti, if there were as many Ganges Rivers as the number of grains of sand of the Ganges and there was a Buddha land for each grain of sand in all those Ganges Rivers, would those Buddha lands be many?"

"Yes, World-Honored One, very many."

The Buddha said, "Subhuti, however many living beings there are in all these Buddha lands, though they each have a different mentality, the Tathagata understands them all. Why is that? Subhuti, what the Tathagata calls different mentalities are not in fact different mentalities. That is why they are called different mentalities."

"Why? Subhuti, the past mind cannot be grasped, neither can the present mind or the future mind."

19

"What do you think, Subhuti? If someone were to fill the 3,000 chiliocosms with precious treasures as an act of generosity, would that person bring great happiness by his virtuous act?" "Yes, very much, World-Honored One."

"Subhuti, if such happiness were conceived as an entity separate from everything else, the Tathagata would not have said it to be great, but because it is ungraspable, the Tathagata has said that the virtuous act of that person brought about great happiness."

20

"Subhuti, what do you think? Can the Tathagata be perceived by his perfectly formed body?"

"No, World-Honored One. What the Tathagata calls a perfectly formed body is not in fact a perfectly formed body. That is why it is called a perfectly formed body."

"What do you think, Subhuti? Can the Tathagata be perceived by his perfectly formed physiognomy?"

"No, World-Honored One. It is impossible to perceive the Tathagata by any perfectly formed physiognomy. Why? Because what the Tathagata calls perfectly formed physiognomy is not in fact perfectly formed physiognomy. That is why it is called perfectly formed physiognomy."

21

"Subhuti, do not say that the Tathagata conceives the idea 'I will give a teaching'. Do not think that way. Why? If anyone says that the Tathagata has something to teach, that person slanders the Buddha because he does not understand what I say. Subhuti, giving a Dharma talk in fact means that no talk is given. This is truly a Dharma talk."

Then, Insight-Life Subhuti said to the Buddha, "World-Honored One, in the future, will there be living beings who will feel complete confidence when they hear these words?"

The Buddha said, "Subhuti, those living beings are neither living beings nor non-living beings. Why is that? Subhuti, what the Tathagata calls non-living beings are truly living beings."
22

Subhuti asked the Buddha, "World-Honored One, is the highest, most fulfilled, awakened mind that the Buddha attained the unattainable?"

The Buddha said, "That is right, Subhuti. Regarding the highest, most fulfilled, awakened mind, I have not attained anything. That is why it is called the highest, most fulfilled, awakened mind."

23

"Furthermore, Subhuti, that mind is everywhere equally. Because it is neither high nor low, it is called the highest, most fulfilled, awakened mind. The fruit of the highest, most fulfilled, awakened mind is realized through the practice of all wholesome actions in the spirit of non-self, nonperson, non-living being, and non-life span. Subhuti, what are called wholesome actions are in fact not wholesome actions. That is why they are called wholesome actions."

24

"Subhuti, if someone were to fill the 3,000 chiliocosms with piles of the seven precious treasures as high as Mount Sumeru as an act of generosity, the happiness resulting from this is much less than that of another person who knows how to accept, practice, and explain the Vajracchedika Prajnaparamita Sutra to others. The happiness resulting from the virtue of a person who practices this sutra, even if it is only a gatha of four lines, cannot be described by using examples or mathematics."

25

"Subhuti, do not say that the Tathagata has the idea, 'I will bring living beings to the shore of liberation.' Do not think that way, Subhuti. Why? In truth there is not one single being for the Tathagata to bring to the other shore. If the Tathagata were to think there was, he would be caught in the idea of a self, a person, a living being, or a life span. Subhuti, what the Tathagata calls a self essentially has no self in the way that ordinary persons think there is a self. Subhuti, the Tathagata does not regard anyone as an ordinary person. That is why he can call them ordinary persons."

26

"What do you think, Subhuti? Can someone meditate on the Tathagata by means of the thirty-two marks?"

Subhuti said, "Yes, World-Honored One. We should use the thirty-two marks to meditate on the Tathagata."

The Buddha said, "If you say that you can use the thirty-two marks to see the Tathagata, then the Cakravartin is also a Tathagata?"

Subhuti said, "World-Honored One, I understand your teaching. One should not use the thirty-two marks to meditate on the Tathagata."

Then the World-Honored One spoke this verse:

"Someone who looks for me in form or seeks me in sound
is on a mistaken path and cannot see the Tathagata."

27

"Subhuti, if you think that the Tathagata realizes the highest, most fulfilled, awakened mind and does not need to have all the marks, you are wrong. Subhuti, do not think in that way. Do not think that when one gives rise to the highest, most fulfilled, awakened mind, one needs to see all objects of mind as nonexistent, cut off from life. Please do not think in that way. One who gives rise to the highest, most fulfilled, awakened mind does not contend that all objects of mind are nonexistent and cut off from life."

"Subhuti, if a bodhisattva were to fill the 3,000 chiliocosms with the seven precious treasures, as many as the number of sand grains in the Ganges as an act of generosity, the happiness brought about by his or her virtue is less than that brought about by someone who has understood and wholeheartedly accepted the truth that all dharmas are of selfless nature and is able to live and bear fully this truth. Why is that, Subhuti? Because a bodhisattva does not need to build up virtue and happmess."

Subhuti asked the Buddha, "What do you mean, World-Honored One, when you say that a bodhisattva does not need to build up virtue and happiness?"

"Subhuti, a bodhisattva gives rise to virtue but is not caught in the idea of virtue and happiness. That is why the Tathagata has said that a bodhisattva does not need to build up virtue and happiness."

"Subhuti, if someone says that the World-Honored One comes, goes, sits, and lies down, that person has not understood what I have said. Why? The meaning of Tathagata is 'does not come from anywhere and does not go anywhere[1]. That is why he is called a Tathagata."

"Subhuti, if a daughter or son of a good family were to grind the 3,000 chiliocosms to particles of dust, do you think there would be many particles?"

Subhuti replied, "World-Honored One, there would be many indeed. Why? If particles of dust had a real self-existence, the Buddha would not have called them particles of dust. What the Buddha calls particles of dust are not, in essence, particles of dust. That is why they can be called particles of dust. World-Honored One, what the Tathagata calls the 3,000 chiliocosms are not chiliocosms. That is why they are called chiliocosms. Why? If chiliocosms are real, they are a compound of particles under the conditions of being assembled into an object. That which the Tathagata calls a compound is not essentially a compound. That is why it is called a compound."

"Subhuti, what is called a compound is just a conventional way of speaking. It has no real basis. Only ordinary people are caught up in conventional terms."

"Subhuti, if anyone says that the Buddha has spoken of a self view, a person view, a living-being view, or a life span view, has that person understood my meaning?"

"No, World-Honored One. Such a person has not understood the Tathagata. Why? What the Tathagata calls a self view, a person view, a living-being view, or a life span view are not in essence a self view, a person view, a living-being view, or a life span view. That is why they are called a self view, a person view, a living-being view, or a life span view."

"Subhuti, someone who gives rise to the highest, most fulfilled, awakened mind should know that this is true of all dharmas, should see that all dharmas are like this, should have confidence in the understanding of all dharmas without any conceptions about dharmas. Subhuti, what is called a conception of dharmas, the Tathagata has said, is not a conception of dharmas. That is why it is called a conception of dharmas."

"Subhuti, if someone were to offer an immeasurable quantity of the seven treasures to fill the worlds as infinite as space as an act of generosity, the happiness resulting from that virtuous act would not equal the happiness resulting from a son or daughter of a good family who gives rise to the awakened mind and reads, recites, accepts, and puts into practice this sutra, and explains it to others, even if only a gatha of four lines. In what spirit is this explanation given? Without being caught up in signs, just according to things as they are, without agitation. Why is this?

"All composed things are like a dream,
a phantom, a drop of dew, a flash of lightning.
That is how to meditate on them,
that is how to observe them."

After they heard the Lord Buddha deliver this sutra, the Venerable Subhuti, the bhiksus and bhiksunis, laymen and laywomen, and gods and asuras, filled with joy and confidence, undertook to put these teachings into practice.

The Sutra Of Innumerable Meanings

Chapter I: Virtues

Thus Have I Heard. Once the Buddha was staying at the city of royal palaces on mount Grdhrakuta with a great assemblage of great Bhikkhus, in all twelve thousand. There were eighty thousand Bodhisattva-Mahasattvas. There were gods, dragons, yakshas, gandharvas, asuras, garudas, kimnaras, and mahoragas, besides all the bhikshus(monks), Bhikshunis(nuns), upasakas(laymen), and upasikas(laywomen). There were Great wheel rolling kings, small wheel rolling kings, and kings of the golden wheel, silver wheel, and other wheels; further kings and princes, ministers and people, men and women, and great rich persons, each encompassed by a hundred thousand myriad followers. They went up to the Buddha, made obeisance at his feet, burned incense, and scattered flowers. After they variously worshipped, they retired and sat to one side.

Those Bodhisattvas' names were Son of the Law-King Manjushri, Son of the Law-King Great Dignity Treasury, Son of the Law-King Great Eloquence Treasury, The Bodhisattva Maitreya, The Bodhisattva Leader, The Bodhisattva Medicine King, The Bodhisattva Medicine Lord, The Bodhisattva Flower Light Banner, The Bodhisattva King Commanding Dharanis At Will, The Bodhisattva Regarder Of The Cries Of The World, The Bodhisattva Great Power Obtained, The Bodhisattva Ever Zealous, The Bodhisattva Precious Stick, The Bodhisattva Above The Triple World, The Bodhisattva Vimabhara, The Bodhisattva Scented Elephant, The Bodhisattva Great Scented Elephant, The Bodhisattva King Of The Lions Roar, The Bodhisattva Lion's Playing In The World, The Bodhisattva Lion's Force, The Bodhisattva Lion's Assiduity, The Bodhisattva Brave Power, The Bodhisattva Lion's Overbearing, The Bodhisattva Adornment, And The Bodhisattva Great Adornment: such Bodhisattva-Mahasattvas as these, eighty thousand in all.

Of these Bodhisattvas there is none who is not a great saint of the Law Body. They have attained commands, meditations, Wisdom, emancipation and the knowledge of emancipation. With Tranquil minds and constantly in contemplation they are peaceful, Indifferent, non active, and free from desires. They are immune from any kind of delusion or distraction. Their minds are calm and clear, profound and infinite. They remain in this state for hundreds of thousands of kotis of kalpas, and all of the innumerable teachings have been revealed to them. Having obtained the great wisdom, they penetrate all things, they completely understand the reality of their nature and form, and clearly discriminate existing and non-existing, long and short.

Moreover, well knowing the capacities, natures, and inclinations of all, with Dharanis and the unhindered power of discourse, they roll the law wheel just as Buddhas do. First, dipping the dust of desire in a drop of the teachings, they remove the fever of the passions of life and realize the serenity of the law by opening the gate of nirvana, and fanning the wind of emancipation. Next, raining the profound law of the twelve causes, they pour it on the violent and intense rays of suffering—ignorance, old age, illness, death and so on; then pouring abundantly the supreme Mahayana, they dip all the good roots of living beings in it, scatter the seeds of goodness over the fields of merits, and make all put forth the sprout of Buddha hood. With their wisdom brilliant as the sun and the moon and their timely tactfulness, they promote the work of the Mahayana and make all accomplish Perfect Enlightenment speedily; and with eternal pleasure wonderful and true, and through infinite compassion, they relieve all from suffering.

These are the true good friends for all living beings, these are the great field of blessings for all living beings, these are the unsummoned teachers for all living beings, and these are the peaceful place of pleasure, relief, protection, and great support for all living beings. They become great good leaders or great leaders for living beings everywhere. They serve as eyes for blind beings, and as ears, nose, or tongue for those who are deaf, who have no nose, or who are dumb; make deficient organs complete; turn the deranged to the great right thought. As the master of a ship or the great master of a ship, they carry all living beings across the river of life and death to the shore of Nirvana. As the king of medicine or the great king of medicine, they discriminate the phases of a disease, know well the properties of medicines, dispense medicines according to the disease, and make people take them. As the controller or the great controller, they have no dissolute conduct; they are like a trainer of elephants and horses who never fails to train well, or like a majestic and brave lion that inevitably subdues and overpowers all beasts.

Bodhisattvas, playing in all the paramitas, being firm and immovable at the stage of Tathagata, and purifying the Buddha-country with the stability of their vow power, will rapidly accomplish Perfect Enlightenment. All these Bodhisattvas-mahasattvas have such wonderful merit as seen above.

Those bhikshus names were Great Wisdom Shariputra, Supernatural Power Maudgalyayana, Wisdom Life Subhuti, Maha-Katayana, Maitrayani's son Purna, Ajnata-Kaundinya, Divine Eye Aniruddha, Precept Keeping Upali, Attendant Ananda, Buddha's son Rahula, Upananda, revada, Kapphina, Vakkula, Acyuta, Svagata, Dhuta Maha-Kasyapa, Uruvilva-Kasyapa, Gaya-Kasyapa, and Nadi-Kasyapa. There are twelve thousand bhikshus such as these. All are Arhats, unrestricted by all bonds of faults, free from attachment, and truly emancipated.

At that time the Bodhisattva-Mahasattva Great Adornment, seeing that all the groups sat in settled mind, rose up from his seat, went up to the Buddha with the eighty thousand bodhisattvas-mahasattvas in the assembly, made obeisance at his feet, a hundred thousand times made procession round him, burned celestial incense, scattered celestial flowers, and presented the Buddha with celestial robes, garlands, and jewels of priceless value which came rolling down from the sky and gathered over all like clouds. The celestial bins and bowls were filled with all sorts of celestial delicacies, which satisfied just by the sight of their color and the smell of their perfume. They placed celestial banners, flags, canopies, and playthings everywhere; pleased the Buddha with celestial music; then went forth to kneel with folded hands, and praised him in verse, saying with one voice and one mind:

"Great! The Great Enlightened, The Great Holy Lord,
In Him there is no defilement, no contamination, no attachment.
The Trainer of Gods and men, elephants and horses,
His moral breeze and virtuous fragrance
Deeply permeate all.
Serene is his wisdom, calm his emotion,
And stable his prudence.
His thought is settled, his consciousness extinct,
And thus his mind is quiet.
Long since, he removed false thoughts
And conquered all the laws if existence.
His body is neither existing nor non-existing;
Without cause or condition,
Without self or others;
Neither square nor round,
Neither long nor short;
Without appearance or disappearance,
Without birth or death;
Neither created nor emanating,
Neither made nor produced;
Neither sitting nor lying,
Neither walking nor stopping;
Neither moving nor rolling,
Neither calm nor quiet;
Without advance or retreat,
Without safety or danger;
Without right or wrong,
Without merit or demerit;
Neither that nor this,
Neither going nor coming;
Neither blue nor yellow,
Neither red nor white;

Neither crimson nor purple,
Without a variety of colour.
Born of commandments, meditation,
Wisdom, Emancipation, and Knowledge;
Merit of contemplation, the six divine facilities,
And the practice of the way;
Sprung of benevolence and compassion,
The ten powers, and fearlessness;
He has come in response
To good karmas of living beings.
He reveals his body,
Ten feet, six inches in height,
Glittering with purple gold,
Well proportioned, brilliant,
And highly bright.
The mark of hair curls as the moon,
In the nape of the neck there is a light as of the sun.
The curling hair is deep blue,
On the head there is there is a protuberance.
The pure eyes, like a stainless mirror,
Blink up and down.
The eyebrows trail in dark blue,
The mouth and cheeks are well formed.
The lips and tongue appear pleasantly red,
Like a scarlet flower.
The White teeth, forty in number,
Appear as snowy agate.
Broad the forehead, high bridged the nose,
And majestic the face.
The chest, with a swastika mark,
Is like a lion's breast.
The hands and feet are flexible,
With the mark of a thousand spokes.
The sides and palms are well rounded,
And show in fine lines.
The arms are elongated,
And the fingers are straight and slender.
The skin is delicate and smooth,
And the hair curls to the right.
The ankles and knees are well defined,
And the male organ is hidden
Like that of a horse.
The fine muscles and collarbone,
And the thigh bones are slim
Like those of a deer.
The chest and back are shining,
Pure and without blemish,
Untainted by any muddy water,
Unspotted by any speck of dust.
There are thirty two such signs,
The eighty kinds of excellence are visible,
And truly there is nothing
Of form or non-form.
All visible forms are transcended;
His body is formless and yet has form.
This is also true

Of the form of the body of all living beings.
Living beings adore him joyfully,
Devote their minds to him,
And pay their respects wholeheartedly.
By cutting off arrogance and egotism,
He has accomplished such a wonderful body.
Now we, the assemblage of eighty thousand,
Making obeisance all together,
Submit ourselves to the saint of nonattachment,
The Trainer of Elephants and horses,
Detached from the state of thinking,
Mind, thought, and perception.
We make obeisance,
And submit ourselves to the Law Body,
To all commands, meditation and wisdom,
Emancipation and knowledge.
We make obeisance,
And submit ourselves to the wonderful character.
We make obeisance,
And submit ourselves to the unthinkable.
The sacred voice sounds eight ways,
As the thunder sounds.
It is sweet, pure, and greatly profound.
He preaches the four noble truths,
The six paramitas, the twelve causes,
According to the working of the minds of living beings.
One never hears without opening one's mind
And breaking the bonds of the infinite chain of life and death.
One never hears without reaching srota-apanna,
Sakrdagamin, Ana gamin, and arhat;
Reaching the state of pratyekabuddha,
Of non-fault and noncondition;
Reaching the state of Bodhisattva,
Of non life and non death;
Of obtaining infinite dharani
And the unhindered power of discourse,
With which ones recites profound and wonderful verses,
Plays and bathes in the pure pond on the law,
Or displays supernatural motion
By jumping and flying up,
Or freely goes in or out of water and fire,
The aspect of the Tathagata's Law-wheel is like this.
It is pure, boundless, and unthinkable.
Making obeisance all together,
We submit ourselves to him
When he rolls the Law-wheel.
We make obeisance ,
And submit ourselves to the sacred voice.
We make obeisance,
And submit ourselves to the Causes, Truths, and Paramitas.
For infinite past kalpas,
The World Honored One has practiced
All manner of virtues with effort
To Bring benefits to us human beings,
Heavenly beings, and dragon kings,
Universally to all living beings.

He abandoned all things hard to abandon,
His treasures, wife, and child,
His country, and his palace.
Unsparing of his person and possessions,
He gave all, his head, eyes, and brain,
To people as alms.
Keeping the Buddha's precepts of purity,
He never did any harm,
Even at the cost of his life.
He never became angry,
Even though beaten with swords and staff,
Or though cursed and abused.
He never became tired,
In spite of long exertion.
He kept his mind at peace both day and night,
And was always in meditation.
Learning all the law ways,
With his deep wisdom
He has seen into the capacity of living beings.
As a result, obtaining free power,
He became the law king,
Who is free in the Law.
Making obeisance again all together,
We submit ourselves to the one who has completed all hard things."

Chapter II : Preaching

AT THAT TIME the Bodhisattva-Mahasattva Great Adornment, with the eighty thousand Bodhisattva-Mahasattvas, finished praising the Buddha with this verse and said to the Buddha in unison: "World Honored One, we, the assemblage, of the eighty thousand Bodhisattvas, want to ask you about the Tathagata 's law.

We are anxious That the World Honored One should hear us with sympathy."

The Buddha Addressed the Bodhisattva Great Adornment and the eighty thousand Bodhisattvas: "Excellent! Excellent! Good sons, you have well known that this is the time. Ask me what you like. Before long, the Tathagata will enter Pari-nirvana. After Nirvana, there shall not be a doubt left to anybody. I will answer any question you wish to ask."

Thereupon the Bodhisattva Great Adornment, with the eighty thousand Bodhisattvas, said to the Buddha in unison, with one voice: "World Honored One! If the Bodhisattva-Mahasattvas want to accomplish perfect enlightenment quickly, what doctrine should they practice? What doctrine makes Bodhisattva-Mahasattvas attain perfect enlightenment quickly?"

The Buddha addressed the Bodhisattva Great Adornment and the eighty thousand Bodhisattvas: "Good Sons, there is one doctrine which makes Bodhisattvas attain perfect enlightenment quickly. If a Bodhisattva learns this doctrine, then he will accomplish perfect enlightenment."

"World Honored One! What is this doctrine called? What is it's meaning? How does the Bodhisattva practice it?"

The Buddha said "Good Sons! This one doctrine is called the doctrine of Innumerable Meanings. A Bodhisattva, If he wants to learn and master the doctrine the doctrine of Innumerable Meanings, should observe that all laws were originally, will be, and are in themselves void in nature and form; They are Neither great nor small, Neither appearing nor disappearing, Neither fixed or movable, and neither advancing nor retreating; they are non dualistic, just emptiness. All living beings, however, discriminate falsely: "It is this" or "it is that", and "It is advantageous" or "It is disadvantageous"; they entertain evil thoughts, make various evil karmas, and thus transmigrate within the six realms of existence; and they suffer all manner of miseries, and cannot escape from there during infinite kotis of kalpas. Bodhisattva-Mahasattvas, observing rightly like this, should raise the mind of compassion, display the great mercy desiring to relieve others of suffering, and once again penetrate deeply into all laws. According to the nature of a law, such al law settles. According to the nature of a law, such a laws changes. According to the nature of a law, such a law vanishes. According to the nature of a law, such an evil law emerges. According to the nature of a law, such a good law appears. Settling, changing, and vanishing are also like this. Bodhisattvas, having completely observed and known these four aspects from beginning to end, should next observe that none of the laws settle down for even a moment, but all emerge and vanish anew every moment; and observe that they emerge, settle, change, and vanish instantly. After such observation, we see all manner of natural desires of living beings. As natural desires are innumerable, preaching is innumerable, and as preaching is innumerable, meanings are innumerable. The Innumerable Meanings originate from one law. This one law is, namely, non form. Such non form is formless, and not form. Being not form, and formless, it is called the real aspect of things. The mercy which Bodhisattva-Mahasattvas display after stabilizing themselves in such a real aspect is real, and not vain. They excellently relieve living beings from sufferings. Having given relieve from suffering they preach the law again, and let all living beings obtain pleasure.

"Good Sons! A Bodhisattva, if he practices completely the doctrine of Innumerable Meanings like this, will soon accomplish Perfect Enlightenment without fail. Good sons! The Sutra of Innumerable Meanings, such a profound and supreme Great-vehicle, is reasonable in its logic, unsurpassed in its worth, and protected by all the Buddhas of the three worlds. No kind of demon or heretic can break into it, nor can any wrong view of life and death destroy it . Therefore, good sons! Bodhisattva-mahasattvas, if you want to accomplish supreme Buddha hood quickly, you should learn and master the Sutra of Innumerable Meanings, such a profound and supreme great vehicle.

"At that time the Bodhisattva Great Adornment said to the Buddha again: World-honored one! The preaching of the World-honored one is incomprehensible, the natures of living beings are also incomprehensible, and the doctrine of emancipation is also incomprehensible. Though we have no doubt about the laws preached by the Buddha, we repeatedly ask the World-honored one for fear that all living beings should be perplexed. For more then forty years since the Tathagata attained enlightenment, you have continuously preached all the laws to living beings—the four aspects, suffering, void ness, transience, selflessness, non-large, non-small, non-birth, non-death, one aspect, no-aspect, the nature of the law, the form of the law, void from the beginning, non-coming, non-going, non-appearance, and non-disappearance. Those who have heard it have obtained the law of warming, the law of the highest, the law of the best in the world(The law of warming, highest, and best in the world are three stages passed through by disciples not yet free of desire when they try to understand the Four Noble Truths.), the merit of srota-apanna, the merit of sakrdagamin, the merit of Ana gamin, the merit of arhat, and the way of pratyekabuddha; have aspired to enlightenment; and ascending the first stage, the second stage, and the third stage, have attained the tenth stage. Because of what difference between your past and present preaching on laws do you say that if a bodhisattva practices only the Sutra of Innumerable Meanings, a profound and Great-vehicle, he will soon accomplish supreme Buddha hood without fail? World-honored one! Be pleased to discriminate the Law widely for living beings out of compassion for all, and to leave no doubt to all Law-hearers in the present and future.

"Hereupon the Buddha said to the Bodhisattva Great Adornment: Excellent! Excellent! Great good sons, you have well questioned the Tathagata about such a wonderful meaning of the profound and supreme Great-vehicle. Do you know that you will bring many benefits, please men and gods, and relieve living beings from sufferings. It is truly the great benevolence, and the truth without falsehood. For this reason you will surely and quickly accomplish supreme Buddha hood. You will also make all living beings in the present and future accomplish supreme Buddha hood.

"Good Sons! After six years right sitting under the Bodhi tree of the wisdom throne, I could accomplish Perfect Enlightenment. With the Buddha's eye I saw all the laws and understood that they were inexpressible. Wherefore? I knew that the natures of all living beings were not equal. As their natures and desires were not equal, I preached the law variously. It was with tactful power that I preached the law variously. In forty years and more, the truth has not been revealed yet. Therefore living beings' powers of attainment are too different to accomplish supreme Buddha hood quickly.

"Good sons! The law is like water that washes off dirt. As a well, a pond, a stream, a river, a valley stream, a ditch, or a great sea each alike effectively washes off all kinds of dirt, so the law-water effectively washes off the dirt of all delusions of living beings.

"Good sons! The nature of water is one, but a stream, a river, a well, a pond, a valley stream, a ditch, and a great sea are different from one another. The nature of the law is like this. There is equality and no differentiation in washing off the dirt of delusions, but the three laws, the four merits, the and the two ways are not one and the same.

"Good Sons! Though each washes equally as water, a well is not a pond, a pond is not a stream or a river, nor is a valley stream or ditch a sea. As the Tathagata, the worlds hero, is free in the law, all the laws preached by him are also like this. Though preaching at the beginning, the middle, and the end all alike, effectively wash off the delusions of living beings, the beginning is not the middle, and the middle is not the end. Preaching at the beginning, in the middle, and at the end are the same in expression, but different in one another in meaning.

"Good Sons!" When I rolled the law wheel of the four noble truths for the five men, Ajnata-Kaundinya and the others, at the deer park in Varanasi after leaving the king of trees, I preached that the laws are naturally vacant, ceaselessly transformed, and instantly born and destroyed. When I discoursed explaining the twelve causes and the six paramitas for all the Bhikshus and Bodhisattvas in various places during the middle period, I preached also that all laws are naturally vacant, ceaselessly transformed, and instantly born and destroyed. Now in explaining the Sutra of Innumerable Meanings, a Great Vehicle, at the this time, I preach also that all laws are naturally vacant, ceaselessly transformed, and instantly born and destroyed. Good Sons! Therefore the preaching at the beginning, in the middle, and at the end are the same in expression but different from one another in meaning. As the meaning varies, the understanding of living beings varies. As the understanding varies, the attainment of the law, the merit, and the way also varies.

"Good sons! At the beginning, though I preached the Four Truths for those who sought to be sravakas, eight Kotis of heavenly beings came down to hear the law and raised the desire for enlightenment. In the middle, though I preached in various places, the profound Twelve Causes, for those who sought to be Pratyekabuddha, Innumerable living beings raised the aspiration for enlightenment, or, remained in the stage of Sravaka. Next, although I explained the long term practice of Bodhisattvas (Religious exercises extending over billions of years), through preaching the twelve types of sutras of Great Extent, The Maha-Prajna, and the void ness of the Garland Sea, a hundred thousand Bhikshus, Myriad Kotis of men and gods, and innumerable living beings could remain in the merits of Srota-apanna, Sakrdagamin, Ana Gamin, and Arhat, or in the law appropriate to the pratyekabuddha. Good Sons! For this reason, it is known that the preaching is the same, but the meaning varies, as the meaning varies, the understanding of living beings varies. As the understanding varies, the attainment of the law, merit, and the way also varies. So Good Sons! Since I attained the way, and stood to preach the law for the first time, till I spoke the Sutra Of Innumerable Meanings, The Great-vehicle, today, I have never ceased from preaching suffering, void ness, transience, selflessness, non truth, non reality, non large, non small, non birth and origin and also non death at present, one aspect, non aspect, the form of the law, the nature of the law, non coming, non going, and the four aspects by which all the living are driven.

"Good Sons! For this reason, all the Buddhas, without a double tongue, answer widely all voices with one word, though having one body, reveal bodies innumerable, and numberless as the sands of the Ganges of a hundred thousand myriad Kotis Nayutas; in each body, display various forms, countless as the sands of some hundred thousand myriad kotis nayutas asamkhyeya Ganges, and in each form show shapes countless as the sands of some hundred thousand myriad kotis nayutas asamkhyeya Ganges. Good Son! This is, namely, the incomprehensible and profound world of Buddhas. Men of the two vehicles cannot apprehend it, and even Bodhisattvas of the Ten stages cannot attain it. Only a Buddha, together with a Buddha can fathom it well.

"Good Sons! Thereupon I say: The Sutra Of Innumerable meanings, the wonderful, profound, and supreme Great vehicle, is reasonable in it's logic, unsurpassed in it's worth, and protected by all the Buddhas of the three worlds. No kind of demon or heretic can break into it, nor can any wrong view of life or death destroy it. Bodhisattva-Mahasattvas, if you want to accomplish supreme Buddha hood quickly, you should learn and master the Sutra of Innumerable Meanings, such a profound and supreme Great-vehicle.

"After the Buddha had finished explaining this, the three-thousand-great-thousand fold world was shaken in the six ways; various kinds of celestial flowers, such as utpala, padma, kumuda, and pundarika, rained down naturally from the sky; and innumerable kinds of celestial perfumes, robes, garlands, and treasures of priceless value also rained and came rolling down from the sky, and they were offered to the Buddha, all the Bodhisattvas and sravakas, and the great assembly. So, too, was it in the southern, western, and northern quarters, in the four intermediate directions, in the zenith and the nadir.

"At this time thirty two thousand Bodhisattva-mahasattvas in the assembly attained to the contemplation of the innumerable meaning. Thirty four thousand Bodhisattva-Mahasattvas obtained the numberless and infinite realms of dharani and came to roll the never retrogressing law wheel of Buddhas all over the three worlds. All the Bhikshus and Bhikshunis, upasakas, upasikas, gods, dragons, yakshas, gandharvas, asuras, garudas, kimnaras, mahoragas, great wheel rolling kings, small wheel rolling kings, kings of the silver wheel, iron wheel, and other wheels, kings and princes, ministers and people, men and women, and great rich persons, and all the groups of a hundred thousand followers, hearing together, the Buddha, Tathagata preaching this sutra, obtained the law of warming, the law of the highest, the law of the best in the world, the merit of srota-apanna, the merit of sakrdagamin, the merit of Ana gamin, the merit of Arhat, and the merit of Pratyekabuddha; attained to the Bodhisattvas assurance of the law of no birth; acquired one Dharani, two

Dharanis, three Dharanis, four Dharanis, five, six, seven, eight, nine, ten Dharanis, a hundred thousand myriad kotis of Dharanis, and asamkhyeya Dharanis as innumerable as the sands of the Ganges; and all came to roll the never retrogressing law wheel rightly. Infinite living beings gained the aspiration to perfect enlightenment.

Chapter III: Ten Merits

AT THAT TIME the Bodhisattva-Mahasattva Great Adornment said to the Buddha again: "World Honored One! The World Honored One has preached this sutra of Innumerable Meanings, a wonderful, profound, and supreme Great Vehicle. It is truly profound. Wherefore? In this assembly, all the Bodhisattva-Mahasattvas, all the four groups, gods, dragons, demons, kings, subjects, and all the living beings, hearing this Sutra Of Innumerable Meanings, a profound and supreme great vehicle, never fail to obtain the realm of Dharanis, the three laws, the four merits, and the aspiration to enlightenment. It should be known that this law is reasonable in it's logic, unsurpassed in it's worth, and protected by all the Buddhas of the three worlds. No kind of demon or heretic break into it, nor an any wrong view of life and death destroy it. Wherefore? Because hearing it but once is keeping all the laws.

"If a living being can hear this sutra, he will acquire a great benefit. Wherefore? If he practices it sincerely, he will quickly accomplish supreme Buddha hood without fail. If a living being cannot hear it should be known that he loses a great benefit. He will never accomplish supreme Buddha hood even a after a lapse of infinite boundless, inconceivable asamkhyeya kalpas. Wherefore? Because he does not know the great way to enlightenment, he meets with many sufferings in walking steep ways.

"World Honored One! This sutra is inconceivable. World Honored One! Be pleased to explain the profound and inconceivable matter of this sutra out of benevolence for all the people. World Honored One! From What Place does this sutra come? From what place does it leave? At what place does it stay? Whereupon does this sutra make people quickly accomplish perfect enlightenment, having such infinite merits and inconceivable powers?

"At that time the World Honored One Addressed the Bodhisattva-Mahasattva Great Adornment: Excellent! Excellent! Good Sons; Just So, Just So, Just as you say. Good Sons! I preach this sutra as profound, profound, and truly profound. Wherefore? Because it makes people quickly accomplish supreme Buddha Hood; hearing it but once is keeping all the laws; it greatly benefits all the living; There is no suffering practicing the great direct way. Good Sons! You ask where this sutra comes from, where it leaves for, and where it stays. Do listen attentively. Good Sons! This sutra originally comes from the abode of all the Buddhas, leaves for the aspiration of all the living, and stays at the place where all the Bodhisattvas practice. Good Sons! This sutra comes like this, leaves like this, and stays like this. Therefore this sutra, having such infinite merits and inconceivable power, makes people quickly accomplish supreme Buddha hood.

"Good Sons! Do you want to hear how this sutra has ten inconceivable merit powers? The Bodhisattva Great Adornment Said: "we heartily want to hear. And the Buddha said: Good Sons! First, this sutra makes the un-awakened Bodhisattva aspire to Buddha hood, makes a merciless one raise the mind of mercy, Makes a homicidal one raise the mind of great compassion, makes a jealous one raise the mind of joy, makes an attached one raise the mind of detachment, makes a miserly one raise the mind of donation, makes an arrogant one raise the mind of keeping the commandments, makes an irascible one raise the mind of perseverance, makes an indolent one raise the mind of assiduity, makes a distracted one raise the mind of meditation, makes an ignorant one raise the mind of wisdom, makes one who lacks concern for saving others raise the mind of saving others, makes one who commits the ten evils raise the mind of the ten virtues, makes one who wishes for existence aspire to the mind of non existence, makes one who has an inclination toward apostasy build the mind of non retrogression, makes one who commits defiled acts raise the mind of un defilement, and makes one who suffers from delusions raise the mind of detachment. Good Sons! This is called the first inconceivable merit power of this sutra.

"Good Sons! Secondly the inconceivable merit power of this sutra is as follows: If a living being can hear this sutra but once, or only one verse and phrase, he will penetrate into a hundred thousand kotis of meanings, and the law kept by him cannot be explained fully even in infinite kalpas. Wherefore? It is because this sutra has innumerable meanings.

"Good Sons! Suppose that from one seed, a hundred thousand myriad seeds grow, from each of a hundred thousand myriad seeds, another hundred thousand myriad seeds grow, and in such a process seeds increase to an unlimited extent. This sutra is like this. From one law a hundred thousand meanings grow, from each of a hundred thousand meanings, a hundred thousand myriad meanings grow, and in such a process meanings increase to an unlimited and boundless extent. Such being the case, this sutra is called innumerable meanings. Good Sons This is the second inconceivable merit power of this sutra.

"Good Sons! Thirdly, the inconceivable merit power of this sutra is as follows: If a living being can hear this sutra but once, or only one verse and phrase, he will penetrate into a hundred thousand myriad kotis of meanings. After that, his delusions, even though existent, will become as if non existent; he will not be seized with fear, though he moves between birth and death; he will raise the mind of compassion for all of the living, and obtain the spirit of bravery to obey all the laws. A powerful wrestler can shoulder and hold any heavy thing. The keeper of this sutra is also like this. He can shoulder the heavy treasure of supreme Buddha hood, and carry living beings on his back out of the way of birth and death. He will be able to relieve others, even though he can not yet relieve himself. Just as a ferry master though he stays on this shore owing to his serious illness and unsettled body, can be made to cross over by means of a good and solid ship that has the quality of carrying anyone without fail, so also is it with the keeper of this sutra. Although he stays on this shore of ignorance, old age and death, owing to the hundred and eight kinds of serious illness (the one hundred and eight illusions, or obstacles to enlightenment), with which his body under the existence of all the five states is seized and ever afflicted, he can deliver from birth and death this strong Mahayana Sutra of Innumerable Meanings as it is preached, which realizes the deliverance of living beings. Good Sons! This is called the third inconceivable merit power of this sutra.

"Good Sons! Fourthly the inconceivable merit power of this sutra is as follows: if a living being can hear this sutra but once, only one verse and phrase, he will obtain the spirit of bravery, and relieve others, even though he cannot yet relieve himself. He will become the attendant of the Buddhas together with all of the Bodhisattvas, and all the Buddha-Tathagatas will always preach the law to him. On hearing it, he will keep the law entirely and follow it without disobeying. Moreover, he will interpret it for people extensively as occasion calls.

"Good Sons! Suppose that a new prince is born of a king and queen. A day, two days, or seven days, and a month, two months, or seven months passing away, he attain the age of one, two, or seven. Although he can not yet manage national affairs, he will come to be revered by people and take all the great kings sons into his company. The King And Queen will always stay and converse with him, with special and deep affection because he is their little child. Good Sons! The keeper of this sutra is also like this. The King--The Buddha-- and the queen--this sutra--come together, and this son--a Bodhisattva-- is born of them. If the Bodhisattva can hear one phrase or verse of this sutra once, twice, ten times, a hundred times, a thousand time, myriad times, myriad kotis of time, or innumerable and numberless times like the sands of the Ganges, he will come to shake the Three-Thousand Great Thousand fold world, though he can not yet realize the Ultimate Truth, and will take all great Bodhisattvas into his attendance, while being admired by all of the four classes and eight guardians, though he can not yet roll the great law wheel, with the sacred voice like the roll of thunder. Entering deeply into the secret law of the Buddhas, he will interpret it without error or fault. He will always be protected by all of the Buddhas, and especially covered with affection, because he is a beginner in learning. Good Sons! This is called the fourth inconceivable merit power of this sutra.

"Good Sons! Fifthly, the inconceivable merit power of this sutra is as follows: If good sons or good daughters keep, read, and recite and copy the Sutra Of Innumerable Meanings, such a profound and supreme great vehicle, either during the Buddhas lifetime or after his extinction, they will realize the way of great Bodhisattvas though they cannot yet be delivered from all the faults of an ordinary man, and are still wrapped in delusions. They will fill with joy and convince those living beings, extending a day to a hundred Kalpas, or shortening a hundred Kalpas to a day. Good Sons! These good sons or good daughters are just like a dragon's son who can raise clouds and cause a rainfall seven days after his birth. Good Sons! This is called the fifth inconceivable merit power of this sutra.

"Good Sons! Sixthly, the inconceivable merit power of this sutra is as follows: if good sons or good daughters keep, read, and recite this sutra either during the Buddhas lifetime, or after his extinction, even though clothed in delusions, they will deliver living beings from the life and death of delusions, and make them overcome all sufferings, by preaching the law for them. After hearing it, living beings will put it into practice, and attain the law, the merit, and the way, where there will be equality, and no difference from the Buddha Tathagata. Suppose that a king, in journeying, or falling ill, leaves the management of national affairs to his prince, though he is an infant. Then the prince, by order of the great king, leads all of the government officials according to the law, and propagates the right policy, so that every citizen of the country follows his orders exactly as if the king were governing. It is the same with good sons or good daughters keeping this sutra. During the Buddhas lifetime, or after his extinction, these good sons will propagate the doctrine, preaching exactly as the Buddha did, though they themselves cannot live in the first stage of immobility, and if living beings, after hearing their preaching, practice it intently, they will cut off delusions, and attain the law, the merit, and the way. Good Sons! This is called the sixth inconceivable merit power of this sutra.

"Good Sons! Seventhly, the inconceivable merit power of this sutra is as follows: If good sons or good daughters, hearing this sutra either during the Buddhas lifetime or after his extinction, rejoice, believe, and raise the rare mind; keep, read, recite, copy, and expound it; practice it as it has been preached; aspire to Buddha hood; cause all the good roots to sprout; raise the mind of great compassion; and want to relieve all living beings of sufferings, the six paramitas will be naturally present in them, though they cannot yet practice the six paramitas. They will attain the assurance of the law of no birth in their bodies; life and death, and delusions will be instantly destroyed; and they will rise to the seventh stage of Bodhisattva.

"Suppose there is a vigorous man who tries to destroy an enemy on behalf of his king, and after the enemy has been destroyed, with great joy, the king gives him half the kingdom as a prize. Good Sons or Good Daughters who keep this sutra are like this. They are the most vigorous of all ascetics. They come to attain the law treasure of the six paramitas, even though they are not consciously seeking it. The enemy of death and life will be naturally destroyed, and they will be made comfortable by the prize of a fief, realizing the assurance of no birth as the treasure of half the Buddha-country. Good Sons! This is called the seventh inconceivable merit power of this sutra.

"Good Sons! Eighthly the inconceivable merit power of this sutra is as follows: If good sons or good daughters, either during the Buddhas lifetime, or after his extinction, see someone who has received this sutra, they will make him revere and believe it exactly as if he saw the body of the Buddha; they will keep, read, recite, copy and worship this sutra with joy; serve and practice it as the law; firmly keep the commandments and perseverance; they will also practice almsgiving; raise a deep benevolence; and explain the sutra of Innumerable Meanings, this supreme great vehicle, widely to others. To one who for a long time does not at all recognize the existence of sinfulness and blessedness, they will show this sutra, and force him to have faith in it with all sorts of expedients. By the strong power of the sutra, he will be made to stir up faith and to convert suddenly. After stirring up faith, he will endeavor so valorously that he can acquire the virtue and power of this sutra, and attain the way and the merit. In this way, these good sons or good daughters will attain they assurance of the law of no birth in their bodies of men or women by the merit of having been enlightened, reach the upper stage, become the attendants of the Buddhas, together with all the Bodhisattvas convert living beings, quickly, purify Buddha lands, and attain supreme Buddha hood before long. Good Sons! This is called the eight inconceivable merit power of this sutra.

"Good Sons! Ninthly, the inconceivable merit power of this sutra is as follows: If good sons or good daughters, receiving this sutra either during the Buddhas lifetime or after his extinction, leap for joy; acquire the unprecedented; keep, read, recite, copy, and adore this sutra; and explain it's meaning discriminately and widely for living beings, they will instantly destroy the heavy barrier of sins resulting from previous karma and become purified, acquire great eloquence, gradually realize all paramitas, accomplish all Samadhis and Suramgama-samadhi, enter the great gate of dharani and rise up to the upper stage quickly with strenuous efforts. They will spread their divided bodies in all of the lands of ten directions, and relieve and emancipate entirely all living beings who suffer greatly in the twenty five abodes. Thus such a power can be seen in this sutra. Good Sons, This is called the ninth inconceivable merit power of this sutra.

"Good Sons! Tenthly, the inconceivable merit power of this sutra is as follows: if good sons or good daughters, receiving this sutra either during the Buddhas lifetime or after his extinction, greatly rejoice; raise the rare mind; keep, read, recite, copy, adore, and expound this sutra, and practice it as the law, these good sons or good daughters will obtain the innumerable realms of Dharani in their bodies because it is wholly by the merciful and friendly instruction of these good sons or good daughters that other people obtain the way and the merit through the power of the practice of this sutra. They will make vast oaths and great vows of numberless asamkhyeya naturally and from the beginning in the stage of ordinary men, and raise a deep desire to relieve all living beings. They will realize the great compassion, thoroughly abolish all sufferings, gather many good roots, and bring benefit to all. They will explain the flavor of the law, and greatly enliven the withered; give all living beings the medicine of the law and set all at ease; gradually elevate their view, to live in the stage of the Law-Cloud(The stage of the Law-Cloud is the tenth and highest stage of the Bodhisattva-Way). They will spread favor extensively, grant mercy to all suffering living beings, and lead them to the Buddha way. Thereupon these persons (Good sons and daughters) will accomplish Perfect Enlightenment before long. Good Sons! This is called the tenth inconceivable merit power of this sutra.

Good sons! The sutra of innumerable meanings, such a supreme Great-Vehicle, has an extremely great divine power and is unsurpassed in it's worth. It makes all ordinary men accomplish the sacred merit, and makes them free from life and death forever. Thereupon this sutra is called Innumerable Meanings. It makes all the living sprout the innumerable ways of all the Bodhisattvas in the stage of ordinary men, and makes the tree of merit grow dense, thick, and tall. Therefore this sutra is called inconceivable merit power.

At that time the Bodhisattva-Mahasattva Great Adornment, with the eighty thousand Bodhisattva-Mahasattvas, said to the Buddha with one voice: "World Honored One! The Sutra of Innumerable Meanings, Such a profound, Wonderful, and supreme great vehicle preached by the Buddha, is reasonable in it's logic, unsurpassed in it's worth and protected by all the Buddhas of the three worlds. No kind of demon or heretic can break into it, nor can any wrong view of life or death destroy it. Thereupon this sutra has ten such inconceivable merit powers. It greatly benefits innumerable living beings, makes all Bodhisattva-Mahasattvas attain the contemplation of innumerable meanings, a hundred thousand realms of Dharani, all the stages and assurances of Bodhisattva, and the accomplishments of the four way merits of pratyekabuddha and arhat. The World Honored One has preached such a law willingly for us in compassion, and made us attain the benefits of the law abundantly. This is immensely marvelous and unprecedented. It is difficult to repay the merciful favor of the World Honored One.

At the close of these words, the three thousand, Great thousand fold world was shaken in the six ways; various kinds of celestial flowers, such as utpala, padma, kumuda, and Pundarika rained down from the sky; and numberless kinds of celestial perfumes, robes, garlands, and treasures of priceless value also rained and came rolling down from the sky, and they were offered to the Buddha, all the Bodhisattvas and sravakas, and the great assembly. The celestial bins and bowls were filled with all manner of celestial delicacies, which gave satisfaction naturally to anyone who just saw them and smelled their perfume. The celestial banners, flags, canopies, and playthings, were placed everywhere, and celestial music was played in praise of the Buddha.

Also the Buddha worlds, as numerous as the sands of the Ganges, in the east were shaken in the six ways; celestial flowers, perfumes, robes, garlands, and treasures of priceless value rained down; the celestial bins and bowls, and all sorts of celestial delicacies gave satisfaction to anyone who just saw them and smelled their perfume. The celestial banners, flags, canopies, and playthings were placed everywhere, and celestial music was played in praise of those Buddhas, those Bodhisattvas and sravakas, and the great assembly. So, too, was it in the southern, western, and northern quarters, in the four intermediate directions, and in the Zenith, and Nadir.

At that time the Buddha addressed the Bodhisattva-Mahasattva Great Adornment and the eighty thousand Bodhisattva-mahasattvas: You should entertain a deep respect for this sutra, practice it as the law, instruct all widely, and propagate it earnestly. You should protect it heartily day and night, and make all living beings attain the benefits of the law. This is truly great mercy, and great compassion, so, offering the divine power of a vow, you should protect this sutra and not let anybody put obstacles in it's way. Then you should have it practiced widely in Jambudvipa, and make all the living observe, read, recite, copy, and adore it without fail. Because of this you will be made to attain perfect enlightenment rapidly.

At that time the Bodhisattva-Mahasattva Great Adornment rose up from his seat, went up to the Buddha with the eighty thousand Bodhisattva-Mahasattvas, made obeisance at his feet, a hundred thousand times made procession around him, and then going forth to kneel, said to the Buddha with one voice: World Honored One! We have been placed under the mercy of the World Honored One to our delight. The sutra of Innumerable Meanings, This profound, wonderful, and supreme great vehicle, has been preached for us. We will widely propagate this sutra after the Tathagatas extinction in obedience to the Buddhas command, and let all keep, read, recite, copy, and adore it. Be pleased to have no anxiety! With the vow-power, we will let all the living observe, read, recite, copy, and adore this sutra, and acquire the marvelous merit of this sutra. At that time the Buddha said in praise: Excellent! Excellent! All good sons; you are really and truly the Buddhas sons. You are persons who abolish sufferings and remove calamities thoroughly with great mercy and great compassion. You are the good field of blessings for all living beings. You have been the great good leaders extensively for all. You are the great support for all living beings. You are the great benefactors of all living beings. Always bestow the benefits of the law extensively on all.

At that time all in the great assembly, greatly rejoicing together, made salutation to the Buddha and, taking possession of the sutra, withdrew.

The Lotus Sutra
Translated by Burton Watson

Chapter One: Introduction

This is what I heard:

At one time the Buddha was in Rajagriha, staying on Mount Gridhrakuta. Accompanying him were a multitude of leading monks numbering twelve thousand persons. All were arhats whose outflows had come to an end, who had no more earthly desires, who had attained what was to their advantage and had put an end to the bonds of existence, and whose minds had achieved a state of freedom.

Their names were Ajnata Kaundinya, Mahakashyapa, Uruvilvakashyapa, Gayakashyapa, Nadikashyapa, Shariputra, Great Maudgaly~yana, Mahakatyayana, Aniruddha, Kapphina, Gavampati, Revata, Pilindavatsa, Bakkula, Mahakaushthila, Nanda, Sundarananda, Purna Maitrayaniputra, Subhuti, Ananda, and Rahula. All were like these, great Arhats who were well known to others. There were also two thousand persons, some of whom were still learning and some who had completed their learning. There was the nun Mahaprajapati with her six thousand followers. And there was Rahula's mother, the nun Yashodhara, with her followers. There were bodhisattvas and mahasattvas, eighty thousand of them, none of them ever regressing in their search for anuttara-samyak-sambodhi. All had gained dharanis, delighted in preaching, were eloquent, and turned the wheel of the Law that knows no regression. They had made offerings to immeasurable hundreds and thousands of Buddhas, in the presence of various Buddhas had planted numerous roots of virtue, had been constantly praised by the Buddhas, had trained themselves in compassion, were good at entering the Buddha wisdom, and had fully penetrated the great wisdom and reached the farther shore. Their fame had spread throughout immeasurable worlds and they were able to save countless hundreds of thousands of living beings.

Their names were Bodhisattva Manjushri, Bodhisattva Perceiver of the World's Sounds, Bodhisattva Gainer of Great Authority, Bodhisattva Constant Exertion, Bodhisattva Never Resting, Bodhisattva Jeweled Palm, Bodhisattva Medicine King, Bodhisattva Brave Donor, Bodhisattva Jeweled Moon, Bodhisattva Moonlight, Bodhisattva Full Moon, Bodhisattva Great Strength, Bodhisattva Immeasurable Strength, Bodhisattva Transcending the Threefold World, Bodhisattva Bhadrapala, Bodhisattva Maitreya, Bodhisattva Jeweled Accumulation, and Bodhisattva Guiding Leader. Bodhisattvas and mahasattvas such as these numbering eighty thousand were in attendance.

At that time Shakra Devanam Indra with his followers, twenty thousand sons of gods, also attended. There were also the sons of gods Rare Moon, Pervading Fragrance, Jeweled Glow, and the Four Great Heavenly Kings, along with their followers, ten thousand sons of gods.

Present were the sons of gods Freedom and Great Freedom and their followers, thirty thousand sons of gods, Present were King Brahma, lord of the saha world, the great Brahma Shikhin, and the great Brahma Light Bright, and their followers, twelve thousand sons of gods.

There were eight dragon kings, the dragon king Nanda, the dragon king Upananda, the dragon king Sagara, the dragon king Vasuki, the dragon king Takshaka, the dragon king Anavatapta, the dragon king Manasvin, the dragon king Utpalaka, each with several hundreds of thousands of followers.

There were four kimnara kings, the kimnara king Great Law, and the kimnara king Upholding the Law, each with several hundreds of thousands of followers.

There were four gandharva kings, and gandharva king Pleasant, the gandharva king Pleasant Sound, the gandharva Beautiful Sound, each with several hundreds of thousands of followers.
There were four asura kings, the asura king Balin, the asura king Kharaskandha, the asura king Vemachitrin, and the asura king Rahu, each with several hundreds of thousands of followers.

There were four garuda kings, the garuda king Great Majesty, the garuda king Great Body, the garuda king Great Fullness, and the garuda king As One Wishes, each with several hundreds of thousands of followers. And there was King Ajatashatru, the son of Vaidehi, with several hundreds of thousands of followers.

Each of these, after bowing in obeisance before the Buddha's feet, withdrew and took a seat to one side.

At that time the World-Honored One, surrounded by the four kinds of believers, received offerings and tokens of respect and was honored and praised. And for the sake of the bodhisattvas he preached the Great Vehicle sutra entitle Immeasurable Meanings, a Law to instruct the bodhisattvas, one that is guarded and kept in mind by the Buddhas.

When the Buddha had finished preaching this Sutra, he sat with his legs crossed in lotus position and entered into the samadhi of the place of immeasurable meanings, his body and mind never moving. At that time heaven rained down mandarava flowers, great mandarava flowers, manjushaka flowers, and great manjushaka flowers, scattering them over the Buddha and over the great assembly, and everywhere the Buddha world quaked and trembled in six different ways.

At that time the monks, nuns, laymen, laywomen, heavenly beings, dragons, yakshas, gandharvas, asuras, garudas, kimnaras, mahoragas, human and nonhuman beings in the assembly, as well as the petty kings and wheel-turning sage kings - all those in the great assembly, having gained what they had never had before, were filled with joy and, pressing their palms together, gazed at the Buddha with a single mind.

At that time the Buddha emitted a ray of light from the tuft of white hair between his eyebrows, one of his characteristic features, lighting up eighteen thousand worlds in the eastern direction. There was no place that the light did not penetrate, reaching downward as far as the Avichi hell and upward to the Akanishtha heaven. From this world one could see the living beings in the six paths of existence in all of those other lands. One could likewise see the Buddhas present at that time in those other lands and could hear the sutra teachings which those Buddhas were expounding. At the same time one could see the monks, nuns laymen, and laywomen who had carried out religious practices and attained the way. One could also see the bodhisattvas and mahasattvas who, through various causes and conditions and various types of faith and understanding and in various forms and aspects were carrying out the way of the bodhisattva. And one could also see the Buddhas who had entered parinirvana, towers adorned with the seven treasures were erected for the Buddha relics.

At that time the Bodhisattva Maitreya had this thought: Now the World-Honored One has manifested these miraculous signs. But what is the cause of these auspicious portents? Now the Buddha, the World Honored One, has entered into samadhi. An unfathomable event such as this is seldom to be met with. Whom shall I question about this? Who can give me an answer?

And again he had this thought: this Manjushri, son of a Dharma King, has already personally attended and given offerings to immeasurable numbers of Buddhas in the past. Surely he must see these rare signs. I will now question him.

At this time the monks, nuns, laymen and laywomen, as well as the heavenly beings, dragons, spirits, and the others all had this thought: this beam of brightness from the Buddha, these signs of transcendental powers - now whom shall we question about them?

At that time Bodhisattva Maitreya wished to settle his doubts concerning the matter. And in addition he could see what was in the minds of the four kinds of believers, the monks, nuns, laymen and laywomen, as well as the heavenly beings, dragons, spirits and the others who made up the assembly. So he questioned Manjushri, saying, "What is the cause of these auspicious portents, these signs of transcendental powers, this emitting of a great beam of brightness that illumines the eighteen thousand lands in the eastern direction so we can see all the adornments of the Buddha worlds there?"

Then Bodhisattva Maitreya, wishing to state his meaning once more, asked the question in verse form:

Manjushri,
Why from the white tuft between the eyebrows
of our leader and teacher
does this great light shine all around?
Why do mandarava
and manjushaka flowers rain down
and breezes scented with sandalwood
delight the hearts of the assembly?
Because of these
the earth is everywhere adorned and purified
and this world
quakes and trembles in six different ways.
At this time the four kinds of believers
are all filled with joy and delight,
they rejoice in body and mind,
having gained what they never had before.
The beam of brightness from between the eyebrows
illumines the eastern direction
and eighteen thousand lands
are all the color of gold.
From the Avichi hell
upward to the Summit of Being,
throughout the various worlds
the living beings in the six paths,
the realm to which their births and deaths are tending,
their good and bad deeds,
and the pleasing or ugly recompense they receive -
all these can be seen from here.
We can also see Buddhas,
those sage lords, lions,
expounding and preaching sutras
that are subtle, wonderful and foremost.
Their voices are clear and pure,
issuing in soft and gentle sounds,
as they teach bodhisattvas
in numberless millions.
Their Brahma sounds are profound and wonderful,
making people delight in hearing them.
Each in his own world
preaches the correct Law,
following various causes and conditions
and employing immeasurable similes,
illuminating the Law of the Buddha,
guiding living beings to enlightenment.
If a person should encounter troubles,
loathing old age, sickness and death,
the Buddhas preach to him on nirvana,
explaining how he may put an end to all troubles.
If a person should have good fortune,
having in the past made offerings to the Buddhas,
determined to seek a superior Law,
the Buddhas preach the way of the pratyekabuddha.
If there should be Buddha sons
who carry out various religious practices,
seeking to attain the unsurpassed wisdom,
the Buddhas preach the way of purity.

Manjushri,
I have been dwelling here,
seeing and hearing in this manner
many things numbering in the thousands of millions.
Numerous as they are,
I will now speak of them in brief.
I see in these lands
bodhisattvas numerous as Ganges sands,
according with various causes and conditions
and seeking the way of the Buddha.
Some of them give alms,
gold, silver, coral,
pears, mani jewels,
seashell, agate,
diamonds and other rarities,
men and women servants, carriages,
jeweled hand carriages and palanquins,
gladly presenting these donations.
Such gifts they give to the Buddha way,
desiring to achieve the vehicle
that is foremost in the threefold world
and praised by the Buddhas.
There are some bodhisattvas
who give jeweled carriages drawn by teams of four,
with railings and flowered canopies
adorning their top and sides.
Again I see bodhisattvas
who give their own flesh, hands and feet,
or their wives and children,
seeking the unsurpassed way.
I also see bodhisattvas
who happily give
heads, eyes, bodies and limbs
in their search for the Buddha wisdom.
Manjushri,
I see kings
going to visit the place of the Buddha
to ask him about the unsurpassed way.
They put aside their happy lands,
their palaces, their men and women attendants,
shave their hair and beard
and don the clothes of the Dharma.
Or I see bodhisattvas
who become monks,
living alone in quietude,
delighting in chanting the sutras.
Again I see bodhisattvas
bravely and vigorously exerting themselves,
entering the deep mountains,
their thoughts on the Buddha way.
And I see them removing themselves from desire,
constantly dwelling in emptiness and stillness,
advancing deep into the practice of mediation
until they have gained the five transcendental powers.
And I see bodhisattvas
resting in meditation, palms pressed together,

with a thousand, ten thousand verses
praising the king of the doctrines.
Again I see bodhisattvas,
profound in wisdom, firm in purpose,
who know how to question the Buddhas
and accept and abide by all they hear.
I see Buddha sons
proficient in both meditation and wisdom,
who use immeasurable numbers of similes
to expound the Law to the assembly,
delighting in preaching the Law,
converting the bodhisattvas,
defeating the legions of the devil
and beating the Dharma drum.
And I see bodhisattvas
profoundly still and silent,
honored by heavenly beings and dragons
but not counting that a joy.
And I see bodhisattvas
living in forests, emitting light,
saving those who suffer in hell,
causing them to enter the Buddha way.
And I see Buddha sons
who have never once slept,
who keep circling through the forest
diligently seeking the Buddha way.
And I see those who observe the precepts,
no flaw in their conduct,
pure as jewels and gems,
and in that manner seeking the Buddha way.
And I see Buddha sons
abiding in the strength of fortitude,
taking the abuse and blows
of persons of overbearing arrogance,
willing to suffer all these,
and in that manner seeking the Buddha way.
I see bodhisattvas
removing themselves form frivolity and laughter
and from foolish companions,
befriending persons of wisdom,
unifying their minds, dispelling confusion,
ordering their thoughts in mountain and forest
for a million, a thousand, ten thousand years
in that manner seeking the Buddha way.
Or I see bodhisattvas
with delicious things to eat and drink
and a hundred kinds of medicinal potions,
offering them to the Buddha and his monks;
fine robes and superior garments
costing in the thousands or ten thousands,
or robes that are beyond cast,
offering them to the Buddha and his monks;
a thousand, ten thousand, a million kinds
of jeweled dwellings made of sandalwood
and numerous wonderful articles of bedding,
offering them to the Buddha and his monks;

immaculate gardens and groves
where flowers and fruit abound,
flowing springs and bathing pools,
offering them to the Buddha and his monks;
offerings of this kind,
or many different wonderful varieties
presented gladly and without regret
as they seek the unsurpassed way.
Or there are bodhisattvas
who expound the Law of tranquil extinction,
giving different types of instruction
to numberless living beings.
Or I see bodhisattvas
viewing the nature of all phenomena
as having no dual characteristics,
as being like empty space.
And I see Buddha sons
whose minds have no attachments,
who use this wonderful wisdom
to seek the unsurpassed way.
Manjushri,
there are also bodhisattvas
who after the Buddha has passed into extinction
make offerings to his relics.
I see Buddha sons
building memorial towers
as numberless as Ganges sands,
ornamenting each land with them,
jeweled towers lofty and wonderful,
five thousand yojanas high,
their width and depth
exactly two thousand yojanas,
each of these memorial towers
with its thousand banners and streamers,
with curtains laced with gems like dewdrops
and jeweled bells chiming harmoniously.
There heavenly beings, dragons, spirits,
human and nonhuman beings,
with incense, flowers and music
constantly making offerings.
Manjushri,
these Buddha sons
in order to make offerings to the relics
adorn the memorial towers
so that each land, just as it is,
is as outstandingly wonderful and lovely
as the heavenly king of trees
when its flowers open and unfold.
When the Buddha emits a beam of light
I and the other members of the assembly
can see these lands
in all their various outstanding wonders.
The supernatural powers of the Buddhas
and their wisdom are rare indeed;
by emitting one pure beam of light,
the Buddhas illuminate countless lands.

I and the others have seen this,
have gained something never known before.
Buddha son, Manjushri,
I beg you to settle the doubts of the assembly.
The four kinds of believers look up in happy anticipation,
gazing at you and me.
Why does the World-Honored One
emit this beam of brightness?
Buddha son, give a timely answer,
settle these doubts and occasion joy!
What rich benefits will come
from the projecting of this beam of brightness?
It must be that the Buddha wishes to expound
the wonderful Law he gained
when he sat in the place of practice.
He must have prophecies to bestow.
He has showed us Buddha lands
with their adornment and purity of manifold treasures,
and we have seen their Buddhas -
this is not done for petty reasons.
Manjushri, you must know.
The four kinds of believers, the dragons and spirits
gaze at you in surmise,
wondering what explanation you will give.

At that time Manjushri said to the bodhisattva and mahasattva Maitreya and the other great men: "Good men, I suppose that the Buddha, the World Honored One, wishes now to expound the great Law, to rain down the rain of the great Law, to blow the conch of the great Law, to beat the drum of the great Law, to elucidate the meaning of the great Law. Good men, in the past I have seen this auspicious portent among the Buddhas. They emitted a beam of light like this, and after that they expounded the great Law. Therefore we should know that now, when the present Buddha manifests this light, we will do likewise. He wishes to cause all living beings to hear and understand the Law, which is difficult for all the world to believe. Therefore he has manifested this auspicious portent.

"Good men, once, at a time that was an immeasurable, boundless, inconceivable number of asamkhya kalpas in the past, there was a Buddha named Sun Moon Bright, Thus Come One, worthy of offerings, of right and universal knowledge, perfect clarity and conduct, well gone, understanding the world, unexcelled worthy, trainer of people, teacher of heavenly and human beings, Buddha, World-Honored One, who expounded the correct Law. His exposition was good at the beginning, good in the middle, good at the end. The meaning was profound and far-reaching, the words were skillful and wondrous. It was pure and without alloy, complete, clean and spotless, and bore the marks of Brahma practice."

"For the sake of those seeking to become voice-hearers he responded by expounding the Law of the four noble truths, so that they could transcend birth, old age, sickness and death and attain nirvana. For the sake of those seeking to become pratyekabuddhas he responded by expounding the Law of the twelve-linked chain of causation. For the sake of the bodhisattvas he responded by expounding the six paramitas, causing them to gain anuttara-samyak-sambodhi and to acquire the wisdom that embraces all species."

"Then there was another Buddha who was also named Sun Moon Bright, and then another Buddha also named Sun Moon Bright. There were twenty thousand Buddhas like this, all with the same appellation, all named Sun Moon Bright. And all had the same surname, the surname Bharadvaja. Maitreya, you should understand that from the first Buddha to the last, all had the same appellation, all were named Sun Moon Bright. They were worthy of all the ten epithets and the Law they expounded was good at the beginning, in the middle, and at the end."

"The last Buddha, when he had not yet left family life, had eight princely sons. The first was named Having Intention, the second Good Intention, the third Immeasurable intention, the fourth jeweled intention, the fifth Increased Intention, the sixth Cleansed of Doubt Intention, the seventh Echoing Intention, and the eighth Law Intention. Dignity and virtue came easily to them, and each presided over a four-continent realm."

"When these princes heard that their father had left family life and had gained anuttara-samyak-sambodhi, they all cast aside their princely positions and followed him by leaving family life. Conceiving a desire for the Great Vehicle, the constantly carried out Brahma practices, and all became teachers of the Law. They had already planted good roots in the company of a thousand, ten thousand Buddhas."

"At that time the Buddha Sun Moon Bright preached the Great Vehicle sutra entitled Immeasurable Meanings, a Law to instruct the Bodhisattvas, one that is guarded and kept in mind by the Buddhas. When he had finished preaching the sutra, he sat cross-legged in the midst of the great assembly and entered into the samadhi of the place of immeasurable meanings, his body and mind never moving. At this time heaven rained down mandarava flowers, great mandarava flowers, manjushaka flowers, and great manjushaka flowers, scattering them over the Buddha and the great assembly, and everywhere the Buddha world quaked and trembled in six different ways."

"At that time the monks, nuns, laymen and laywomen , heavenly beings, dragons, yakshas, gandharvas, asuras, garudas, kimnaras, and mahoragas, the human and nonhuman beings in the assembly, as well as the petty kings and wheel-turning sage kings - all those in this great assembly gained what they had never had before and, filled with joy, pressed their palms together and gazed at the Buddha with a single mind.

"At that time the Thus Come One emitted a ray of light from the tuft of white hair between his eyebrows, one of his characteristic features, lighting up eighteen thousand Buddha lands in the eastern direction. There was no place that the light did not penetrate, just as you have seen it light up these Buddha lands now."

"Maitreya, you should understand this. At that time in the assembly there were twenty million bodhisattvas who were happy and eager to hear the Law. When these bodhisattvas saw this beam of light that illuminated the Buddha lands everywhere, they gained what they had never had before. They wished to know the causes and conditions that had occasioned this light."

"At that time there was a bodhisattva named Wonderfully Bright who had eight hundred disciples. At this time the Buddha Sun Moon Bright arose from his samadhi and, because of the bodhisattva Wonderfully Bright, preached the Great Vehicle sutra called the Lotus of the Wonderful Law, a Law to instruct the bodhisattvas, one that is guarded and kept in mind by the Buddhas. For sixty small kalpas the Buddha remained in his seat without rising, and the listeners in the assembly at that time also remained seated there for sixty small kalpas, their bodies and minds never moving. And yet it seemed to them that they had been listening to the Buddha peach for no more than the space of a meal. At this time in the assembly there was not a single person who in body or mind had the least feeling of weariness."

"When the Buddha Sun Moon Bright had finished preaching this sutra over a period of sixty small kalpas, he spoke these words to the Brahmas, devils, shramanas and Brahmans, as well as to the heavenly and human beings and asuras in the assembly, saying, 'tonight at midnight the Thus Come One will enter the nirvana of no remainder."

"At this time there was a bodhisattva named Virtue Storehouse. The Buddha Sun Moon Bright bestowed a prophecy on him, announcing to the monks, "This bodhisattva Virtue Storehouse will be the next to become a Buddha. He will be called Pure Body, tathagata, arhat, samyak-sambuddha."

"After the Buddha had finished bestowing this prophecy, at midnight he entered the nirvana of no remainder."

"After the Buddha had passed away, Bodhisattva Wonderfully Bright upheld the Sutra of the Lotus of the Wonderful Law, for a period of fully eighty small kalpas expounding it for others. The eight sons of the Buddha Sun Moon Bright all acknowledged Wonderfully Bright as their teacher. Wonderfully Bright taught and converted them and roused in them a firm determination to gain anuttara-samyak-sambodhi. Those princely sons gave offerings to immeasurable hundreds, thousands, ten thousands, millions of Buddhas, and after that all were able to achieve the Buddha way. The last to become a Buddha was named Burning Torch."

"Among the eight hundred disciples of Wonderfully Bright was one named Seeker of Fame. He was greedy for gain and support, and though he read and recited numerous sutras, he could not understand them, but for the most part forgot them. Hence he was called Seeker of Fame. Because this man had in addition planted various good roots, however, he was able to encounter immeasurable hundreds, thousands, ten thousands, millions of Buddhas, to make offerings to them, revere, honor and praise them."

"Maitreya, you should understand this. Bodhisattva Wonderfully Bright who lived then-could he be known to you? He was no other than I myself. And Bodhisattva Seeker of Fame was you."

"Now when I see this auspicious portent, it is no different from what I saw before. Therefore I suppose that now the Thus Come One is about to preach the Great Vehicle sutra called the Lotus of the Wonderful Law, a Law to instruct the bodhisattvas, one that is guarded and kept in mind by the Buddhas."

At that time Manjushri, wishing in the presence of the great assembly to state his meaning once more, spoke in verse form, saying:

I recall that in a past age
immeasurable, innumerable kalpas ago
there was a Buddha, most honored of men,
named Sun Moon Bright.
This World-Honored One expounded the Law,
saving immeasurable living beings
and numberless millions of bodhisattvas,
causing them to enter the Buddha wisdom.
The eight princely sons whom this Buddha sired
before taking leave of family life,
when they saw that the great sage had left his family
did likewise, carrying out Brahma practices.
At that time the Buddha preached the Great Vehicle,
a sutra named Immeasurable Meanings,
and in the midst of a great assembly
for the sake of the people established broad distinctions.
When the Buddha had finished preaching this sutra
he sat in the seat of the Law,
sitting cross-legged in the samadhi
called the place of immeasurable meanings.
The heavens rained mandarava flowers,
heavenly drums sounded of themselves,
and the heavenly beings, dragons and spirits
made offerings to the most honored of men.
All the Buddha lands
immediately quaked and trembled greatly.
The Buddha emitted a light from between his eyebrows,
manifesting signs that are rarely seen.
This light illumined the eastern direction,
eighteen thousand Buddha lands,
showing how all the living beings there
were recompensed in birth and death for their past deed.
That one could see how these Buddha lands,
adorned with numerous jewels,
shone with hues of lapis lazuli and crystal
was due to the illumination of the Buddha's light.

One could also see the heavenly and human beings,
dragons, spirits, many yakshas,
gandharvas and kimnaras,
each making offerings to his respective Buddha.
One could also see Thus Come Ones
naturally attaining the Buddha way,
their bodies the color of golden mountains,
upright, imposing, very subtle and wonderful.
It was as though in the midst of pure lapis lazuli
there should appear statues of real gold.
In the midst of the great assembly the World-Honored Ones
expounded the principles of the profound Law.
In one after another of the Buddha lands
the voice-hearers in countless multitudes
through the illumination of the Buddha's light
all became visible with their great assemblies.
There were also monks
residing in the midst of forests,
exerting themselves and keeping the pure precepts
as though they were guarding a bright jewel.
One could also see bodhisattvas
carrying out almsgiving, forbearances, and so forth,
their number like Ganges sands,
due to the illumination of the Buddha's light.
One could also see bodhisattvas
entering deep into meditation practices,
their bodies and minds still and unmoving,
in that manner seeking the unsurpassed way.
One could also see bodhisattvas
who knew that phenomena are marked by tranquility and extinction,
each in his respective land
preaching the Law and seeking the Buddha way.
At that time the four kinds of believers
seeing the Buddha Sun Moon Bright
manifest his great transcendental powers,
all rejoiced in their hearts,
and each one asked his neighbor
what had caused these events.
The one honored by heavenly and human beings
just then arose from his samadhi
and praised Bodhisattva Wonderfully Bright, saying,
"You are the eyes of the world,
one whom all can take faith in and believe,
able to honor and uphold the storehouse of the Dharma.
The law that I preach-
you alone know how to testify to it."
The World-Honored One, having bestowed this praise,
causing Wonderfully Bright to rejoice,
preached the Lotus Sutra
for fully sixty small kalpas.
He never rose from this seat,
and the supreme and wonderful Law that he preached
was accepted and upheld in its entirety
by the Dharma teacher Wonderfully Bright.
After the Buddha had preached the Lotus,
causing all the assembly to rejoice,

on that very same day
he announced to the assembly of heavenly and human beings,
"I have already expounded for you
the meaning of the true entity of all phenomena.
Now when midnight comes
I will enter nirvana.
You must strive with all your hearts
and remove yourselves from indulgence and laxity,
it is very difficult to encounter a Buddha—
you meet one once in a million kalpas."
When the children of the World-Honored One
heard that the Buddha was to enter nirvana,
each one was filled with sorrow and distress,
wondering why the Buddha should so quickly seek extinction.
The sage lord, king of the Law,
comforted and reassured the countless multitude,
saying, "When I enter extinction
you must not be concerned or fearful!
This bodhisattva Virtue Storehouse
has already fully understood in his mind
the true entity that is without outflows.
He will be next to become a Buddha,
bearing the name Pure Body,
and he too will save immeasurable multitudes."
That night the Buddha entered extinction,
as a fire dies out when the firewood is exhausted.
They divided and apportioned his relics
and built immeasurable numbers of towers,
and the monks and nuns
whose number was like Ganges sands
redoubled their exertions,
thereby seeking the unsurpassed way.
This Dharma teacher Wonderfully Bright
honored and upheld the Buddha's storehouse of the Dharma
throughout eighty small kalpas,
broadly propagating the Lotus Sutra.
These eight princely sons
whom Wonderfully Bright converted
held firmly to the unsurpassed way
and were thus able to encounter innumerable Buddhas.
And after they had made offerings to these Buddhas
they followed them in practicing the great way
and one after the other succeeded in becoming a Buddha,
each in turn bestowing a prophecy on his successor.
The last to become a heavenly being among heavenly beings
was named the Buddha Burning Torch.
As leader and teacher of seers
he saved immeasurable multitudes.
This Dharma teacher Wonderfully Bright
at that time had a disciple
whose mind was forever occupied with laziness and sloth,
who was greedy for fame and profit.
He sought fame and profit insatiably,
often amusing himself among clansmen and those of other surnames.
He threw away what he had studied and memorized,
neglected and forgot it, failed to understand it.

Because of this
he was named Seeker of Fame.
But he had also carried out many good actions
and thus was able to meet with innumerable Buddhas.
He made offerings to the Buddhas
and followed them in practicing the great way,
carrying out all the six paramitas,
and now he has met the lion of the Shakyas.
Hereafter he will become a Buddha
whose name will be Maitreya,
who will save living beings extensively
in numbers beyond calculation.
After that Buddha passed into extinction,
that lazy and slothful one-he was you,
and the Dharma teacher Wonderfully Bright-
that was the person who is now I myself.
I saw how the Buddha Torch Bright (Sun Moon Bright)
earlier manifested an auspicious portent like this.
And so I know that now this present Buddha
is about to preach the Lotus Sutra.
The signs now are like those of the earlier auspicious portent,
this is an expedient means used by the Buddhas.
Now when the Buddha emits this beam of brightness
he is helping to reveal the meaning of the true entity of
phenomena.
Human beings now will come to know it.
Let us press our palms together and wait with a single mind.
The Buddha will rain down the rain of the Law to fully satisfy all seekers of the way.
You who seek the three vehicles,
if you have doubts and regrets,
the Buddha will resolve them for you,
bringing them to an end so that nothing remains.

Chapter Two: Expedient Means

At that time the World-Honored One calmly arose from his samadhi and addressed Shariputra, saying: "The wisdom of the Buddhas is infinitely profound and immeasurable. The door to this wisdom is difficult to understand and difficult to enter. Not one of the voice-hearers or pratyekabuddhas is able to comprehend it.

"What is the reason for this? A Buddha has personally attended a hundred, a thousand, ten thousand, a million, a countless number of Buddhas and has fully carried out an immeasurable number of religious practices. He has exerted himself bravely and vigorously, and his name is universally known. He has realized the Law that is profound and never known before, and preaches it in accordance with what is appropriate, yet his intention is difficult to understand.

"Shariputra, ever since I attained Buddhahood I have through various causes and various similes widely expounded my teachings and have used countless expedient means to guide living beings and cause them to renounce attachments. Why is this? Because the Thus Come One is fully possessed by both expedient means and the paramita of wisdom.

"Shariputra, the wisdom of the Thus Come One is expansive and profound. He has immeasurable [mercy], unlimited [eloquence], power, fearlessness, concentration, emancipation, and samadhis, and has deeply entered the boundless and awakened to the Law never before attained.

"Shariputra, the Thus Come One knows how to make various kinds of distinctions and to expound the teachings skillfully. His words are soft and gentle and delight the hearts of the assembly.

"Shariputra, to sum it up: the Buddha has fully realized the Law that is limitless, boundless, never attained before.

"But stop, Shariputra, I will say no more. Why? Because what the Buddha has achieved is the rarest and most difficult-to-understand Law. The true entity of all phenomena can only be understood and shared between Buddhas. This reality consists of the appearance, nature, entity, power, influence, inherent cause, relation, latent effect, manifest effect, and their consistency from beginning to end."

At that time the World-Honored One, wishing to state his meaning once more, spoke in verse form, saying:

The hero of the world is unfathomable.
Among heavenly beings or the people of the world,
among all living beings,
none can understand the Buddha.
The Buddha's power, fearlessness,
emancipation and samadhis
and the Buddha's other attributes
no one can reckon or fathom.
Earlier, under the guidance of countless Buddhas
he fully acquired and practiced various ways,
profound, subtle and wonderful doctrines
that are hard to see and hard to understand.
For immeasurable millions of kalpas
he has been practicing these ways
until in the place of practice he achieved the goal.
I have already come to see and know completely
this great goal and recompense,
the meaning of these various natures and characteristics.
I and the other Buddhas of the ten directions
can now understand these things.
This Law cannot be described,

words fall silent before it.
Among the other kinds of living beings
there are none who can comprehend it,
except the many bodhisattvas
who are firm in the power of faith.
The many disciples of the Buddhas
in the past have given offerings to the Buddhas,
have already cut off all outflows
and now are dwelling in their last incarnation.
But even such persons as they
have not the power needed.
Even if the whole world
were filled with men like Shariputra,
though they exhausted their thoughts and pooled there capacities,
they could not fathom the Buddha's knowledge.
Even if ten directions were all filled with men like Shariputra
or like the other disciples,
though they filled the lands in the ten directions
and exhausted their thoughts and pooled their capacities,
still they could not understand it.
If pratyekabuddhas, acute in understanding,
without outflows, in their last incarnation,
should fill the worlds in the ten directions,
as numerous as bamboos in a grove,
though they should join together with one mind
for a million or for countless kalpas,
hoping to conceive of the Buddha's true wisdom,
they could not understand the smallest part of it.
If bodhisattvas newly embarked on their course
should give offerings to numberless Buddhas,
completely mastering the intent of the various doctrines
and also able to preach the Law effectively,
like so many rice and hemp plants, bamboos or reeds,
filling the lands in the ten directions,
with a single mind, with their wonderful knowledge,
for kalpas numerous as Ganges sands
should all together pool their thoughts and capacities,
they could not understand the Buddha's knowledge.
If bodhisattvas who never regress,
their number like Ganges sands,
with a single mind should join in pondering and seeking,
they could not understand it either.
I also announce to you, Shariputra,
that this profound subtle and wonderful Law
without outflows, incomprehensible,
I have now attained in full.
Only I understand its characteristics,
and the Buddhas of the ten directions do likewise.
Shariputra, you should know
that the words of the various Buddhas never differ.
Toward the Law preached by the Buddhas
you must cultivate a great power of faith.
The world-honored One has long expounded his doctrines
and now must reveal the truth.
I announce this to the assembly of voice-hearers
and to those who seek the vehicle of the pratyekabuddha;

I have enabled people to escape the bonds of suffering
and to attain nirvana.
The Buddha, through the power of expedient means,
has shown them the teachings of the three vehicles
prying living beings loose from this or that attachment
and allowing them to attain release.

At that time among the great assembly there were voice-hearers, Arhats whose outflows had come to an end, Ajnata Kaundinya and the others, twelve hundred persons. And there were monks, nuns, laymen and laywomen who had conceived a desire to become voice-hearers or pratyekabuddhas. Each of these had this thought: Now for what reason does the World-Honored One so earnestly praise expedient means and state that the Law attained by the Buddha is profound and difficult to understand, that it is very difficult to comprehend the meaning of the words he preaches, that not one of the voice-hearers or pratyekabuddhas can do so? If the Buddha preaches but one doctrine of emancipation, then we too should be able to attain this Law and reach the state of Nirvana. We cannot follow the gist of what he is saying now.

At that time Shariputra understood the doubts that were in the minds of the four kinds of believers, and he himself had not fully comprehended. So he addressed the Buddha, saying, "World-Honored One, what causes and conditions lead you to earnestly praise expedient means, the foremost device of the Buddhas, the profound, subtle and wonderful Law that is difficult to understand? From times past I have never heard this kind of preaching from the Buddha. Now the four kinds of believers all have doubts. We beg that the World-Honored One earnestly praise this Law that is profound, subtle and wonderful, difficult to understand?"

At that time Shariputra, wishing to state his meaning once more, spoke in verse from, saying:

Sun of wisdom, great sage and venerable one,
at long last you preach this Law.
You yourself declare you have attained
power, fearlessness, samadhis,
concentration, emancipation, and these other attributes,
and the Law that is beyond comprehension.
This Law attained in the place of practice
no one is capable of questioning you about.
'My intention is hard to fathom,
and no one can question me."
No one questions, yet you yourself preach,
praising the path you walk on.
Your wisdom is very subtle and wonderful,
that which all the Buddhas attain.
The arhats who are without outflows
and those who seek nirvana
now have all fallen into the net of doubt,
wondering for what reason the Buddha preaches this.
Those who seek to become pratyekabuddhas,
monks and nuns,
heavenly beings, dragons and spirits,
along with the gandharvas and others,
look at one another, filled with perplexity,
gazing upward at the most honored of two-legged beings.
What is the meaning of all this?
I beg the Buddha to explain it for us.
Among the assembly of voice-hearers
the Buddha has said I am foremost,
yet now I lack the wisdom
to solve these doubts and perplexities.
Have I in fact grasped the ultimate Law,

or am I still on the path of practice?
The sons born from the Buddha's mouth
press palms together, gaze upward and wait.
We beg you to put forth subtle and wonderful sounds
and at this time explain to us how it really is.
The heavenly beings, dragons, spirits, and the others,
their numbers like Ganges sands,
the bodhisattvas seeking to be Buddhas
in a great force of eighty thousand,
as well as the wheel-turning sage kings
come from ten thousands of millions of lands,
all press their palms and with reverent minds
wish to hear the teaching of perfect endowment.

At that time the Buddha addressed Shariputra, saying, "Stop, stop! There is no need to speak further. If I speak of this matter, then the heavenly and human beings throughout the worlds will all be astonished and doubtful."

Shariputra once more spoke to the Buddha, saying, "World-Honored One, we beg you to preach! We beg you to preach! What is the reason? Because this assembly of countless hundreds, thousands, ten thousands, millions of asamkhayas of living beings in the past have seen the Buddhas; their faculties are vigorous and acute and their wisdom is bright. If they hear the Buddha preach, they will be capable of reverent belief."

At that time Shariputra, wishing to state his meaning once more, spoke in verse form, saying:

Dharma King, none more highly honored,
speak, we beg you, without reserve!
In this assembly of numberless beings
are those capable of reverent belief.

The Buddha repeated, "Stop, Shariputra! If I speak of this matter, the heavenly and human beings and asuras throughout the worlds will all be astonished and doubtful. The monks who are overbearingly arrogant will fall into a great pit."

At that time the World-Honored One repeated what he had said in verse form:

Stop, stop, no need to speak!
My Law is wonderful and difficult to ponder.
Those who are overbearingly arrogant
when they hear it will never show reverent belief.

At that time Shariputra once more spoke to the Buddha, saying, "World-Honored One, we beg you to preach! We beg you to preach! In this assembly at present the persons like myself number in the hundreds, thousands, ten thousands, millions. In age after age we have already attended the Buddhas and received instruction. People of this kind are certain to be capable of reverent belief. Throughout the long night they will gain peace and rest and will enjoy many benefits."

At that time Shariputra, wishing to state his meaning once more, spoke in verse form, saying:

Supremely honored among two-legged beings,
we beg you to preach this foremost Law.
I who am regarded as the Buddha's eldest son
ask you to favor us by preaching distinctions.
The countless members of this assembly
are capable of according reverent belief to this Law
The Buddhas have already in age after age

taught and converted them in this manner.
All with a single mind and palms pressed together
desire to hear and receive the Buddha's words.
I and the other twelve hundred of our group,
as well as the others who seek to become Buddhas,
beg that for the sake of this assembly
you will favor us by preaching distinctions.
When we hear this Law
we will be filled with great joy.

At that time the World-Honored One said to Shariputra, "Three times you have stated your earnest request. How can I do other than preach? Now you must listen attentively and carefully ponder. For your sake I will now analyze and explain the matter."

When he had spoken these words, there were some five thousand monks, nuns, laymen and laywomen in the assembly who immediately rose from their seats, bowed to the Buddha, and withdrew. What was the reason for this? These persons had roots of guilt that were deep and manifold, and in addition they were overbearingly arrogant. What they had not attained they supposed they had attained, what they had not understood they supposed they had understood. And because they had this failing, they did not remain where they were.

The World-Honored One was silent and did not try to detain them.

At this time the Buddha said to Shariputra, "Now this assembly of mine is free of branches and leaves, made up solely of the steadfast and truthful. Shariputra, it is well that these persons of overbearing arrogance have withdrawn. Now listen carefully and I will preach for you."

Shariputra said, "So be it, World-Honored One. We are eager to listen!"

The Buddha said to Shariputra, "A wonderful Law such as this is preached by the Buddhas, the Thus Come Ones, at certain times. But like the blooming of the udumbara, such times come very seldom. Shariputra, you and the others must believe me. The words that the Buddhas preach are not empty or false.

"Shariputra, the Buddhas preach the Law in accordance with what is appropriate, but the meaning is difficult to understand. Why is this? Because we employ countless expedient means, discussing causes and conditions and using words of simile and parable to expound the teachings. This Law is not something that can be understood through pondering or analysis. Only those who are Buddhas can understand it. Why is this? Because the Buddhas, the World-Honored Ones, appear in the world for one great reason alone. Shariputra, what does it mean to say that the Buddhas, the World-Honored Ones, appear in the world for one great reason alone?

"The Buddhas, the World-Honored Ones , wish to open the door of Buddha wisdom to all living beings, to allow them to attain purity. That is why they appear in the world. They wish to show the Buddha wisdom to living beings, and therefore they appear in the world. They wish to cause living beings to awaken to the Buddha wisdom, and therefore they appear in the world. They wish to induce living beings to enter the path of Buddha wisdom, and therefore they appear in the world. Shariputra, this is the one great reason for which the Buddhas appear in the world."

The Buddha said to Shariputra, "The Buddhas, the Thus Come Ones, simply teach and convert the Bodhisattvas. All the things they do are at all times done for this one purpose. They simply wish to show the Buddha wisdom to living beings and enlighten them to it.

"Shariputra, the Thus Come Ones have only a single Buddha vehicle which they employ in order to preach the Law to living beings. They do not have any other vehicle a second one or a third one 1. Shariputra, the Law preached by all the Buddhas of the ten directions is the same as this.

"Shariputra, the Buddhas of the past used countless numbers of expedient means, various causes and conditions, and words of simile and parable in order to expound the doctrines for the sake of living beings. These doctrines are all for the sake of the one Buddha vehicle. These living beings, by listening to the doctrines of the Buddhas, are all eventually able to attain wisdom embracing all species.

Shariputra, when the Buddhas of the future make their appearance in the world, they too will use countless numbers of expedient means, various causes and conditions, and words of simile and parable in order to expound the doctrines for the sake of living beings. These doctrines will all be for the sake of the one Buddha vehicle. And these living beings, by listening to the doctrines of the Buddhas, will all eventually be able to attain wisdom embracing all species.

"Shariputra, the Buddhas, the World-Honored Ones, who exist at present in the countless hundreds, thousands, ten thousands, and millions of Buddha lands in the ten directions, benefit and bring peace and happiness to living beings in large measure, these Buddhas too use countless numbers of expedient means, various causes and conditions, and words of simile and parable in order to expound the doctrines for the sake of living beings. These doctrines are all for the sake of the one Buddha vehicle. And these living beings, by listening to the doctrines of the Buddhas, are all eventually able to attain wisdom embracing all species.

"Shariputra, these Buddhas simply teach and convert the Bodhisattvas. They do it because they wish to show the Buddha wisdom to living beings. They do it because they wish to use the Buddha wisdom to enlighten living beings. They do it because they wish to cause living beings to enter the path of Buddha wisdom.

"Shariputra, I too will now do the same, I know that living beings have various desires. Attachments that are deeply implanted in their minds. Taking cognizance of this basic nature of theirs, I will therefore use various causes and conditions, words of simile and parable, and the power of expedient means and expound the Law for them. Shariputra, I do this so that all of them may attain the one Buddha vehicle and wisdom embracing all species.

"Shariputra, when the age is impure and the times are chaotic, then the defilements of living beings are grave, they are greedy and jealous and put down roots that are not good. Because of this, the Buddhas, utilizing the power of expedient means, apply distinctions to the one Buddha vehicle and preach as though it were three.

"Shariputra, if any of my disciples should claim to be an arhat or a pratyekabuddha and yet does not heed or understand that the Buddhas, the Thus Come Ones, simply teach and convert the bodhisattvas, then he is no disciple of mine, he is no arhat or pratyekabuddha.

"Again, Shariputra, if there should be monks or nuns who claim that they already have attained the status of arhat, that this is their last incarnation, that they have reached the final nirvana, and that therefore they have no further intention of seeking anuttara-samyak-sambodhi, then you should understand that such as these are all persons of overbearing arrogance. Why do I say this? Because if they are monks who have truly attained the status of arhat, then it would be unthinkable that they should fail to believe this Law. The only exception would be in a time after the Buddha had passed away, when there was no Buddha present in the world. Why is this? Because after the Buddha has passed away it will be difficult to find anyone who can embrace, recite, and understand the meaning of sutras such as this. But if persons at that time encounter another Buddha, then they will attain decisive understanding with regard to this Law.

"Shariputra, you and the others should with a single mind believe and accept the words of the Buddha. The words of the Buddhas, the Thus Come Ones, are not empty or false. There is no other vehicle, there is only the one Buddha vehicle.

"At that time the World-Honored One, wishing to state his meaning once more, spoke in verse form, saying:

There are monks and nuns
who behave with overbearing arrogance,
laymen full of self-esteem,
laywomen who are lacking in faith.

Among the four kinds of believers, the likes of these
number five thousand.
They fail to see their own errors,
are heedless and remiss with regard to the precepts,
clinging to their shortcomings, unwilling to change.
But these persons of small wisdom have already left;
the chaff among this assembly
has departed in the face of the Buddha's authority.
These persons were of paltry merit and virtue,
incapable of receiving this Law.
This assembly is now free of branches and leaves,
made up only of those steadfast and truthful.
Shariputra, listen carefully,
for the Law which the Buddhas have attained,
through the power of countless expedient means
they preach for the benefit of living beings.
The thoughts that are in the minds of living beings,
the different types of paths they follow,
their various desires and natures,
the good and bad deeds they have done in previous existences--
all these the Buddha takes cognizance of,
and then he employs causes, similes and parables,
words that embody the power of expedient means,
in order to gladden and please them all.
Sometimes he preaches sutras,
verses, stories of the previous lives of disciples,
stories of the previous lives of the Buddha, of unheard-of things.
At other times he preaches regarding causes and conditions,
uses similes, parables, passages of poetry
or discourses.
For those of dull capacities who delight in a little Law,
who greedily cling to birth and death,
who, despite the innumerable Buddhas,
fail to practice the profound and wonderful way
but are perplexed and confused by a host of troubles--
for these I preach nirvana.
I devise these expedient means
and so cause them to enter into the Buddha wisdom.
Up to now I have never told you
that you were certain to attain the Buddha way.
The reason I never preached in that manner
was that the time to preach so had not yet come.
But now is the very time
when I must decisively preach the Great Vehicle.
I use these nine devices,
adapting them to the living beings when I preach
my basic aim being to lead them into the Great Vehicle,
and that is why I preach this sutra.
There are sons of the Buddha who minds are pure,
who are gentle and of acute capacities,
who under innumerable Buddhas
have practiced the profound and wonderful way.
For these sons of the Buddha
I preach this sutra of the Great Vehicle.
And I predict that these persons
in a future existence will attain the Buddha way.

Because deep in their minds they think of the Buddha
and practice and uphold the pure percepts,
they are assured they will attain Buddhahood,
and hearing this, their whole bodies are filled with great joy.
The Buddha knows their minds and their practices
and therefore preaches for them the Great Vehicle.
When the voice-hearers and bodhisattvas
hear this Law that I preach,
as soon as they have heard one verse
they will all without doubt be certain of attaining Buddhahood.
In the Buddha lands of the ten directions
there is only the Law of the one vehicle,
there are not two, there are not three,
except when the Buddha preaches so as an expedient means,
merely employing provisional names and terms
in order to conduct and guide living beings
and preach to them the Buddha wisdom.
The Buddhas appear in the world
solely for this one reason, which is true;
the other two are not the truth.
Never do they use a lesser vehicle
to save living beings and ferry them across.
The Buddha himself dwells in this Great Vehicle,
and adorned with the power of meditation and wisdom
that go with the Law he has attained,
he uses it to save living beings.
He himself testifies to the unsurpassed way,
the Great Vehicle, the Law in which all things are equal.
If I used a lesser vehicle
to convert even one person,
I would be guilty of stinginess and greed,
but such a thing would be impossible.
If a person will believe and take refuge in the Buddha,
the Thus Come One will never deceive him,
nor will he ever show geed or jealousy,
for he has rooted out evil from among the phenomena.
Therefore throughout the ten directions
the Buddha alone is without fear.
I adorn my body with the special characteristics
and shine my light upon the world.
I am honored by numberless multitudes
and for them I preach the emblem of the reality of things.
Shariputra, you should know
that at the start I took a vow,
hoping to make all persons
equal to me, without any distinction between us,
and what I long ago hoped for
has now been fulfilled.
I have converted all living beings
and caused them all to enter the Buddha way.
If when I encounter living beings
I were in all cases to teach them the Buddha way,
those without wisdom would become confused
and in their bewilderment would fail to accept my teachings.
I know that such living beings have never in the past cultivated good roots
but have stubbornly clung to the five desires,

and their folly and craving have given rise to affliction.
Their desires are the cause
whereby they fall into the three evil paths,
revolving wheel-like through the six realms of existence
and undergoing every sort of suffering and pain.
Having received a tiny form in the womb,
in existence after existence they constantly grow to maturity.
Persons of meager virtue and small merit,
they are troubled and beset by manifold sufferings.
They stray into the dense forest of mistaken views,
debating as to what exists and what does not,
and in the end cling to such views,
embracing all sixty-two of them 2.
They are profoundly committed to false and empty doctrines,
holding firmly to them, unable to set them aside.
Arrogant and puffed up with self-importance,
fawning and envious, insincere in mind,
for a thousand, ten thousand, a million kalpas
they will not hear the Buddha's name,
nor will they hear the correct Law--
such people are difficult to save.
For these reasons, Shariputra,
I have for their sake established expedient means,
preaching the way that ends all suffering.
And showing them nirvana.
But although I preach nirvana,
this is not a true extinction.
All phenomena from the very first
have of themselves constantly borne the marks of
tranquil extinction.
Once the sons of the Buddha have carried out this path,
then in a future existence they will be able to become Buddhas.
I have employed the power of expedient means
to unfold and demonstrate this doctrine of three vehicles,
but the World-Honored Ones, every one of them,
all preach the single vehicle way.
Now before this great assembly
I must clear away all doubts and perplexities.
There is no discrepancy in the words of the Buddhas,
there is only the one vehicle, not two.
For numberless kalpas in the past
countless Buddhas who have now entered extinction,
a hundred, thousand, ten thousand, million types
in numbers incapable of calculation-
such World-Honored Ones,
using different types of causes, similes, and parables,
the power of countless expedient means,
have expounded the characteristics of teachings.
These World-Honored Ones
have all preached the doctrine of the single vehicle,
converting countless living beings
and causing them to enter the Buddha way.
And these great sage lords,
knowing what is desired deep in the minds
of the heavenly and human beings and the other living things
throughout all the worlds,

have employed still other expedient means
to help illuminate the highest truth.
If there are living beings
who have encountered these past Buddhas,
and if they have listened to their Law, presented alms,
or kept the precepts, shown forbearance,
been assiduous, practiced meditation and wisdom, and so forth,
cultivating various kinds of merit and virtue,
then persons such as these
all have attained the Buddha way.
After the Buddhas have passed into extinction,
if persons are of good and gentle mind,
then living beings such as these
have all attained the Buddha way.
After the Buddhas have passed into extinction,
if persons make offerings to the relics,
raising ten thousand or a million kinds of towers,
using gold, silver and crystal,
seashell and agate,
carnelian, lapis lazuli, pearls
to purify and adorn them extensively,
in this way erecting towers;
or if they raise up stone mortuary temples
or those of sandalwood or aloes,
hovenia or other kinds of timber,
or of brick, tile clay or earth;
if in the midst of the broad fields
they pile up earth to make a mortuary temple for the Buddhas,
or even if little boys at play
should collect sand to make a Buddha tower,
then persons such as these
have all attained the Buddha way.
If there are persons who for the sake of the Buddha
fashion and set up images,
carving them with many distinguishing characteristics,
then all have attained the Buddha way.
Or if they make things out of the seven kinds of gems,
of copper, red or white copper,
pewter, lead, tin
iron wood, or clay,
or use cloth soaked in lacquer or resin
to adorn and fashion Buddha images,
then persons such as these have all attained the Buddha way.
If they employ pigments to paint Buddha images,
endowing them with the characteristics of hundredfold merit,
if they make them themselves or have other make them,
then all have attained the Buddha way.
Even if little boys in play
should use a piece of grass or wood or a brush,
or perhaps a fingernail
to draw an image of the Buddha,
such persons as these
bit by bit will pile up merit
and will become fully endowed with a mind of
great compassion;
they all have attained the Buddha way.

Merely by converting the bodhisattvas
they bring salvation and release to numberless multitudes.
And if persons, in the presence of such memorial towers,
such jeweled images and painted images,
should with reverent minds make offerings
of flowers, incense, banners or canopies,
or if they should employ persons to make music,
striking drums or blowing horns or conch shells,
playing pipes, flutes, zithers, harps,
balloon guitars, cymbals and gongs,
and if these many kinds of wonderful notes
are intended wholly as an offering;
or if one with a joyful mind
sings a song in praise of the Buddha's virtue,
even if it is just one small note,
then all who do these things have attained the Buddha way.
If someone with a confused and distracted mind
should take even one flower
and offer it to a painted image,
in time he would come to see countless Buddhas.
Or if a person should bow or perform obeisance,
or should merely press his palms together,
or even should raise a single hand,
or give no more than a slight nod of the head,
and if this were done in offering to an image,
then in time he would come to see countless Buddhas.
And if he himself attains the unsurpassed way
and spreads salvation abroad to countless multitudes,
he will enter the nirvana of no remainder
as a fire dies out when the firewood is exhausted.
If persons with confused and distracted minds
should enter a memorial tower
and once exclaim, "Hail to the Buddha!"
Then all have attained the Buddha way.
If from past Buddhas
when they were in the world or after their extinction,
they should be those who heard this Law,
then all have attained the Buddha way.
The World-Honored Ones of the future,
whose numbers will be incalculable,
these Thus Come Ones
will also employ expedient means to preach the Law,
and all these Thus Come Ones
through countless expedient means
will save and bring release to living beings
so that they enter the Buddha's wisdom which is free
of outflows.
If there are those who hear the Law,
then not one will fail to attain Buddhahood.
The original vow of the Buddhas
was that the Buddha way, which they themselves practice,
should be shared universally among living beings
so that they too may attain this same way.
The Buddhas of future ages,
although they preach hundreds, thousands, millions
a countless number of doctrines,

in truth do so for the sake of the single vehicle.
The Buddhas, most honored of two-legged beings,
know that phenomena have no constantly fixed nature,
that the seed of Buddhahood sprout through causation,
and for this reason they preach the single vehicle.
But that these phenomena are part of an abiding Law,
that the characteristics of the world are constantly abiding--
this they have come to know in the place of practice
and as leaders and teachers they preach expedient means.
The presently existing Buddhas of the ten directions,
whom heavenly and human beings make offerings to,
who in number are like Ganges sands,
they have appeared in the world
in order to bring peace and comfort to living beings,
and they too preach the Law in this way.
They understand the foremost truth of tranquil extinction
and therefore employ the power of expedient means,
and though they point out various different paths,
in truth they do so for the sake of the Buddha vehicle.
They understand the actions of living beings,
the thoughts that lie deep in their minds,
the deeds they have carried out in the past,
their desires, their nature, the power of their exertions,
and whether their capacities are acute or dull,
and so they employ various causes and conditions,
similes, parables, and other words and phrases,
adapting what expedient means are suitable to their preaching.
Now I too am like this;
in order to bring peace and comfort to living beings
I employ various different doctrines
to disseminate the Buddha way.
Through the power of my wisdom
I know the nature and desires of living beings
and through expedient means I preach these doctrines,
causing all living beings to attain joy and gladness.
Shariputra, you should understand
that I view things through the Buddha eye,
I see the living beings in the six paths,
how poor and distressed they are, without merit or wisdom,
how they enter the perilous road of birth and death,
their sufferings continuing with never a break,
how deeply they are attached to the five desires,
like a yak enamored of it's tail,
blinding themselves with greed and infatuation,
their vision so impaired they can see nothing.
They do not seek the Buddha, with his great might,
or the Law that can end their sufferings,
but enter deeply into erroneous views,
hoping to shed suffering through great suffering.
For the sake of these living beings
I summon up a mind of great compassion.
When I first sat in the place of practice
and gazed at the tree and walked around it,
for the space of three times seven days
I pondered the matter in this way.
The wisdom I have attained, I thought,

is subtle, wonderful, the foremost.
But living beings, dull incapacity,
are addicted to pleasure and blinded by stupidity.
With persons such as this,
what can I say, how can I save them?
At that time the Brahma kings,
along with the heavenly king Shakra,
the Four Heavenly Kings who guard the world,
and the heavenly king Great Freedom,
in company with other heavenly beings
and their hundreds and thousands
of followers,
reverently pressing their palms together and bowed,
begging me to turn the wheel of the Law.
Immediately I thought to myself
that if I merely praised the Buddha vehicle,
then the living beings, sunk in their suffering,
would be incapable of believing in this Law.
And because they rejected the Law and failed to believe it,
they would fall into the three evil paths.
It would be better if I did not preach the Law
but quickly entered into nirvana.
Then my thoughts turned to the Buddhas of the past
and the power of expedient means they had employed,
and I thought that the way I had now attained
should likewise be preached as three vehicles.
When I thought in this manner,
the Buddhas of the ten directions all appeared
and with Brahma sounds comforted and instructed me.
"Well done, Shakyamuni!" they said.
"Foremost leader and teacher,
you have attained the unsurpassed Law.
But following the example of all other Buddhas,
you will employ the power of expedient means.
We too have all attained
the most wonderful, the foremost Law,
but for the sake of living beings
we make distinctions and preach the three vehicles.
People of small wisdom delight in a small Law,
unable to believe that they themselves could becomes Buddhas.
Therefore we employ expedient means,
making distinctions and preaching various goals.
But though we preach the three vehicles,
we do it merely in order to teach the bodhisattvas."
Shariputra, you should understand this.
When I heard these saintly lions
and their deep, pure subtle, wonderful sounds,
I rejoiced, crying "Hail to the Buddhas!"
Then I thought to myself,
I have come into this impure and evil world,
and as these Buddhas have preached,
I too must follow that example in my actions.
After I had thought of the matter in this way,
I set out at once for Varanasi.
The marks of tranquil extinction borne by all phenomena
cannot be explained in words,

and therefore I used the power of expedient means
to preach to the five ascetics.
This I termed turning the wheel of the Law,
and also with regard to "the sound of nirvana,"
and "arhat," "Dharma" and Samgha,"
I used these terms to indicate distinctions.
"From infinite kalpas in the past
I have extolled and taught the Law of nirvana,
ending the long sufferings of birth and death."
This is how I customarily preached.
Shariputra, you should know this.
When I looked at the Buddha sons,
I saw incalculable thousands, ten thousands, millions
who had determined to seek the way of the Buddha,
everyone with a respectful and reverent mind,
all coming to the place of the Buddha,
persons who in the past had listened to other Buddhas
and heard the Law preached through expedient means.
Immediately the thought came to me
that the reason the Thus Come One has appeared
is so he may preach the Buddha wisdom.
Now is precisely the time to do so.
Shariputra, you should understand
that persons of dull capacity and small wisdom,
who are attached to appearances, proud and overbearing,
are incapable of believing in this Law.
Now I, joyful and fearless,
in the midst of the bodhisattvas,
honestly discarding expedient means,
will preach only the unsurpassed Way.
When the bodhisattvas hear this Law,
they will be released from all entanglements of doubt.
The twelve hundred Arhats,
they too will all attain Buddhahood.
Following in the same fashion that the Buddhas of the
three existences
employ in preaching the Law,
I now will do likewise,
preaching a Law that is without distinctions.
The times when the Buddhas appear in the world are far apart and difficult to encounter.
And even when they appear in the world
it is difficult for them to preach this Law.
Throughout incalculable, innumerable kalpas
it is rare that one may hear this Law,
and a person capable of listening to this Law,
such a person is likewise rare.
It is like the udumbara flower
which all the world loves and delights in,
which heavenly and human beings look on as something rare,
but which appears only once in many ages.
If a person hears this Law, delights and praises it,
even if he utters just one word,
then he has made offerings
to all the Buddhas of the three existences.
But a person like this is very rarely found,
rarer than the udumbara flower.

You should have no doubts.
I being king of the doctrines,
make this announcement to the entire great assembly.
I employ only the single vehicle way
to teach and convert the bodhisattvas,
I have no voice-hearer disciples.
You, Shariputra,
and the voice-hearers and bodhisattvas,
you should understand that this wonderful Law
is the secret crux of the Buddhas.

In this evil world of the five impurities
those who merely delight in and are attached to the desires,
living beings such as this
in the end will never seek the Buddha way.
When evil persons in ages to come
hear the Buddha preach the single vehicle,
they will be confused, will not believe or accept it,
will reject the Law and fall into the evil paths.
But when there are those with sense of shame, persons of purity
who have determined to seek the Buddha way,
then for the sake of such as these
one should widely praise the way of the single vehicle.
Shariputra, you should understand this.
The Law of the Buddhas is like this.
Employing ten thousand, a million expedient means,
they accord with what is appropriate in preaching the Law.
Those who are not versed in this matter
cannot fully comprehend this.
But you and the others already know
how the Buddhas, the teachers of the world,
accord with what is appropriate in employing expedient means.
You will have no more doubts or perplexities
but, your minds filled with great joy,
will know that you yourselves will attain Buddhahood.

Chapter Three: Simile and Parable

At that time Shariputra's mind danced with joy. Then he immediately stood up, pressed his palms together, gazed up in reverence at the face of the Honored-One, and said to the Buddha, "Just now, when I heard from the World-Honored One, this voice of the Law, my mind seemed to dance and I gained what I had never had before. Why do I say this? Because in the past when I heard a Law of this kind from the Buddha and saw how the bodhisattvas received prophecies that in time they would attain Buddhahood, I and the others felt that we had no part in the affair. We were deeply grieved to think we would never gain the immeasurable insight of the Thus Come One.

"World-Honored One, I have constantly lived in the mountain forest or alone under the trees, sometimes sitting, sometimes walking around, and always I have thought to myself, since I and the others all alike have entered into the nature of the Law, why does the Thus Come One use the Law of the Lesser Vehicle to bring us salvation?

"But the fault is ours, not that of the World-Honored One. Why do I say this? If he had been willing to wait until the true means for attaining anuttara-samyak-sambodhi was preached, then we would surely have obtained release through the Great Vehicle. But we failed to understand that the Buddha was employing expedient means and preaching what was appropriate to the circumstances. So when we first heard the Law of the Buddha, we immediately believed and accepted it, supposing that we had gained understanding.

"World-Honored One, for a long time now, all day and throughout the night, I have repeatedly taxed myself with this thought. But now I have heard from the Buddha what I had never heard before, a Law never known in the past, and it has ended all my doubts and regrets. My body and mind are at ease and I have gained a wonderful feeling of peace and security. Today at last I understand that truly I am the Buddha's son, born from the Buddha's mouth, born through conversion to the Law, gaining my share of the Buddha's Law!"

At that time Shariputra, wishing to state his meaning once more, spoke in verse form, saying:

When I heard the sound of this Law,
I gained what I had never had before.
My mind was filled with great joy,
I was released from all bonds of the net of doubt.
From past times I have received the Buddha's teachings
and have not been denied the Great Vehicle.
The Buddha's sound is very rarely heard,
but it can free living beings from distress.
Already I have put an end to outflows,
and hearing this, am freed from care and distress.
I lived in the mountain valleys
or under the forest trees,
sometimes sitting, sometimes walking around,
and constantly I thought of this matter--
how severely I taxed myself!

"Why have I been deceived?" I said.
"I and the others are sons of the Buddha too,
all alike have entered the Law that is without outflows,
yet in times to come we will never be able
to expound the unsurpassed way.
The golden body, the thirty-two features,
the ten powers, the various emancipations--
though all alike share a single Law,
these we will never attain!
The eighty types of wonderful characteristics,

the eighteen unshared properties--
merits such as these
are all lost to us!"
When I was walking around alone,
I saw the Buddha among the great assembly,
his fame filling the ten directions,
bringing benefit far and wide to living beings,
and I thought to myself, I am deprived of such benefits!
How greatly have I been deceived!
Constantly, day and night,
whenever I pondered over this,
I wanted to ask the World-Honored One
whether I had indeed been deprived or not.
Constantly, when I saw the World-Honored One
praising the bodhisattvas,
then day and night
I would mull this matter over.
But now as I listen to the voice of the Buddha,
I see he preaches the Law in accordance with what
is appropriate,
using this hard-to-conceive doctrine of no outflows
to lead people to the place of practice.
Formerly I was attached to erroneous views,
acting as teacher to the Brahmans.
But the World-Honored One, knowing what was in my mind,
rooted out my errors and preached nirvana.
I was freed of all my errors
and gained understanding of the Law of emptiness.

At that time my mind told me
I had reached the stage of extinction,
but now I realize
that was not true extinction. If the time should come when I can become a Buddha,
then I will possess all the thirty-two features
and heavenly and human beings, the many yakshas,
dragons, spirits and others will hold me in reverence.
When that time comes, then I can say
that at last all has been wiped out without residue.
In the midst of the great assembly, the Buddha
declared that I will become a Buddha.
When I heard the sound of the this Law
my doubts and regrets were all wiped away.
At first, when I heard the Buddha's preaching,
there was great astonishment and doubt in my mind.
Is this not a devil pretending to be the Buddha,
trying to vex and confuse my mind? I thought.
But the Buddha employed various causes,
similes, and parables, expounding eloquently.
His mind was peaceful as the sea,
and as I listened, I was freed from the net of doubt.
The Buddha said that in past ages
the countless Buddhas who have passed into extinction
rested and abided in the midst of expedient means,
and all likewise preached this Law.
The Buddhas of the present and future,
whose numbers are beyond calculation,

they too will use expedient means
in expounding this same Law.
Thus the present World-Honored One,
being born and later leaving his family,
attaining the way and turning the wheel of the Law,
likewise employs expedient means in preaching.
The World-Honored One preaches the true way.
Papiyas would not do that.
Therefore I know for certain
this is not a devil pretending to be the Buddha.
But because I fell into the net of doubt
I supposed this to be the devil's work.
Now I hear the Buddha's soft and gentle sound,
profound, far-reaching, very subtle and wonderful,
expounding and discoursing on the pure Law,
and my mind is filled with great joy.
My doubts and regrets are forever ended,
I will rest and abide in true wisdom.
I am certain I will become a Buddha,
to be revered by heavenly and human beings,
turning the wheel of the unsurpassed Law
and teaching and converting the bodhisattvas.

At that time the Buddha said to Shariputra, "Now, in the midst of this great assembly of heavenly and human beings, shramanas, Brahmans and so forth, I say this. In the past, under twenty thousand million Buddhas, for the sake of the unsurpassed way I have constantly taught and converted you. And you throughout the long night followed me and accepted my instruction.. Now , because I want to make you recall to mind the way that you originally vowed to follow, for the sake of the voice-hearers I am preaching this Great Vehicle sutra called the Lotus of the Wonderful Law, a Law to instruct the bodhisattvas, one that is guarded and kept in mind by the Buddhas.

"Shariputra, in ages to come, after a countless, boundless inconceivable number of kalpas have passed, you will make offerings to some thousands, ten thousands millions of Buddhas, and will honor and uphold the correct Law. You will fulfill every aspect of the way of the bodhisattva and will be able to become a Buddha with the name Flower Glow Thus Come One, worthy of offerings, of right and universal knowledge, perfect clarity and conduct, well gone, understanding the world, unexcelled worthy, trainer of people, teacher of heavenly and human beings, Buddha, World-Honored One.

"Your realm will be called Free from Stain, the land will be level and smooth, pure and beautifully adorned, peaceful, bountiful and happy. Heavenly and human beings will flourish there. The ground will be of lapis lazuli, roads will crisscross it in eight directions, and ropes of gold will mark their boundaries. Beside each road will grow rows of seven-jeweled trees which will constantly flower and bear fruit. And this Flower Glow Thus Come One will employ the three vehicles to teach and convert living beings.

"Shariputra, when this Buddha appears, although it will not be an evil age, because of his original vow he will preach the Law through the three vehicles. His kalpa will be called Great Treasure Adornment. Why will it be called Great Treasure Adornment? Because in that land bodhisattvas will be looked on as a great treasure. Those bodhisattvas will be countless, boundless, inconceivable in number, beyond the reach of reckoning or of simile and parable. Without the power of Buddha wisdom, one cannot understand how many.. Whenever these bodhisattvas wish to walk anywhere, jeweled flowers will uphold their feet.

'These bodhisattvas will not have just conceived the desire for enlightenment, but all will have spent a long time planting the roots of virtue. Under countless hundreds, thousands, tens of thousands, millions of Buddhas they will have carried out Brahma practices in a flawless manner, and will have been perpetually praised by the Buddhas. Constantly they will have cultivated Buddha wisdom, acquiring great transcendental powers and thoroughly understanding the gateways to all the doctrines. They will be upright in character, without duplicity, firm in intent and thought. Bodhisattvas such as this will abound in that land.

"Shariputra, the life span of the Buddha Flower Glow will be twelve small kalpas, not counting the times when he is still a prince and before he becomes a Buddha. The people of his land will have a life span of eight small kalpas. When Flower Glow Thus Come One has lived for twelve small kalpas, he will prophesy that the bodhisattva Firm Full will attain anuttara-samyak-sambodhi. He will announce to the monks, 'This bodhisattva Firm Full will be the next to become a Buddha. He will be named Flower feet Safely Walking, tathagata, arhat, samyak-sambuddha. His Buddha land will be like mine.'

"Shariputra, after the Buddha Flower Glow has passed into extinction, the era of the Correct Law will last for thirty-two small kalpas, and the era of the Counterfeit Law will last for another thirty-two small kalpas."

At that time the World-Honored One, wishing to state his meaning once more, spoke in verse form, saying:

Shariputra, in ages to come
you will become a Buddha, of universal wisdom, venerable,
bearing the name Flower Glow,
and you will save countless multitudes.
You will make offerings to numberless Buddhas,
be endowed with all the Bodhisattva practices,
the ten powers and other blessings,
and will realize the unsurpassed way.
After countless kalpas have passed,
your kalpa will be named Great Treasure Adornment.
Your world will be called Free from Stain,
pure, without flaw or defilement.
Its land will be made of lapis lazuli,
its roads bounded by ropes of gold,
and seven-jeweled trees in a jumble of colors
will constantly bear blossoms and fruit.
The bodhisattvas of that realm
will always be firm in intent and thought.
Transcendental powers and paramitas--
each will be endowed with all of these,
and under numberless Buddhas
they will diligently study the bodhisattva way.
Thus these great men
will be converted by the Buddha Flower Glow.
When that Buddha was still a prince,
he gave up his country, abandoned worldly glory,
and in his final incarnation
left his family and attained the Buddha way.
Flower Glow Buddha will continue in the world
for a life span of twelve small kalpas.
The numerous people of his land
will have a life span of eight small kalpas.
After that Buddha has passed into extinction,
the Correct Law will endure in the world
for thirty-two small kalpas,
saving living beings far and wide.
When the correct law has passed away,
the Counterfeit Law will endure for thirty-two kalpas.
The Buddha's relics will circulate widely;
heavenly and human beings everywhere will make offerings to them.
The actions of Flower Glow Buddha

will all be as I have said.
This most saintly and venerable of two-legged beings
will be foremost and without peer.
And he will be none other than you--
you should rejoice and count yourself fortunate!

At that time, when the four kinds of believers, namely, monks, nuns, laymen and laywomen, and the heavenly beings, dragons, yakshas, gandharvas, asuras, garudas, kimnaras, mahoragas, and others in the great assembly saw how Shariputra received from the Buddha this prophecy that he would attain anuttara-samyak-sambodhi, their hearts were filled with great joy and danced without end. Each one removed the upper robe that he or she was wearing and presented it a an offering to the Buddha. Shakra Devanam Indra, King Brahma, and the countless sons of gods likewise took their wonderful heavenly robes, heavenly mandarava flowers and great mandarava flowers and offered them to the Buddha. The heavenly robes they had scattered remained suspended in the air and turned round and round of themselves. Heavenly beings made music, a hundred, a thousand, ten thousand varieties, all at the same time in the midst of the air, raining down quantities of heavenly flowers and speaking these words: "In the past at Varanasi the Buddha first turned the wheel of the Law. Now he turns the wheel again, the wheel of the unsurpassed, the greatest Law of all!"

At that time the sons of gods, wishing to state their meaning once more, spoke in verse form, saying:

In the past at Varanasi
you turned the wheel of the Law of the four noble truths,
making distinctions, preaching that all things
are born and become extinct, being made up of the
five components.
Now you turn the wheel of the most wonderful,
the unsurpassed great Law.
This Law is very profound and abstruse;
there are few who can believe it.
Since times past often we have heard
the World-Honored One's preaching,
but we have never heard this kind of profound, wonderful and superior Law.
Since the World-Honored One preaches this Law,
we all welcome it with joy.
Shariputra with his great wisdom
has now received this venerable prophecy.
We too in the same way
will surely be able to attain Buddhahood,
throughout all the many worlds
the most venerable, the unsurpassed goal.
The Buddha way is difficult to fathom,
but you will preach with expedient means,
according to what is appropriate.
The meritorious deeds we have done
in this existence or past existences,
and the blessings gained from seeing the Buddha--
all these we will apply to the Buddha way.

At that time Shariputra said to the Buddha: "World-Honored One, now I have no mere doubts or regrets. In person I have received from the Buddha this prophecy that I will attain anuttara-samyak-sambodhi. These twelve hundred persons here whose minds are free -- in the past they remained at the level of learning, and the Buddha constantly taught and converted them, saying, 'My Law can free you from birth, old age, sickness and death and enable you at last to achieve nirvana.' These persons, some of whom were still learning and some who had completed their learning, each believed that, because he had shed his views of 'self,' and also his views of 'existing' and 'not existing,' he had attained nirvana. But now from the World-Honored One they hear what they had never heard before, and all have fallen into doubt and perplexity.

"Very well, World-Honored One. I beg that for the sake of the four kinds of believers you will explain the causes and conditions and make it possible for them to shed their doubts and regrets."

At that time the Buddha said so Shariputra, "Did I not tell you earlier that when the Buddhas, the World-Honored Ones, cite various causes and conditions and use similes, parables, and other expressions, employing expedient means to preach the Law, it is all for the sake of anuttara-samyak-sambodhi? Whatever is preached is all for the sake of converting the bodhisattvas.

"Moreover, Shariputra, I too will now make use of similes and parables to further clarify this doctrine. For through similes and parables those who are wise can obtain understanding.

"Shariputra, suppose that in a certain town in a certain country there was a very rich man. He was far along in years and his wealth was beyond measure. He had many fields, houses and menservants. His own house was big and rambling, but it had only one gate. A great many people--a hundred, two hundred, perhaps as many as five hundred--lived in the house. The halls and rooms were old and decaying, the walls crumbling, the pillars rotten at their base, and the beams and rafters crooked and aslant.

"At that time a fire suddenly broke out on all sides, spreading through the rooms of the house. The sons of the rich man, ten, twenty perhaps thirty, were inside the house. When the rich man saw the huge flames leaping up on every side, he was greatly alarmed and fearful and thought to himself, I can escape to safety through the flaming gate, but my sons are inside the burning house enjoying themselves and playing games, unaware, unknowing, without alarm or fear. The fire is closing in on them, suffering and pain threaten them, yet their minds have no sense of loathing or peril and they do not think of trying to escape!

"Shariputra, this rich man thought to himself, I have strength in my body and arms. I can wrap them in a robe or place them on a bench and carry them out of the house. And then again he thought, this house has only one gate, and moreover it is narrow and small.

My sons are very young, they have no understanding, and they love their games, being so engrossed in them that they are likely to be burned in the fire. I must explain to them why I am fearful and alarmed. The house is already in flames and I must get them out quickly and not let them be burned up in the fire!

"Having thought in this way, he followed his plan and called to all his sons, saying, 'You must come out at once!' But though the father was moved by pity and gave good words of instruction, the sons were absorbed in their games and unwilling to heed them. They had no alarm, no fright, and in the end no mind to leave the house. Moreover, they did not understand what the fire was, what the house was, what the danger was. They merely raced about this way and that in play and looked at their father without heeding him.

"At that time the rich man had this thought: the house is already in flames from this huge fire. If I and my sons do not get out at once, we are certain to be burned. I must now invent some expedient means that will make it possible for the children to escape harm.

"The father understood his sons and knew what various toys and curious objects each child customarily liked and what would delight them. And so he said to them, 'The kind of playthings you like are rare and hard to find. If you do not take them when you can, you will surely regret it later. For example, things like these goat-carts, deer-carts and ox-carts. They are outside the gate now where you can play with them. So you must come out of this burning house at once. Then whatever ones you want, I will give them all to you!'

"At that time, when the sons heard their father telling them about these rare playthings, because such things were just what they had wanted, each felt emboldened in heart and, pushing and shoving one another, they all came wildly dashing out of the burning house.

"At that time the rich man, seeing that his sons had gotten out safely and all were seated on the open ground at the crossroads and were no longer in danger, was greatly relieved and his mind danced for joy. At that time each of the sons said to his father, "the playthings you promised us earlier, the goat-carts and deer-carts and ox-carts--please give them to us now!"

"Shariputra, at that time the rich man gave to each of his sons a large carriage of uniform size and quality. The carriages were tall and spacious and adorned with numerous jewels. A railing ran all around them and bells hung from all four sides. A canopy was stretched over the top, which was also decorated with an assortment of precious jewels. Ropes of jewels twined around, a fringe of flowers hung down, and layers of cushions were spread inside, on which were placed vermilion pillows. Each carriage was drawn by a white ox, pure and clean in hide, handsome in form and of great strength, capable of pulling the carriage smoothly and properly at a pace fast as the wind. In addition, there were many grooms and servants to attend and guard the carriage.

"What was the reason for this? This rich man's wealth was limitless and he had many kinds of storehouses that were all filled and overflowing. And he thought to himself, 'There is no end to my possessions. It would not be right if I were to give my sons small carriages of inferior make. These little boys are all my sons and I love them without partiality. I have countless numbers of large carriages adorned with seven kinds of gems. I should be fair-minded and give one to each of my sons. I should not show any discrimination. Why? Because even if I distributed these possessions of mine to every person in the whole country I would still not exhaust them, much less could I do so by giving them to my sons!

"At that time each of the sons mounted his large carriage, gaining something he had never had before, something he had originally never expected. Shariputra, what do you think of this? When this rich man impartially handed out to his sons these big carriages adorned with rare jewels, was he guilty of falsehood or not?"

Shariputra said, "No, World-Honored One. This rich man simply made it possible for his sons to escape the peril of fire and preserve their lives. He did not commit a falsehood. Why do I say this? Because if they were able to preserve their lives, then they had already obtained a plaything of sorts. And how much more so when, through an expedient means, they are rescued from that burning house! World-Honored One, even if the rich man had not given the tiniest carriage, he would still not be guilty of falsehood. Why? Because this rich man had earlier made up his mind that he would employ an expedient means to cause his sons to escape. Using a device of this kind was no act of falsehood. How much less so, then, when the rich man knew that his wealth was limitless and he intended to enrich and benefit his sons by giving each of them a large carriage."

The Buddha said to Shariputra, "Very good, very good. In is just as you have said. And Shariputra, the Thus Come One is like this. That is, he is a father to all the world. His fears, cares and anxieties, ignorance and misunderstanding, have long come to an end, leaving no residue. He has fully succeeded in acquiring measureless insight, power and freedom from fear and gaining great supernatural powers and the power of wisdom. He is endowed with expedient means and the paramita of wisdom, his great pity and great compassion are constant and unflagging; at all times he seeks what is good and will bring benefit to all.

'He is born into the threefold world, a burning house, rotten and old. In order to save living beings from the fires of birth, old age, sickness and death, care suffering, stupidity, misunderstanding, and the three poisons; to teach and convert them and enable them to attain anuttara-samyak-sambodhi.

"He sees living beings seared and consumed by birth, old age, sickness and death, care and suffering, sees them undergo many kinds of pain because of their greed and attachment and striving they undergo numerous pains in their present existence, and later they undergo the pain of being reborn in hell or as beasts or hungry spirits. Even if they are reborn in the heavenly realm or the realm of human beings, they undergo the pain of poverty and want, the pain of parting from loved ones, the pain of encountering those they detest--all these many different kinds of pain.

"Yet living beings drowned in the midst of all this, delight and amuse themselves, unaware, unknowing, without alarm or fear. They feel no sense of loathing and make no attempt to escape. In this burning house which is the threefold world, they race about to east and west, and though they encounter great pain, they are not distressed by it.

Shariputra, when the Buddha sees this, then he thinks to himself, I am the father of living beings and I should rescue them from their sufferings and give them the joy of the measureless and boundless Buddha wisdom so that they may find their enjoyment in that.

"Shariputra, the Thus Come One also has this thought: if I should merely employ supernatural powers and the power of wisdom; if I should set aside expedient means and for the sake of living beings should praise the Thus Come One's insight, power and freedom from fear, then living beings would not be able to gain salvation. Why? Because these living beings have not yet escaped from birth, old age, sickness, death, care and suffering, but are consumed by flames in the burning house that is the threefold world. How could they be able to understand the Buddha's wisdom?

"Shariputra, that rich man, though he had strength in his body and arms, did not use it. He merely employed a carefully contrived expedient means and thus was able to rescue his sons from the peril of the burning house, and afterward gave each of them a large carriage adorned with rare jewels. And the Thus Come One does the same. Though he possesses power and freedom from fear, he does not use these. He merely employs wisdom and expedient means to rescue living beings from the burning house of the threefold world, expounding to them the three vehicles, the vehicle of the voice-hearer, that of pratyekabuddha, and that of the Buddha.

"He says to them, 'You must not be content to stay in this burning house of the threefold world! Do not be greedy for its coarse and shoddy forms, sounds, scents, tastes and sensations! If you become attached to them and learn to love them, you will be burned up! You must come out of this threefold world at once so that you can acquire the three vehicles, the vehicles of the voice-hearer, the pratyekabuddha and the Buddha. I promise you now that you will get them, and that promise will never prove false. You have only to apply yourselves with diligent effort!'

"The Thus Come One employs this expedient means to lure living beings into action. And then he says to them, 'You should understand that these doctrines of the three vehicles are all praised by the sages. They are free, without entanglements, leaving nothing further to depend upon or seek. Mount these three vehicles, gain roots that are without outflows, gain powers, awareness, the way, meditation, emancipation, samadhis, and then enjoy yourselves. You will gain the delight of immeasurable peace and safety.'

"Shariputra, if there are living beings who are inwardly wise in nature, and who attend the Buddha, the World-Honored One, hear the Law, believe and accept it, and put forth diligent effort, desiring to escape quickly from the threefold world and seeking to attain nirvana, they shall be called [those who ride] the vehicle of the voice hearer.

They are like those sons who left the burning house in the hope of acquiring goat-carts.

"If there are living beings who attend the Buddha, the World-Honored One, hear the Law, believe and accept it, and put forth diligent effort, seeking wisdom that comes of itself, taking solitary delight in goodness and tranquility, and profoundly understanding the causes and conditions of all phenomena, they shall be called [those who ride] the vehicle of the pratyekabuddha. They are like the sons who left the burning house in the hope of acquiring deer-carts.

"If there are living beings who attend the Buddha, the World-Honored One, hear the Law, believe and accept it, and put forth diligent effort, seeking comprehensive wisdom, the insight of the Thus Come One, powers and freedom from fear, who pity and comfort countless living beings, bring benefit to heavenly and human beings, and save them all, they shall be called [those who ride] the Great Vehicle. Because the bodhisattvas seek this vehicle, they are called mahasattvas. They are like the sons who left the burning house in the hope of acquiring ox-carts.

"Shariputra, that rich man, seeing that his sons had all gotten out of the burning house safely and were no longer threatened, recalled that his wealth was immeasurable and presented each of his sons with a large carriage. And the Thus Come One does likewise. He is the father of all living beings. When he sees that countless thousands of millions of living beings, through the gateway of the Buddha's teaching, can escape the pains of the threefold world, the fearful and perilous road, and gain the delights of nirvana, the Thus Come One at that time has this thought: I possess measureless, boundless wisdom, power, fearlessness, the storehouse of the Law of the Buddhas. These living beings are all my sons. I will give the Great Vehicle to all of them equally so that there will not be those who gain extinction by themselves, but that all may do so through the extinction of the Thus Come One.

"To all the living beings who have escaped from the threefold world he then gives the delightful gifts of the meditation, emancipation, and so forth, of the Buddhas. All these are uniform in characteristics, uniform in type, praised by the sages, capable of producing pure, wonderful, supreme delight.

"Shariputra, that rich man first used three types of carriages to entice his sons, but later he gave them just the large carriage adorned with jewels, the safest, most comfortable kind of all. Despite this, that rich man was not guilty of falsehood. The Thus Come One does the same, and he is without falsehood. First he preaches the three vehicles to attract and guide living beings, but later he employs just the Great Vehicle to save them. Why? The Thus Come One possesses measureless wisdom, power, freedom from fear, the storehouse of the Law. He is capable of giving to all living beings the Law of the Great Vehicle. But not all of them are capable of receiving it.

"Shariputra, for this reason you should understand that the Buddhas employ the power of expedient means. And because they do so, they make distinctions in the one Buddha vehicle and preach it as three."

The Buddha, wishing to state his meaning once more, spoke in verse form, saying:

Suppose there was a rich man
who had a large house.
This house was very old,
and decayed and dilapidated as well.
The halls, though lofty, were in dangerous condition
beams and rafters were slating and askew,
foundations and steps were crumbling.
Walls were cracked and gaping
and the plaster had fallen off of them.
The roof thatch was in disrepair or missing,
the tips of the eaves had dropped off.
The fences surrounding it were crooked or collapsed
and heaped rubbish was piled all around.
Some five hundred persons
lived in the house.
Kites, owls, hawks, eagles,
crows, magpies, doves, pigeons,
lizards, snakes, vipers, scorpions,
centipedes and millipedes,
newts and ground beetles,
weasels, raccoon dogs, mice, rats,
hordes of evil creatures
scurried this way and that.
Places that stank of excrement
overflowed in streams of filth
where dung beetles and other creatures gathered.
Foxes, wolves and jackals
gnawed and trampled in the filth
or tore apart dead bodies,
scattering bones and flesh about.
Because of this, packs of dogs
came racing to the spot to snatch and tear,

driven by hunger and fear,
searching everywhere for food,
fighting, struggling and seizing,
baring their teeth, snarling and howling.
That house was fearful, frightening,
so altered was its aspect.
In every part of it
there were goblins and trolls,
yakshas and evil spirits
who feed on human flesh
or on poisonous creatures.
The various evil birds and beasts
bore offspring, hatched and nursed them,
each hiding and protecting its young,
but the yakshas outdid one another
in their haste to seize and eat them.
And when they had eaten their fill,
their evil hearts became fiercer than ever;
the sound of their wrangling and contention
was terrifying indeed.
Kumbhanda demons
crouched on clumps of earth
or leaped one or two feet
off the ground,
idling, wandering here and there,
amusing themselves according to their whims.

Sometimes they seized a dog by two of its legs
and beat it till it had lost its voice,
or planted their feet on the dog's neck,
terrifying it for their own delight.
Again there were demons
with large tall bodies,
naked in form, black and emaciated
constantly living there,
who would cry out in loud ugly voices,
shouting and demanding food.
There were other demons
whose throats were like needles,
or still other demons
with heads like the head of an ox,
some feeding on human flesh,
others devouring dogs.
Their hair like tangled weeds,
cruel, baleful, ferocious,
driven by hunger and thirst,
they dashed about shrieking and howling.
The yakshas and starving spirits
and the various evil birds and beasts
hungrily pressed forward in all directions,
peering out at the windows.
Such were the perils of this house,
threats and terrors beyond measure.
This house, old and rotting,
belonged to a certain man
and that man had gone nearby

and he had not been out for long
when a fire
suddenly broke out in the house.
In one moment from all four sides
the flames rose up in a mass.
Ridgepoles, beams, rafters, pillars
exploded with a roar, quivering, splitting,
broke in two and came rumbling down
as walls and partitions collapsed.

The various demons and spirits
lifted their voices in a great wail,
the hawks, eagles and other birds,
the kumbhanda demons,
were filled with panic and terror,
not knowing how to escape.
The evil beasts and poisonous creatures
hid in their holes and dens,
and the pishacha demons,
who were also living there,
because they had done so little that was good,
were oppressed by the flames
and attacked one another,
drinking blood and gobbling flesh.
The jackals and their like
were already dead by this time
and the larger of the evil beasts
vied in devouring them.
Foul smoke swirled and billowed up,
filling the house on every side.
The centipedes and millipedes,
the poisonous snakes and their kind,
scorched by the flames,
came scurrying out of their lairs,
whereupon the kumbhanda demons
pounced on them and ate them.
In addition, the starving spirits,
the fire raging about their heads,
hungry, thirsty, tormented by the heat,
raced this way and that in terror and confusion.
Such was the state of that house,
truly frightening and fearful;
malicious injury, the havoc of fire-
many ills, not just one, afflicted it.
At this time the owner of the house
was standing outside the gate
when he heard someone say,
"A while ago your various sons,
in order to play their games,
went inside the house.
They are very young and lack understanding
and will be wrapped up in their amusements."
When the rich man heard this,
he rushed in alarm into the burning house,
determined to rescue his sons
and keep them from being burned by the flames.

He urged his sons to heed him,
explaining the many dangers and perils,
the evil spirits and poisonous creatures,
the flames spreading all around,
the multitude of sufferings
that would follow one another without end,
the poisonous snakes, lizards and vipers,
as well as the many yakshas
and kumbhanda demons,
the jackals, foxes and dogs,
hawks, eagles, kites, owls,
ground beetles and similar creatures
driven and tormented by hunger and thirst,
truly things to be feared.
His sons could not stay in such a perilous place,
much less when it was all on fire!
But the sons had no understanding
and although they heard their father's warnings,
they continued engrossed in their amusements,
never ceasing their games.
At that time the rich man
thought to himself:
My sons may behave in this manner,
adding to my grief and anguish.
In this house at present
there is not a single joy,
and yet my sons,
wrapped up in their games,
refuse to heed my instructions
and will be destroyed by the fire!

Then it occurred to him
to devise some expedient means,
and he said to his sons,
"I have many kinds
of rare and marvelous toys,
wonderful jeweled carriages,
goat-carts, deer-carts,
carts drawn by big oxen.
They are outside the gate right now
you must come out and see them!
I have fashioned these carts
explicitly for you.
You may enjoy whichever you choose,
play with them as you like!
When the sons heard
this description of the carts,
at once they vied with one another
in dashing out of the house,
till they reached the open ground,
away from all peril and danger.
When the rich man saw that his sons
had escaped from the burning house
and were standing in the crossroads,
he seated himself on a lion seat,
congratulating himself in these words:

"Now I am content and happy.
These sons of mine
have been very difficult to raise.
Ignorant, youthful, without understanding,
they entered that perilous house
with its many poisonous creatures
and its goblins to be feared.
The roaring flames of the great fire
rose up on all four sides,
yet those sons of mine
still clung to their games.
But now I have saved them,
caused them to escape from danger.

That is the reason, good people,
I am content and happy."
At that time the sons,
seeing their father comfortably seated,
all went to where he was
and said to him:
"Please give us
the three kinds of jeweled carriages
you promised us earlier.
You said if we came out of the house
you'd give us three kinds of carts
and we could choose whichever we wished.
Now is the time
to give them to us!"
The rich man was very wealthy
and had many storehouses.
With gold, silver, lapis lazuli,
seashells, agate,
and other such precious things
he fashioned large carriages
beautifully adorned and decorated,
with railings running around them
and bells hanging from all sides.
Ropes of gold twisted and twined,
nets of pearls
stretched over the top,
and fringes of golden flowers
hung down everywhere.
Multicolored decorations
wound around and encircled the carriages,
soft silks and gauzes
served for cushions,
with fine felts of most wonderful make
valued at thousands or millions,
gleaming white and pure,
to spread over them.
There were large white oxen,
sleek, stalwart, of great strength,
handsome in form,
to draw the jeweled carriages,
and numerous grooms and attendants
to accompany and guard them.

These wonderful carriages
the man presented to each of his sons alike.
The sons at that time
danced for joy,
mounting the jeweled carriages,
driving off in all directions,
delighting and amusing themselves
freely and without hindrance.
I say this to you, Shariputra-
I am like this rich man.
I, most venerable of the sages,
am the father of this world
and all living beings
are my children.
But they are deeply attached to worldly pleasures
and lacking in minds of wisdom.
There is no safety in the threefold world;
it is like a burning house,
replete with a multitude of sufferings,
truly to be feared,
constantly beset with the griefs and pains
of birth, old age, sickness and death,
which are like fires
raging fiercely and without cease.
The Thus Come One has already left
the burning house of the threefold world
and dwells in tranquil quietude
in the safety of forest and plain.
But now this threefold world
is all my domain,
and the living beings in it
are all my children.
Now this place
is beset by many pains and trials.

I am the only person
who can rescue and protect others,
but though I teach and instruct them,
they do not believe or accept my teachings,
because, tainted by desires,
they are deeply immersed in greed and attachment.
So, I employ an expedient means,
describing to them the three vehicles,
causing all living beings
to understand the pains of the threefold world,
and then I set forth and expound
a way whereby they can escape from the world.
If these children of mine
will only determine in their minds to do so,
they can acquire all the three understandings
and the six transcendental powers,
can become pratyekabuddhas
or bodhisattvas who never regress.
I say to you, Shariputra,
for the sake of living beings
I employ these similes and parables

to preach the single Buddha vehicle.
If you and the others are capable
of believing and accepting my words,
then all of you are certain
to attain the Buddha way.
This vehicle is subtle, wonderful,
foremost in purity;
throughout all worlds
it stands unsurpassed.
The Buddha delights in and approves it,
and all living beings
should praise it,
offer it alms and obeisance.
There are immeasurable thousands of millions
of powers, emancipations,
meditations, wisdoms,
and other attributes of the Buddha.

But if the children can obtain this vehicle,
it will allow them
day and night for unnumbered kalpas
to find constant enjoyment,
to join the bodhisattvas
and the multitude of voice-hearers
in mounting this jeweled vehicle
and proceeding directly to the place of practice.
For these reasons,
though one should seek diligently in the ten directions,
he will find no other vehicles
except when the Buddha preaches them as an expedient means.
I tell you, Shariputra,
you and the others
are all my children,
and I am a father to you.
For repeated kalpas
you have burned in the flames of manifold sufferings,
but I will save you all
and cause you to escape from the threefold world.
Although earlier I told you
that you had attained extinction,
that was only the end of birth and death,
it was not true extinction.
Now what is needed
is simply that you acquire Buddha wisdom.
If there are bodhisattvas
here in this assembly,
let them with a single mind
listen to the true Law of the Buddhas.
Though the Buddhas, the World-Honored Ones,
employ expedient means,
the living beings converted by them
are all bodhisattvas.
If there are persons of little wisdom
who are deeply attached to love and desire,
because they are that way,
the Buddha preaches for them the rule of suffering.

Then the living beings will be glad in mind,
having gained what they never had before.
The rule of suffering which the Buddha preaches
is true and never varies.
If there are living beings
who do not understand the root of suffering,
who are deeply attached to the causes of suffering
and cannot for a moment put them aside,
because they are that way,
the Buddha uses expedient means to preach the way.
As to the cause of all suffering,
it has its root in greed and desire.
If greed and desire are wiped out,
it will have no place to dwell.
To wipe out all suffering-
this is called the third rule.
For the sake of this rule, the rule of extinction,
one practices the way.
And when one escapes from the bonds of suffering
this is called attaining emancipation.
By what means
can a person attain emancipation?
Separating oneself from falsehood and delusion-
this alone may be called emancipation.
But if a person has not truly
been able to emancipate himself from everything,
then the Buddha will say
he has not achieved true extinction,
because such a person
has not yet gained the unsurpassed way.
My purpose is not to try
to cause them to reach extinction.
I am the Dharma King,
free to do as I will with the Law.
To bring peace and safety to living beings-
that is the reason I appear in the world.
I say to you, Shariputra,
this Dharma seal of mine

I preach because I wish
to bring benefit to the world.
You must not recklessly transmit it
wherever you happen to wander.
If there is someone who hears it,
responds with joy and gratefully accepts it,
you should know that person
is an avivartika.
If there is someone who believes and accepts
the Law of this sutra,
that person has already seen
the Buddhas of the past,
has respectfully offered alms to them
and listened to this Law.
If there is someone who can
believe what you preach

then that person has seen me,
and has also seen you
and the other monks
and the bodhisattvas.
This Lotus Sutra
is preached for those with profound wisdom.
If persons of shallow understanding hear it,
they will be perplexed and fail to comprehend.
As for all the voice-hearers
and pratyekabuddhas,
in this sutra there are things
that are beyond their powers.
Even you, Shariputra,
in the case of this sutra
were able to gain entrance through faith alone.
How much more so, then, the other voice-hearers.
Those other voice-hearers
it is because they have faith in the Buddha's words
that they can comply with this sutra,
not because of any wisdom of their own.
Also, Shariputra,
to persons who are arrogant or lazy
or taken up with views of the self,
do not preach this sutra.
Those with the shallow understandings of ordinary persons,
who are deeply attached to the five desires,
cannot comprehend it when they hear it.
Do not preach it to them.
If a person fails to have faith
but instead slanders this sutra,
immediately he will destroy all the seeds
for becoming a Buddha in this world.
Or perhaps he will scowl with knitted brows
and harbor doubt or perplexity.
Listen and I will tell you
the penalty this person must pay.
Whether the Buddha is in the world
or has already entered extinction,
if this person should slander
a sutra such as this,
or on seeing those who read, recite,
copy and uphold this sutra,
should despise, hate, envy,
or bear grudges against them,
the penalty this person must pay
listen, I will tell you now:
When his life comes to an end
he will enter the Avichi hell,
be confined there for a whole kalpa,
and when the kalpa ends, be born there again.
He will keep repeating this cycle
for a countless number of kalpas.
Though he may emerge from hell,
he will fall into the realm of beasts,
becoming a dog or jackal,
his form lean and scruffy,

dark, discolored, with scabs and sores,
something for men to make sport of.
Or again he will
be hated and despised by men,
constantly plagued by hunger and thirst,
his bones and flesh dried up,
in life undergoing torment and hardship,
in death buried beneath the tiles and stones.
Because he cut off the seeds of Buddhahood
he will suffer this penalty.
If he should become a camel
or be born in the shape of a donkey,
his body will constantly bear heavy burdens
and have the stick or whip laid on it.
He will think only of water and grass
and understand nothing else.
Because he slandered this sutra,
this is the punishment he will incur.
Or he will be born as a jackal
who comes to the village,
body all scabs and sores,
having only one eye,
by the boys
beaten and cuffed,
suffering grief and pain,
sometimes to the point of death.
And after he has died
he will be born again in the body of a serpent,
long and huge in size,
measuring five hundred yojanas,
deaf, witless, without feet,
slithering along on his belly,
with little creatures
biting and feeding on him,
day and night undergoing hardship,
never knowing rest.
Because he slandered this sutra,
this is the punishment he will incur.
If he should become a human being,
his faculties will be blighted and dull,
he will be puny, vile, bent, crippled,
blind, deaf, hunchbacked.

The things he says
people will not believe,
the breath from his mouth will be constantly foul,
he will be possessed by devils,
poor and lowly,
ordered around by others,
plagued by many ailments, thin and gaunt,
having no one to turn to.
Though he attached himself to others,
they would never think of him;
though he might gain something,
he would at once lose or forget it.
Though he might practice the art of medicine

and by its methods cure someone's disease,
the person would grow sicker from some other malady
and perhaps in the end would die.
If he himself had an illness,
no one would aid or nurse him,
and though he took good medicine,
it would only make his condition worse.
If others should turn against him,
he would find himself plundered and robbed.
His sins would be such
that they would bring unexpected disaster on him.
A sinful person of this sort
will never see the Buddha,
the king of the many sages,
preaching the Law, teaching and converting.
A sinful person of this sort
will constantly be born amid difficulties,
crazed, deaf, confused in mind,
and never will hear the Law.
For countless kalpas
numerous as Ganges sands
he will at birth become deaf and dumb,
his faculties impaired,
will constantly dwell in hell,
strolling in it as though it were a garden,
and the other evil paths of existence
he will look on as his own home.
Camel, donkey, pig, dog-
these will be the forms he will take on.
Because he slandered this sutra,
this is the punishment he will incur.
If he should become a human being,
he will be deaf, blind, dumb.
Poverty, want, all kinds of decay
will be his adornment;
water blisters, diabetes,
scabs, sores, ulcers,
maladies such as these
will be his garments.
His body will always smell bad,
filthy and impure.
Deeply attached to views of self,
he will grow in anger and hatred;
aflame with licentious desires,
he will not spurn even birds or beasts.
Because he slandered this sutra,
this is the punishment he will incur.
I tell you, Shariputra,
if I were to describe the punishments that fall
on persons who slander this sutra,
I could exhaust a kalpa and never come to the end.
For this reason
I expressly say to you,
do not preach this sutra
to persons who are without wisdom.
But if there are those of keen capacities,

wise and understanding,
of much learning and strong memory,
who seek the Buddha way,
then to persons such as this
it is permissible to preach it.
If there are persons who have seen
hundreds and thousands and millions of Buddhas,
have planted many good roots
and are firm and deeply committed in mind,
then to persons such as this
it is permissible to preach it.
If there are persons who are diligent,
constantly cultivating a compassionate mind,
not begrudging life or limb,
then it is permissible to preach it.
If there are persons who are respectful, reverent
with minds set on nothing else,
who separate themselves from common folly
to live alone among mountains and waters,
then to persons such as this
it is permissible to preach it.
Again, Shariputra,
if you see a person
who thrusts aside evil friends
and associates with good companions,
then to a person such as this
it is permissible to preach it.
If you see a son of the Buddha
observing the precepts, clean and spotless
as a pure bright gem,
seeking the Great Vehicle Sutra,
then to a person such as this
it is permissible to preach it.
If a person is without anger,
upright and gentle in nature,
constantly pitying all beings,
respectful and reverent to the Buddhas,
then to a person such as this
it is permissible to preach it.
Again, if a son of the Buddha
in the midst of the great assembly
should with a pure mind
employ various causes and conditions,
similes, parables, and other expressions
to preach the Law in unhindered fashion,
to a person such as this
it is permissible to preach it.
If there are monks who,
for the sake of comprehensive wisdom,
seek the Law in every direction,
pressing palms together, gratefully accepting,
desiring only to accept and embrace
the sutra of the Great Vehicle
and not accepting a single verse
of the other sutras,
to persons such as this

it is permissible to preach it.
If a person, earnest in mind,
seeks this sutra
as though he were seeking the Buddha's relics,
and having gained and gratefully accepted it,
that person shows no intention
of seeking other sutras
and has never once given thought
to the writings of the non-Buddhist doctrines,
to a person such as this
it is permissible to preach it.
I tell you Shariputra,
if I described all the characteristics
of those who seek the Buddha way,
I could exhaust a kalpa and never be done.
Persons of this type
are capable of believing and understanding.
Therefore for them you should preach
the Lotus Sutra of the Wonderful Law.

Chapter Four: Belief and Understanding

At that time, when the men of lifelong wisdom Subhuti, Mahakatyayana, Mahakashyapa, and Mahamaudgalyayana heard from the Buddha a Law that they had never known before, and heard the World-Honored One prophesy that Shariputra would attain anuttara-samyak-sambodhi, their minds were moved as seldom before and danced for joy. At once they rose from their seats, arranged their robes, bared their right shoulders and bowed their right knees to the ground. Pressing their palms together with a single mind, they bent their bodies in a gesture of respect and, gazing up in reverence at the face of the Honored One, said to the Buddha: "We stand at the head of the monks and are all of us old and decrepit. We believed that we had already attained nirvana and that we were incapable of doing more, and so we never sought to attain anuttara-samyak-sambodhi.

"It has been a long time since the World-Honored One first began to expound the Law. During that time we have sat in our seats, our bodies weary and inert, meditating solely on the concepts of emptiness, non-form, and non-action. But as to the pleasures and transcendental power of the Law of the bodhisattva or the purifying of Buddha lands and the salvation of living beings-these our minds took no joy in. Why is this? Because the World-Honored One had made it possible for us to transcend the threefold world and to attain the enlightenment of nirvana.

"Moreover, we are old and decrepit. When we heard of this anuttara-samyak-sambodhi, which the Buddha uses to teach and convert the bodhisattvas, our minds were not fill ed with any thought of joy or approval. But now in the presence of the Buddha we have heard this voice-hearer receive a prophecy that he will attain anuttara-samyak-sambodhi and our minds are greatly delighted. We have gained what we have never before. Suddenly we have been able to hear a Law that is rarely encountered, something we never expected up to now, and we look upon ourselves as profoundly fortunate. We have gained great goodness and benefit, an immeasurably rare jewel, something unsought that came of itself.

"World-Honored One, we would be pleased now to employ a parable to make clear our meaning. Suppose there was a man, still young in years, who abandoned his father, ran away, and lived for a long time in another land, for perhaps ten, twenty, or even fifty years. As he drew older, he found himself increasingly poor and in want. He hurried about in every direction, seeking clothing and food, wandering farther and farther a field until by chance he turned his steps in the direction of his homeland.

"The father meanwhile had been searching for his son without success and had taken up residence in a certain city. The father's household was very wealthy, with immeasurable riches and treasures. Gold, silver, lapis Lazuli, coral, amber, and crystal beads all filled and overflowed from his storehouses. He had many grooms and menservants, clerks and attendants, and elephants, horses, carriages, oxen, and goats beyond number. He engaged in profitable ventures at home and in all the lands around, and also had dealings with many merchants and traveling vendors.

"At this time the impoverished son wandered from village to village, passing through various lands and towns, till at last he came to the city where his father was residing. The father thought constantly of his son, but though he had been parted from him for over fifty years, he had never told anyone else about the matter. He merely pondered to himself, his heart filed with regret and longing. He thought to himself that he was old and decrepit. He had great wealth and possessions, gold silver and rare treasures that filled and overflowed from his storehouses, but he had no son, so that if one day he should die, the wealth and possessions would be scattered and lost, for there was no one to entrust them to.

"This was the reason he constantly thought so earnestly of his son. And he also had this thought: If I could find my son and entrust my wealth and possessions to him, then I could feel contented and easy in mind and would have no more worries.

"World-Honored One, at that time the impoverished son drifted from one kind of employment to another until he came by chance to his father's house. He stood by the side of the gate, gazing far off at his father, who was seated on a lion throne, his legs supported by a jeweled footrest, while Brahmans, noblemen, and householders, uniformly deferential, surrounded him. Festoons of pearls worth thousands or tens of thousands adorned his body, and clerks, grooms and menservants holding white fly whisks stood in attendance to left and right. A jeweled canopy covered him, with flowered banners hanging from it, perfumed water had been sprinkled over the ground, heaps of rare flowers were scatted about, and precious objects were ranged here and there, brought out, put away, handed over and received. Such were the many different types of adornments, the emblems of prerogative and marks of distinction.

"When the impoverished son saw how great was his father's power and authority, he was filled with fear and awe and regretted he had ever come to such a place. Secretly he thought to himself; This must be some king, or one who is equal to a king. This is not the sort of place where I can hire out my labor and gain a living. It would be better to go to some poor village where, if I work hard, I will find a place and can easily earn food and clothing. If I stay here for long, I may be seized and pressed into service! Having thought in this way, he raced from the spot.

At that time the rich old man, seated on his lion throne, spied his son and recognized him immediately. His heart was filled with great joy and at once he thought: Now I have someone to entrust my storehouses of wealth and possessions to! My thoughts have constantly been with this son of mine but I had no way of seeing him. Now suddenly he had appeared of himself, which is exactly what I would have wished. Though I am old and decrepit, I still care what becomes of my belongings.

"Thereupon he dispatched a bystander to go after the son as quickly as possible and bring him back. At that time the messenger raced swiftly after the son and laid hold of him. The impoverished son, alarmed and fearful, cried out in an angry voice, 'I have done nothing wrong! Why am I being seized?' But the messenger held on to him more tightly than ever and forcibly dragged him back.

"At that time the son thought to himself, I have committed no crime and yet I am taken prisoner. Surely I am going to be put to death! He was more terrified than ever and sank to the ground, fainting with despair.

"The father, observing this from a distance, spoke to the messenger, saying, 'I have no need of this man. Don't force him to come here, but sprinkle cold water on his face so he will regain his senses. Then say nothing more to him!'

"Why did he do that? Because the father knew that his son was of humble outlook an ambition, and that his own rich and eminent position would be difficult for the son to accept. He knew very well that this was his son, but as a form of expedient means he refrained from saying to anyone, 'this is my son.'

"The messenger said to the son, "I am releasing you now. You may go anywhere you wish.' The impoverished son was delighted, having gained what he had not had before, and picked himself up from the ground and went off to the poor village in order to look for food and clothing.

"At that time the rich man, hoping to entice his son back again, decided to employ an expedient means and send two men as secret messengers, men who were lean and haggard and had no imposing appearance. 'Go seek out that poor man and approach him casually. Tell him you know a place where he can earn twice the regular wage. If he agrees to the arrangement, then bring him here and put him to work. If he asks what sort of work he will be put to, say that he will be employed to clear away excrement, and that the two of you will be working with him.'

"The two messengers then set out at once to find the poor man, and when they had done so, spoke to him as they had been instructed. At that time the impoverished son asked for an advance on his wages and then went with the men to help clear away excrement.

When the father saw his son, he pitied and wondered at him. Another day, when he was gazing out the window, he saw his son in the distance, his body thin and haggard, filthy with excrement, dirt, sweat and defilement. The father immediately took off his necklaces, his soft fine garments and his other adornments and put on clothes that were ragged and soiled. He smeared dirt on his body, took in his right hand a utensil for removing excrement, and assuming a gruff manner, spoke to the laborers, saying, 'Keep at your work! You mustn't be lazy!' By employing this expedient means, he was able to approach his son.

"Later he spoke to his son again, saying, 'Now then, young man! You must keep on at this work and not leave me anymore. I will increase your wages, and whatever you need in the way of utensils, rice, flour, salt, vinegar, and the like you should be in no worry about. I have an old servant I can lend you when you need him. You may set your mind at ease. I will be like a father to you, so have no more worries. Why do I say this? Because I am well along in years, but you are still young and sturdy. When you are at work, you are never deceitful or lazy or speak angry or resentful words. You don't seem to have any faults of that kind the way my other workers do. From now on, you will be like my own son.' And the rich man proceeded to select a name and assign it to the man as though he were his child.

"At this time the impoverished son, though he was delighted at such treatment, still thought of himself as a person of humble station who was in the employ of another. Therefore the rich man kept him clearing away excrement for the next twenty years. By the end of this time, the son felt that he was understood and trusted, and he could come and go at ease, but he continued to live in the same place as before.

"World-Honored One, at that time the rich man fell ill and knew he would die before long. He spoke to his impoverished son, saying, "I now have great quantities of gold, silver, and rare treasures that fill and overflow from my storehouses. You are to take complete charge of the amounts I have and of what is to be handed out and gathered in. This is what I have in mind, and I want you to carry out my wishes. Why is this? Because from now on, you and I will not behave as two different persons. So you must keep your wits about you and see that there are no mistakes or losses.'

"At that time the impoverished son, having received these instructions, took over the surveillance of all the goods, and gold, silver and rare treasures, and the various storehouses, but never thought of appropriated for himself so much as the cost of a single meal. He continued to live where he had before, unable to cease thinking of himself as mean and lowly.

"After some time had passed, the farther perceived that his son was bit by bit becoming more self-assured and magnanimous in outlook, that he was determined to accomplish great things and despised his former low opinion of himself. Realizing that his own end was approaching, he ordered his son to arrange a meeting with his relatives and the king of the country, the high ministers, and the noblemen and householders. When they were all gathered together, he proceeded to make this announcement: "Gentlemen, you should know that this is my son, who was born to me. In such-and-such a city he abandoned me and ran away, and for over fifty years he wandered about suffering hardship. His original name is such-and-such, and my name is such-and-such. In the past, when I was still living in my native city, I worried about him and so I set out in search of him. Sometime after, I suddenly chanced to meet up with him. This is the truth my son, and I will in truth am his father. Now everything that belongs to me, all my wealth and possessions, shall belong entirely to this son of mine. Matters of outlay and income that have occurred in the past this son of mine is familiar with."

"World-Honored One, when the impoverished son heard these words of his father, he was filled with great joy, having gained what he never had before, and he thought to himself, I originally had no mind to covet or seek such things. Yet now these stores of treasures have come of their own accord!

"World-Honored One, this old man with his great riches is none other than the Thus Come One, and we are all like the Buddha's sons. The Thus Come One constantly tells us that we are his sons. But because of the three sufferings, World-Honored One, in the midst of birth and death we undergo burning anxieties, delusions, and ignorance, delighting in and clinging to lesser doctrines. But today the World-Honored One causes us to ponder carefully, to cast aside such doctrines, the filth of frivolous debate.

"We were diligent and exerted ourselves in this matter until we had attained nirvana, which is like one day's wages. And once we had attained it, our hearts were filled with great joy and we considered that this was enough. At once we said to ourselves, "Because we have been diligent and exerted ourselves with regard to the Buddhist Law, we have gained this breadth and wealth of understanding."

"But the World-Honored One, knowing from past times how our minds cling to unworthy desires and delight in lesser doctrines, pardoned us and let us be, not trying to explain to us by saying, You will come to possess the insight of the Thus Come One, your portion of the store of treasures!' Instead the World-Honored One employed the power of expedient means, preaching to us the wisdom of the Thus Come One in such a way that we might heed the Buddha and attain nirvana, which is only day's wages. And because we considered this to be a great gain, we had no wish to pursue the Great Vehicle.

"In addition, though we expounded and set forth the Buddha wisdom for the sake of the Bodhisattvas, we ourselves did not aspire to attain it. Why do I say this? Because the Buddha, knowing that our minds delight in lesser doctrines, employed the power of expedient means to preach in a way that was appropriate for us. So we did not know that we were in truth the sons of the Buddha. But now at least we know it.

"With regard to the Buddha wisdom, the World-Honored One is never begrudging. Why do I say this? From times past we have in truth been the sons of the Buddha, but we delighted in nothing but lesser doctrines. If we had the kind of mind that delighted in great ones, than the Buddha would have preached the Law of the Great Vehicle for us.

"Now in this sutra the Buddha expounds only the one vehicle. And in the past, when in the presence of the bodhisattvas he disparaged the voice-hearers as those who delight in a lesser doctrine, the Buddha was in fact employing the Great Vehicle to teach and convert us. Therefore we say that, though originally we had no mind to covet or seek such a thing, now the great treasure of the Dharma King has come to us of its own accord. It is something that the sons of the Buddha have a right to acquire, and now they have acquired all of it."

At that time, Mahakashyapa, wishing to state his meaning once more, spoke in verse form, saying:

We today have heard
the Buddha's voice teaching
and we dance for joy,
having gained what we never had before.
The Buddha declares that the voice-hearers
will be able to attain Buddhahood.
This cluster of unsurpassed jewels
has come to us unsought.
It is like the case of a boy who.
When still young without understanding,
abandoned his father and ran away,
going far off to another land,
drifting from one country to another
for over fifty years,
his father, distressed in thought,
searched for him in every direction
till, worn out with searching,
he halted in a certain city.
There he built a dwelling
where he could indulge the five desires.
His house was large and costly,
with quantities of gold, silver,
seashell, agate,
pearls, lapis lazuli,
elephants, horses, oxen goats,
palanquins, and carriages,
fields for farming, menservants, grooms,
and other people in great number.
He engaged in profitable ventures
at home and in all the lands around,

and had merchants and traveling vendors
stationed everywhere.
Thousands, ten thousands, millions
surrounded him and paid reverence;
he enjoyed the constant favor
and consideration of the ruler.
The officials and power clans
all joined in paying him honor,
and those who for one reason or another
flocked about him were many.
Such was his vast wealth,
the great power and influence he possessed.
But as he grew old an decrepit
he recalled his son with greater distress than ever,
day and night thinking of nothing else:
"Now the time of my death draws hear.
Over fifty years have passed
since that foolish boy abandoned me.
My storehouses full of goods-
what will become of them?"
At this time the impoverished son
was searching for food and clothing,
going from village to village,
from country to country,
sometimes finding something,
other times finding nothing,
starving and emaciated,
his body broken out in sores and ring worm.
As he moved from place to place
he arrived in time at the city where his father lived,
shifting from one job to another
until he came to his father's house.

At that time the rich man
had spread a large jeweled canopy
inside his gate
and was seated on a lion throne,
surrounded by his dependents
and various attendants and guards.
Some were counting out
gold, silver, and precious objects,
or recording in ledgers
the outlay and income of wealth.
The impoverished son, observing
how eminent and distinguished His father was,
supposed he must be the king of a country
or the equal of a king.
Alarmed and full of wonder,
he asked himself why he had come here.
Secretly he thought to himself,
if I linger here for long
I will perhaps be seized
and pressed into service!
Once this thought had occurred to him,
he raced from the spot,
and inquiring where there was a poor village,

went there in hopes of gaining employment.
The rich man at the time,
seated on his lion throne,
was his son in the distance
and silently recognized who he was.
Immediately he instructed a messenger
to hurry after him and bring him back.
The impoverished son, crying out in terror,
sank to the ground in distress.
"This man has seized me
and is surely going to put me to death!
To think that my search for food and clothing
should bring me to this!"
The rich man knew that his son
was ignorant and self-abasing.

"He will never believe my words,
will never believe I am his father."
So he employed an expedient means,
sending some other men to the son,
a one-eyed man, another puny and uncouth,
completely lacking in imposing appearance,
saying, "Speak to him
and tell him I will employ him
to remove excrement and filth,
and will pay him twice the regular wage."
When the impoverished son heard this
he was delighted and came with the messengers
and worked to clear away excrement and filth
and clean the rooms of the house.
From the window the rich man
would constantly observe his son,
thinking how his son was ignorant and self-abasing
and delighted in such menial labor.
At such times the rich man
would put on dirty ragged clothing,
take in hand a utensil for removing excrement
and go to where his son was,
using this expedient means to approach him,
encouraging him to work diligently.
"I have increased your wages
and given you oil to rub on your feet.
I will see that you have plenty to eat and drink,
mats and bedding that are thick and warm."
At times he would speak severely:
"You must work hard!"
Or again he will say in a gentle voice,
"You are like a son to me."
The rich man, being wise,
gradually permitted his son to come and go in the house.
After twenty years had passed,
he put him in charge of household affairs,
showing him his gold, silver,
pearls, crystal,
and the other things that were handed out or gathered in,
so that he would understand all about them,

though the son continued to live outside the gate,
sleeping in a hut of grass,
for he looked upon himself as poor,
thinking, "None of these things are mine."
The father knew that his son's outlook
was gradually becoming broader and more magnanimous,
and wishing to hand over his wealth and goods,
he called together his relatives,
the king of the country and the high ministers,
the noblemen and householders.
In the presence of this great assembly
he declared, "This is my son
who abandoned me and wandered abroad
for a period of fifty years.
Since I found him again,
twenty years have gone by.
Long ago, in such-and-such a city,
when I lost my son,
I traveled all around searching for him
until eventually I came here.
All that I possess,
my house and people,
I hand over entirely to him
so he may do with them as he wishes."
The son thought now in the past he had been poor,
humble and self-abasing in outlook,
but now he had received from his father
this huge bequest of rare treasures,
along with the father's house
and all his wealth and goods.
He was filled with great joy,
having gained what he never had before.
The Buddha too is like this.
He knows our fondness for the petty,
and so he never told us,
"You can attain Buddhahood."

Instead he explained to us
how we could become free of outflows,
carry out the Lesser Vehicle
and be voice-hearer disciples.
Then the Buddha commanded us
to preach the supreme way
and explain that those who practice this
will be able to attain Buddhahood.
We received the Buddha's teaching
and for the sake of the great bodhisattvas
made use of causes and conditions,
various similes and parables,
a variety of words and phrases,
to preach the unsurpassed way.
When the sons of the Buddha
heard the Law through us,
day and night they pondered,
diligently and with effort practicing it.
At that time the Buddha

bestowed prophecies on them, saying,
"In a future existence
you will be able to attain Buddhahood."
The various Buddhas
in their Law of the secret storehouse
set forth the true facts
for the sake of Bodhisattvas alone;
it is not for our sake
that they expound the true essentials.
The case is like that of the impoverished son
who was able to approach his father.
Though he knew of his father's possessions,
at heart he had no longing to appropriate them.
Thus, although we preached
the treasure storehouse of the Law of the Buddha,
we did not seek to attain it ourselves,
and in this way our case is similar.
We sought to wipe out what was within ourselves,
believing that was sufficient.

We understood only this one concern
and knew nothing of other matters.
Though we might hear
or purifying the Buddha lands,
of teaching and converting living beings,
we took no delight in such things.
Why is this?
Because all phenomena
are uniformly empty, tranquil,
without birth, without extinction,
without bigness, without smallness,
without outflows, without action.
And when one ponders in this way,
one can feel no delight or joy.
Through the long night,
with regard to the Buddha wisdom
we were without greed, without attachment,
without any desire to possess it.
We believed that with regard to the Law
we possessed the ultimate.
Through the long night
we practiced the Law of emptiness,
gaining release from the threefold world
and its burden of suffering and care.
We dwelt in our final existence,
in the nirvana of remainder.
Through the teaching and conversion of the Buddha
we gained a way that was not vain,
and in doing so we repaid
the debt we owed to the Buddha's kindness.
Although for the sake
of the Buddha's sons
we preached the Law of the Bodhisattva,
urging them to seek the Buddha way,
yet we ourselves
never aspired to that Law.

We were thus abandoned by our guide and teacher
because he had observed what was in our minds.

From the first he never encouraged us
or spoke to us of true benefit.
He was like the rich man
who knew that his son's ambitions were lowly
and who used the power of expedient means
to soften and mold his son's mind
so that later he could entrust to him
all his wealth and treasure.
The Buddha is like this,
resorting to a rare course of action.
Knowing that some have a fondness for the petty,
he uses the power of expedient means
to mold and temper their minds,
and only then teaches them the great wisdom.
Today we have gained
what we never had before;
what we previously never hoped for
has now come to us of itself.
We are like the impoverished son
who gained immeasurable treasure.
World-Honored One, now
we have gained the way, gained its fruit;
through the Law of no outflows
we have gained the undefiled eye.
Through the long night
we observed the pure precepts of the Buddha
and today for the first time
we have gained the fruit, the recompense.
In the Law of the Dharma King
we have long carried out Brahma practices;
now we obtain the state of no outflows,
the great unsurpassed fruit.
Now we have become
voice-hearers in truth,
for we will take the voice of the Buddha way
and cause it to be heard by all.
Now we have become
true arhats,
for everywhere among
the heavenly and human beings, devils and Brahmas
of the various worlds
we deserve to receive offerings.
The World-Honored One in his great mercy
makes use of a rare thing,
in pity and compassion teaching and converting,
bringing benefit to us.
In numberless millions of kalpas
who could ever repay him?
Though we offer him our hands and feet,
bow our heads in respectful obeisance,
and present all manners of offerings,
none of us could we pay him.
Though we lift him on the crown of our heads,

bear him on our two shoulders
for kalpas numerous as Ganges sands
reverence him with all our hearts;
though we come with delicate foods,
with countless jeweled robes,
with articles of bedding,
various kinds of potions and medicines;
with ox-head sandalwood
and all kinds of rare gems,
construct memorial towers
and spread the ground with jeweled robes;
though we were to do all this
by way of offering
for kalpas numerous as Ganges sands,
still we could not repay him.
The Buddhas possess rarely known,
immeasurable, boundless,
unimaginable great
transcendental powers.
Free of outflows, free of action,
these kings of the doctrines
for the sake of the humble and lowly
exercise patience in these matters;
to common mortals attached to appearances
they preach in accordance with what is appropriate.
With regard to the Law, the Buddhas
are able to exercise complete freedom.
They understand the various desires and joys
of living beings,
as well as their aims and abilities,
and can adjust to what they are capable of,
employing innumerable similes
to expound the Law for them.
Utilizing the good roots
laid down by living beings in previous existences,
distinguishing between those whose roots are mature
and those whose roots are not yet mature,
they exercise various calculation,
discriminations and perceptions,
and then take the one vehicle way and
in accordance with what is appropriate, preach it as three.

Chapter Five: The Parable of the Medicinal Herbs

At that time the World-Honored One said to Mahakashyapa and the other major disciples: "Excellent, excellent, Kashyapa. You have given an excellent description of the true blessings of the Thus Come One. It is just as you have said. The Thus Come One indeed has immeasurable, boundless, asamkhayas of blessings, and though you and the others were to spend immeasurable millions of kalpas in the effort, you could never finish describing them.

"Kashyapa, you should understand this. The Thus Come One is king of the doctrines. In what he preaches, there is nothing that is vain. With regard to all the various doctrines, he employs wisdom as an expedient means in expounding them. Therefore the doctrines that he expounds all extends to the point where there is comprehensive wisdom. The Thus Come One observes and understands the end to which all doctrines tend. And he also understands the workings of the deepest mind of all living beings, penetrating them completely and without hindrance. And with regard to the doctrines he is thoroughly enlightened, and he reveals to living beings the totality of wisdom.

"Kashyapa, it is like the plants and trees, thickets and groves, and the medicinal herbs, widely ranging in variety, each with its own name and hue, that grow in the hills and streams, the valleys and different soils of the thousand-million fold world. Dense clouds spread over them, covering the entire thousand-million fold world and in one moment saturating it all. The moisture penetrates to all the plants, trees, thickets and groves, and medicinal herbs equally, to their big roots, big stems, big limbs and big leaves. Each of the trees, big and small, depending upon whether it is superior, middling or inferior in nature, receives its allotment. The rain falling from one blanket of clouds accords with each particular species and nature, causing it to sprout and mature, to blossom and bear fruit. Though all these plants and trees grow in the same earth and moistened by the same rain, each has its differences and particulars.

"Kashyapa, you should understand that the Thus Come One is like this. He appears in the world like a great cloud rising up. With a loud voice he penetrates to all the heavenly and human beings and the asuras of the entire world, like a great cloud spreading over the thousand-million fold lands. And in the midst of the great assembly, he addresses these words, saying: " I am the Thus Come One, worthy of offerings, of right and universal knowledge, perfect clarity and conduct, well gone, understanding the world, unexcelled worthy, trainer of people, teacher of heavenly and human beings, Buddha, World-Honored One. Those who have not yet crossed over I will cause to cross over, those not yet freed I will free, those not yet at rest I will put to rest, those not yet in nirvana I will cause to attain nirvana. Of this existence and future existences I understand the true circumstances. I am one who knows all things, sees all things, understands the way, opens up the way, preaches the way. You heavenly and human beings, asuras and others, you must all come here so that I may let you hear the Dharma!"

"At that time living beings of countless thousands, ten thousands, millions of species come to the place where the Buddha is, to listen to the Dharma. The Thus Come One then observes whether they are diligent in their efforts or lazy. And in accordance with each is capable of hearing, he preaches the Law for them in an immeasurable variety of ways so that all of them are delighted and are able to gain excellent benefits therefrom.

"Once these living beings have heard the Law, they will enjoy peace and security in their present existence and good circumstances in future existences, when they will receive joy through the way and again be able to hear the Law. And having heard the Law, they will escape from obstacles and hindrances, and with regard to the various doctrines will be able to exercise their powers to the fullest, so that gradually they can enter into the way. It is like the rain falling from that great cloud upon all the plants and trees, thickets and groves, and medicinal herbs. Each, depending upon its species and nature, receives its full share of moistening and is enabled to sprout and grow.

"The Law preached by the Thus Come One is of one form, one flavor, namely, the form of emancipation, the form of separation, the form of extinction, which in the end comes down to a wisdom embracing all species. When the living beings hear the law of the Thus Come One, though they may embrace, read and recite it, and practice it as it dictates, they themselves do not realize or understand the blessings they are gaining thereby. Why is this? Because only the Thus Come One understands the species, the form, the substance, the nature of these living beings, he knows what things they dwell on, what things they ponder, that things they practice. He knows what Law they dwell on, what Law they ponder, what Law they practice, through what Law they attain what Law.

"Living beings exist in a variety of environments, but only the Thus Come One sees the true circumstances and fully understands them without hindrance. It is like those plants and trees, thickets and groves, and medicinal herbs which do not themselves know whether they are superior, middling or inferior in nature. But the Thus Come One knows that this is the Law of one form, one flavor, namely, the form of emancipation, the form of separation, the form of extinction, the form of ultimate nirvana, of constant tranquility and emptiness. The Buddha understands all this. But because he can see the desires that are in the minds of living beings, he guides and protects them, and for this reason does not immediately preach to them the wisdom that embraces all species.

"You and the others, Kashyapa, have done a very rare thing, for you can understand how the Thus Come One preaches the Law in accordance with what is appropriate, you can have faith in it, you can accept it. Why do I say this? Because the fact that the Buddhas, the World-Honored Ones, preach the Law in accordance with what is appropriate is hard to comprehend, hard to understand."

At that time the World-Honored One, wishing to state his meaning once more, spoke in verse form, saying:

The Dharma King, destroyer of being,
when he appears in the world
accords with the desires of living beings,
preaching the Law in a variety of ways.
The Thus Come One, worthy of honor and reverence,
is profound and far-reaching in wisdom.
For long he remained silent regarding the essential,
in no hurry to speak at once.
If those who are wise hear of it
they can believe and understand it,
but those without wisdom will have doubts and regrets
and for all time will remain in error.
For this reason, Kashyapa,
he adjusts to the person to gain a correct view.
Kashyapa, you should understand
that it is like a great cloud
that rises up in the world
and covers it all over.

This beneficent cloud is laden with moisture,
the lightening gleams and flashes,
and the sound of thunder reverberates afar,
causing the multitude to rejoice.
The sun's rays are veiled and hidden,
a clear coolness comes over the land;
masses of darkness descend and spread-
you can almost touch them.
The rain falls everywhere,
coming down on all four sides,
its flow and saturation are measureless,
reaching to every area of the earth,
to the ravines and valleys of the mountains and streams,
to the remote and secluded places where grow
plants, bushes, medicinal herbs,

trees large and small,
a hundred grains, rice seedlings,
sugar cane, grape vines.
The rain moistens them all,
none ails to receive its full share,
the parched ground is everywhere watered,
herbs and trees alike grow lush.
What falls from the cloud
is water of a single flavor,
but the plants and trees, thickets and groves,
each accept the moisture that is appropriate to its portion.
All the various trees,
whether superior, middling or inferior,
take that is fitting for large or small
and each is enabled to sprout and grow.
Root, stem, limb, leaf,
the glow and hue of flower and fruit-
one rain extends to them
and all are able to become fresh and glossy,
whether their allotment
of substance, form and nature is large or small,
the moistening they receive is one,
but each grows and flourishes in its own way.

The Buddha is like this
when he appears in the world,
comparable to a great cloud
that covers all things everywhere,
Having appeared in the world,
for the sake of living beings
he makes distinctions in expounding
the truth regarding phenomena.
The great sage, the World-Honored One,
to heavenly and human beings,
in the midst of all beings,
pronounces these words:
I am the Thus Come One,
most honored of two-legged beings.
I appear in the world
like a great cloud
that showers moisture upon
all the dry and withered living beings,
so that all are able to escape suffering,
gain the joy of peace and security,
the joys of this world
and the joy of nirvana.
All you heavenly and human beings of this assembly,
listen carefully and with one mind!
All of you should gather around
and observe the one of unexcelled honor.
A am the World-Honored One,
none can rival me.
In order to bring peace and security to living beings
I have appeared it the world
and for the sake of this great assembly
I preach the sweet dew of the pure Law.

This Law is of a single flavor,
that of emancipation, nirvana.
With a single wonderful sound
I expound and unfold its meaning;
constantly for the sake of the Great Vehicle
I create causes and conditions.

I look upon all things
as being universally equal,
I have no mind to favor this or that,
to love one or hate another.
I am without greed or attachment
and without limitation or hindrance.
At all times, for all things
I preach the Law equally;
as I would for a single person,
that same way I do for numerous persons,
constantly I expound and preach the Law,
never have I done anything else,
coming, going, sitting, standing,
never to the end growing weary or disheartened.
I bring fullness and satisfaction to the world,
like rain that spreads its moisture everywhere,
Eminent and lowly, superior and inferior,
observers of precepts, violators of precepts,
those fully endowed with proper demeanor,
those not fully endowed,
those of correct views, of erroneous views,
of keen capacity, of dull capacity-
I cause the Dharma rain on all equally,
never lax or neglectful.
When all the various living beings
hear my Law,
they receive it according to their power,
dwelling in their different environments.
Some inhabit the realm of human and heavenly beings,
of wheel-turning sage kings,
Shakra, Brahma and the other kings-
these are the inferior medicinal herbs.
Some understand the Law of no outflows,
are able to attain nirvana,
to acquire the six transcendental powers
and gain in particular the three understandings,
or live alone in mountain forests,
constantly practicing meditation
and gaining the enlightenment of pratyekabuddhas-
these are the middling medicinal herbs.
Still others seek the place of the World-Honored One,
convinced that they can become Buddhas,
putting forth diligent effort and practicing meditation-
these are the superior medicinal herbs.
Again there are sons of the Buddha
who devote their minds solely to the Buddha way,
constantly practicing mercy and compassion,
knowing that they themselves will attain Buddhahood,
certain of it and never doubting-

these I call small trees.
Those who abide in peace in their transcendental powers,
turning the wheel of non-regression,
saving innumerable millions
of hundreds of thousands of living beings-
bodhisattvas such as these
I call large trees.
The equality of the Buddha's preaching
is like a rain of a single flavor,
but depending upon the nature of the living being,
the way in which it is received is not uniform,
just as the various plants and trees
each receive the moisture in a different manner.
The Buddha employs this parable
as an excellent means to open up and reveal the matter,
using various kinds of words and phrases
and expounding the single Law,
but in terms of the Buddha wisdom
this is no more than one drop of the ocean.
I rain down the Dharma rain,
filling the whole world,
and this single-flavored Dharma
is practiced by each according to the individual's power.
It is like those thickets and groves,
medicinal herbs and trees
which, according to whether they are large or small,
bit by bit grow lush and beautiful.

The Law of the Buddhas
is constantly of a single flavor,
causing the many worlds
to attain full satisfaction everywhere;
by practicing gradually and stage by stage,
all beings can gain the fruits of the way.
The voice-hearers and pratyekabuddhas
inhabit the mountain forests,
dwelling in their final existence,
hearing the Law and gaining its fruits-
we may call them medicinal herbs
that grow and mature each in its own way,
if there are Bodhisattvas
who are steadfast and firm in wisdom,
who fully comprehend the threefold world
and seek the supreme vehicle,
these we call the small trees
that achieve growth and maturity.
Again there are those who dwell in meditation,
who have gained the strength of transcendental powers,
have heard of the emptiness of all phenomena,
greatly rejoice in it in their minds
and emit countless rays of light
to save living beings-
these we call large trees
that have gained growth and maturity
In this way, Kashyapa,
the Law preached by the Buddha

is comparable to a great cloud
which, with a single-flavored rain,
moistens human flowers
so that each is able to bear fruit.
Kashyapa, you should understand
that through various causes and conditions,
various kinds of simile and parable,
I open up and reveal the Buddha way.
This is an expedient means I employ
and the same is true of the other Budd has.

Now for you and the others
I preach the utmost truth:
none in the Multitude of voice-hearers
has entered the stage of extinction.
What you are practicing
is the bodhisattva way,
and as you gradually advance in practice and learning
you are all certain to attain Buddhahood.

Chapter Six: Bestowal of Prophecy

At that time the World-Honored One, having finished reciting these verses, made an announcement to the great assembly, speaking in these words: "This disciple of mine Mahakashyapa in future existences will be able to enter the presence of three thousand billion Buddhas, World-Honored Ones, to offer alms, pay reverence, honor and praise them, widely proclaiming the innumerable great doctrines of the Buddhas. And in his final incarnation he will be able to become a Buddha named Light Bright Thus Come One, worthy of offerings, of right and universal knowledge, perfect clarity and conduct, well gone, understanding the world, unexcelled worthy, trainer of people, teacher of heavenly and human beings, Buddha, World-Honored One.

His land will be called Light Virtue and his kalpa will be called Great Adornment. The life span of this Buddha will be twelve small kalpas. His Correct Law will endure in the world for twenty small kalpas, and his Counterfeit Law for twenty small kalpas.

"His realm will be majestically adorned, free of defilement or evil, shards or rubble, thorns or briers, or the unclean refuse of latrines. The land will be level and smooth, without high places or sags, pits or knolls. The ground will be of lapis lazuli, with rows of jeweled trees and ropes of gold to mark the boundaries of the roads. Jeweled flowers will be scattered around, and everywhere will be pure and clean. The bodhisattvas of that realm will number countless thousands of millions, and the multitude of voice-hearers will likewise be innumerable. There will be no workings of the devil, and although the devil and the devil's people will be there, they will protect the Law of the Buddha."

At that time the World-Honored One, wishing to state his meaning once more, spoke in verse form, saying:

I announce this to the monks:
when I employ the Buddha eye
to observe Kashyapa here,
I see that in a future existence,
after innumerable kalpas have passed,
he will be able to attain Buddhahood.
In future existences
he will offer alms and enter the presence
of three thousand billion
Buddhas, World-Honored Ones.
For the sake of the Buddha wisdom
he will carry out Brahma practices meticulously
and will offer alms to the unexcelled ones,
the most honored of two-legged beings.
After he has done so. And has practiced
all the unsurpassed types of wisdom,
in his final incarnation
he will be able to become a Buddha.
His land will be pure and clean,

the ground of lapis lazuli.
Many jeweled trees
will line the roadsides,
with golden ropes to mark the roads,
and those who see it will rejoice.
It will constantly emit a pleasing fragrance,
with heaps of rare flowers scattered around
and many kinds of strange and wonderful things
for its adornment.
The land will be level and smooth,
without hills or depressions.

The multitude of bodhisattvas
will be beyond calculation,
their minds subdued and gentle,
having attained great transcendental powers,
and they will uphold and embrace
the Great Vehicle scriptures of the Buddhas.
The multitude of voice-hearers
will be free of outflows, in their last incarnation,
sons of the Dharma King,
and their number too will be beyond calculation-
even when one looks with the heavenly eye
one cannot determine their number.
This Buddha will have a life span
of twelve small kalpas,
and his Counterfeit Law
for twenty small kalpas.
Light Bright World-Honored One
will be of this description.

At that time the great Maudgaly~yana, Subhuti and Mahakatyayana, all of them trembling with agitation, pressed their palms together with a single mind and gazed up at the World-Honored One, their eyes never leaving him for an instant. Joining their voices in a single sound, they spoke in verse form, saying:

Great hero and stalwart, World-Honored One,
Dharma King of the Shakyas,
because you have pity on us,
favor us with the Buddha voice!
If, because you understand our innermost minds,
it would be like sweet dew bathing us,
washing away fever and imparting coolness.
Suppose that someone coming from a land of famine
should suddenly encounter a great king's feast.
His heart still filled with doubt and fear,
he would not dare to eat the food at once,
but if he were instructed by the king to do so,
then he would venture to eat.
We now are like such a person,
for whenever we recall the errors of the Lesser Vehicle,
we do not know what we should do
to gain the Buddha's unsurpassed wisdom.
Though we hear the Buddha's voice
telling us that we will attain Buddhahood,
in our hearts we still harbor anxiety and fear,
like that person who did not dare to eat.
But now if the Buddha's prophecy is bestowed upon us,
then joy and peace of mind will quickly be ours.
Great hero and stalwart, World-Honored One,
your constant desire to set the world at ease.
We beg you to bestow such a prophecy on us,
as you would instruct a starving person to eat.

At that time the World-Honored One, understanding the thoughts in the minds of his major disciples, made this announcement to the monks: "Subhuti here in future existences will enter the presence of three hundred ten thousand million nayutas of Buddhas, offering alms, paying reverence, honoring and praising them. He will constantly carry out Brahma practices and fulfill the bodhisattva way, and in his final incarnation he will be able to attain Buddhahood. His title will be Rare Form Thus Come One, worthy of offerings, of right and universal knowledge, perfect clarity and conduct, well gone, understanding the world, unexcelled worthy, trainer of people, teacher of heavenly and human beings, Buddha, World-Honored One. His kalpa will be named Possessed of Jewels and his realm will be named Jewel Born. The land will be level and smooth, the ground made of crystal, it will be adorned with jeweled trees and be free of hills and pits, rubble and thorns and the filth from latrines. Jeweled flowers will cover the ground and everywhere will be pure and clean. The people of his realm will all dwell on jeweled terraces, in rare and wonderful towers and pavilions. His voice-hearer disciples will be countless, boundless, beyond the scope of calculation or simile. The multitude of bodhisattvas will number countless thousands, ten thousands, millions of nayutas. The life span of this Buddha will be twelve small kalpas, his Correct Law will endure in the world for twenty small kalpas, and his Counterfeit Law for twenty small kalpas. This Buddha will constantly dwell in midair, preaching the Law for the assembly and saving numberless multitudes of bodhisattvas and voice-hearers."

At that time the World-Honored One, wishing to state his meaning once more, spoke in verse form, saying:

You multitude of monks,
I now announce this to you.
All of you with a single mind
should hear what I say,
My major disciple
Subhuti
is destined to become a Buddha
with the title Rare Form.
He will offer alms to countless
tens of thousands and millions of Buddhas.
By following the practices of the Buddhas
he will gradually fulfill the great way,
and in his final incarnation
will acquire the thirty-two features.
He will be imposing, exceptional, wonderful,
like a jeweled mountain.
His Buddha land
will be foremost in adornment and purity;
no living beings who sees it
will fail to love and delight in it.
There in the midst, that Buddha
will save unreckonable multitudes.
In that Buddha's Law
will be many bodhisattvas,
all of them with keen capacities,
turning the wheel of non-regression.
That land will constantly
be adorned with bodhisattvas.
The multitude of voice-hearers
will be beyond calculation,
all gaining the three understandings
and exercising the six transcendental powers.
They will dwell in the eight emancipations
and possess great authority and virtue.
The Law preached by that Buddha
will manifest immeasurable
transcendental powers and transformations
of a wondrous nature.
Heavenly and human beings
in numbers like the Ganges sands
will all press their palms together,
listen to and receive the Buddha's words.

That Buddha will have a life span
of twelve small kalpas,
his Correct Law will endure in the world
for twenty small kalpas
and his counterfeit Law
for twenty small kalpas.

At that time the World-Honored One once more spoke to the multitude of monks: "Now I say this to you. Great Katyayana here in future existences will present various articles as offerings and will serve eight thousand million Buddhas, paying honor and reverence to them. After these Buddhas have passed into extinction, he will raise a memorial tower for each one measuring a thousand yojanas in height and exactly five hundred yojanas in both width and depth. It will be made of gold, silver lapis lazuli, seashell, agate, pearl and carnelian, with these seven precious substances joined together. Numerous flowers, necklaces, paste incense, powdered incense, incense for burning, silken canopies, streamers and banners will be presented as offerings to the memorial towers. And after this has been done, he will once more make offerings to twenty thousands of millions of Buddhas, and will repeat the entire process.

"When he has finished offering alms to all the Buddhas, he will fulfill the way of the bodhisattva and will become a Buddha with the title Jambunada Gold Light Thus Come One, worthy of offerings, of right and universal knowledge perfect clarity and conduct, well gone, understanding the world, unexcelled worthy trainer of people, teacher of heavenly and human beings, Buddha, World-Honored One.

"His land will be level and smooth, the ground made of crystal, adorned with jeweled trees, with ropes of gold to mark the boundaries of the roads. Wonderful flowers will cover the ground, everywhere will be pure and clean, and all who see it will rejoice. The four evil paths of existence, hell and the realms of hungry spirits, beasts and asuras, will not exist there. There will be many heavenly and human beings, and multitudes of voice-hearers and bodhisattvas in innumerable tens of thousands of millions will adorn the land. That Buddha's life span will be twelve small kalpas, his Correct Law will endure in the world for twenty small kalpas, and his Counterfeit Law will endure in the world for twenty small kalpas."

At that time the World-Honored One, wishing to state his meaning once more, spoke in verse form, saying:

You multitude of monks,
listen all of you with a single mind,
for in what I speak
there is nothing that departs from the truth.
Katyayana here
will give various kinds
of fine and wonderful articles
as offerings to the Buddhas,
and after the Buddhas have entered extinction
he will raise seven-jeweled towers
and present flowers and incense
as offerings to their relics.

And in his final incarnation
he will gain Buddha wisdom
and achieve impartial and correct enlightenment.
His land will be pure and clean
and he will save innumerable
ten thousands of millions of living beings,
and will receive offerings
from all the ten directions,
This Buddha's brilliance
no one will be able to equal.
His Buddha title will be

Jambu Gold Light.
Bodhisattvas and voice-hearers,
cutting off all forms of existence,
countless and immeasurable in number,
will adorn his land.

At that time the World-Honored One spoke to the great assembly: "Now I say to you. Great Maudgalyayana here will present various kinds of articles as offerings to eight thousand Buddhas, paying honor and reverence to them. After these Buddhas have passed into extinction, for each of them he will raise a memorial tower measuring a thousand yojanas in height and exactly five hundred yojanas in width and depth. It will be made of gold, silver, lapis lazuli, seashell, agate, pearl, and carnelian, with these seven precious substances joined together. Numerous flowers, necklaces, paste incense, and powdered incense, incense for burning, silken canopies, streamers and banners will be presented as offerings. After this has been done, he will also make offerings to two hundred ten thousand million Buddhas, repeating the process.

"Then he will be able to become a Buddha with the title Tamalapatra Sandalwood Fragrance Thus Come One, worthy of offerings, of right and universal knowledge, perfect clarity and conduct, well gone, understanding the world, unexcelled worthy, trainer of people, teacher of heavenly and human beings, Buddha, World-Honored One. His kalpa will be named Joy Replete and his realm Mind Delight. The land will be level and smooth, the ground made of crystal, jeweled trees will adorn it, pearls and flowers will be scattered around, everywhere will be pure and clean, and all who see it will rejoice. There will be many heavenly and human beings, and the bodhisattvas and voice-hearers will be immeasurable in number. That Buddha's life span will be twenty-four small kalpas, his Correct Law will endure in the world for forty small kalpas, and his counterfeit Law for forty small kalpas."

At that time the World-Honored One, wishing to state his meaning once more, spoke in verse form, saying:

This disciple of mine,
the great Maudgalyayana,
when he has cast off his present body,
will be able to see eight thousand,
two hundred ten thousand million
Buddhas, World-Honored Ones,
and for the sake of the Buddha way
will offer alms, honor and reverence them.
Where these Buddhas are
he will constantly carry out Brahma practices
and for immeasurable kalpas
will uphold and embrace the Buddha law,
When these Buddhas have passed into extinction
be will raise seven-jeweled towers,
with golden implements to mark the spot for all time
and flowers, incense and music
presented as offerings
in the memorial towers of the Buddhas.
Step by step he will fulfill
all the duties of the bodhisattva way
and in the land called Mind Delight
will be able to become a Buddha
named Tamalapatra
Sandalwood Fragrance.
This Buddha's life span
will be twenty-four kalpas.
Constantly for the sake of heavenly and human beings
he will expound the Buddha way.
Voice-hearers innumerable

as Ganges sands,
with the three understandings and six transcendental powers,
will display great authority and virtue.
Countless bodhisattvas
will be of firm will, diligent in effort,
and with regard to the Buddha wisdom
non will ever retrogress.
After this Buddha has passed into extinction,
his Correct Law will endure
for forty small kalpas,
and his Counterfeit law will be likewise.
My various disciples,
fully endowed with dignity and virtue,
number five hundred,
and every one will receive such a prophecy.
In a future existence
all will be able to attain Buddhahood.
Concerning the causes and conditions of past existences
as they pertain to me and you
I will now preach.
You must listen carefully.

Chapter Seven: The Parable of the Phantom City

The Buddha made this announcement to the monks: Once in the distant past, an immeasurable, boundless, inconceivable asamkhya number of kalpas ago, there was at that time a Buddha named Great Universal Wisdom Excellence Thus Come One, worthy of offerings, of right and universal knowledge, perfect clarity and conduct, well gone, understanding the world, unexcelled worthy, trainer of people, teacher of heavenly and human beings, Buddha, World-Honored One. His land was named Well Constituted and his kalpa was named Great Form.

"Now monks, since that Buddha passed into extinction, a very great, a very long time had passed. Suppose, for example, that someone took all the earth particles in the thousand-million-fold world and ground the up to make ink powder, and as he passed through the thousand lands of the east, he dropped one grain of the ink powder no bigger in size than a speck of dust. Again., when he passed through another thousand lands, he dropped another grain of ink. Suppose he went on in this way until he had finished dropping all the grains of the ink made from the earth particles. Now what is your opinion? Do you think that, with regard to those lands, the masters of calculation or the disciples of calculation would be able to determine the number of lands that had been visited in the process, or would they not?"

"That would be impossible, World-Honored One."

"Now monks suppose that one should take the earth of all the lands this man had passed through, whether he dropped a grain of ink there or not, and should pound it into dust. And suppose that one particle of dust should represent one kalpa. The kalpas that had elapsed since that Buddha entered extinction would still exceed the number of dust particles by immeasurable, boundless, hundreds, thousands, ten thousands millions of asamkhya kalpas. But because I employ the Thus Come One's power to know and see, when I look at that far-off time it seems like today."

At that time the World-Honored One, wishing to state his meaning once more, spoke in verse form, saying:

When I think of it, in the past,
immeasurable, boundless kalpas ago,
there was a Buddha, most honored of two-legged beings,
named Great Universal Wisdom Excellence.
If a person should use his strength to smash
the ground of the thousand-million-fold world,
should completely crush its earth particles
and reduce them all to powdered ink,
and if when he passed through a thousand lands
he should drop one speck of ink,
and if he continued in this manner
until he had exhausted all the specks of ink,
and if one then took the soil of the lands he had passed through,
both those he dropped a speck in and those he did not,
and once more ground their earth into dust,
and then took one grain of dust to represent one kalpa-
the number of tiny grains of dust would be less
than the number of kalpas in the past when that Buddha lived.
Since that Buddha passed into extinction,
an immeasurable number of kalpas such as this have passed.
The Thus Come One, through his unhindered wisdom,
knows the time when that Buddha passed into extinction
and his voice-hearers and bodhisattvas
as though he were witnessing that extinction right now.
You monks should understand
that the Buddha wisdom is pure, subtle, wonderful,

without outflows, without hindrance,
reaching to and penetrating immeasurable kalpas.

The Buddha announced to the monks: "The Buddha Great Universal Wisdom Excellent had a life span of five hundred and forty ten thousand million nayutas of kalpas. This Buddha at first sat in the place of practice and, having smashed the armies of the devil, was on the point of attaining anuttara-samyak-sambodhi, but the doctrines of the Buddhas did not appear before him. This state continued for one small kalpa, and so on for ten small kalpas, the Buddha sitting with legs crossed, body and mind unmoving, but the doctrines of the Buddhas still did not appear before him.

"At that time the heavenly beings of the Trayastrimsha heaven had earlier spread a lion seat measuring one yojana in height underneath a bodhi tree for the Buddha, intending that the Buddha should sit on this when he attained anuttara-samyak-sambodhi. As soon as the Buddha took his seat there, the Brahma kings caused a multitude of heavenly flowers to rain down, covering the ground for a hundred yojanas around. From time to time a fragrant wind would come up and blow the withered flowers away, whereupon new ones would rain down. This continued without interruption for the space of ten small kalpas as an offering to the Buddha. Up until the time he entered extinction, such flowers constantly rained down. The four Heavenly Kings as their offering to the Buddha constantly beat on heavenly drums, while the other heavenly beings played heavenly musical instruments, all for ten small kalpas. Until the Buddha entered extinction, such was the state of affairs.

"Now, monks, the Buddha Great Universal Wisdom Excellence passed ten small kalpas before him and he was able to attain anuttara-samyak-sambodhi. Before the Buddha left the householder's life, he had sixteen sons, the first of whom was named Wisdom Accumulated. These sons, each had various kinds of rare objects and toys of one kind or another, but when they heard that their father had attained anuttara-samyak-sambodhi, they all threw aside their rare objects and went to where the Buddha was. Their mothers, weeping, followed after them.

"Their grandfather, who was a wheel-turning sage king, along with a hundred chief ministers, as well as hundred, thousand, ten thousand, million of his subjects, all together surrounded the sons and followed to the place of practice, all wishing to draw close to the Great Universal Wisdom Excellence Thus Come One, to offer alms, pay honor, venerate and praise him. When they arrived. They touched their heads to the ground and bowed before his feet. When they had finished circling the Buddha, they pressed their palms together with a single mind, gazed up in reverence at the World-Honored One, and recited these verses of praise, saying:

The World-Honored One, of great authority and virtue,
in order to save living beings
spent immeasurable millions of years
and at last succeeded in becoming a Buddha,
all your vows have now been fulfilled-
it is well--no fortune could be greater!
The World-Honored One is vary rarely met with;
having taken his seat, ten small kalpas pass,
his body and his hands and feet
rest in stillness, never moving,
his mind constantly calm and placid,
never in turmoil or disorder.
In the end he attains eternal tranquility and extinction,
resting in the Law of no outflows.
Now as we observe the World-Honored One
in tranquility, having completed the Buddha way,
we gain excellent benefits
and praise and congratulate him with great joy.
Living beings undergo constant suffering and anguish,
benighted, without teacher or guide,

not realizing there is a way to end suffering,
not knowing how to seek emancipation.
Through the long night increasingly they follow evil paths,
reducing the multitude of heavenly beings;
from darkness they enter into darkness,
to the end never hearing the Buddha's name.
But now the Buddha has attained the unexcelled,
the tranquility of the Law of no outflows.
We and the heavenly and human beings
hereby obtain the greatest benefit.
For this reason all of us bow our heads,
dedicate our lives to the one of unexcelled honor.

At that time the sixteen princes, having praised the Buddha in these verses, urged the World-Honored One to turn the wheel of the Law, speaking all together in these words: "World-Honored One, expound the law. By doing so, you will bring tranquility to and will comfort and benefit heavenly and human beings in large measure." They repeated this request in verse form, saying:

World hero without peer,
you who adorn yourself with a hundred blessings,
you have attained unsurpassed wisdom--
we beg you to preach for the sake of the world.
Save and free us
and other kinds of living beings.
Draw distinctions, enlighten us
and allow us to attain wisdom.
If we can gain Buddhahood,
then all living beings can do likewise.
World-Honored One, you know the thoughts
that living beings hold deep in their minds.
You know the paths they tread

and you know the strength of their wisdom,
their pleasures, the blessings they have cultivated,
the actions they have carried out in past existences,
World-Honored One, all this you know already-
now you must turn the unsurpassed wheel!

The Buddha announced to the monks: "When the Buddha Great Universal Wisdom Excellence attained anuttara-samyak-sambodhi, five hundred ten thousand million Buddha worlds in each of the ten directions trembled and shook in six different ways. The dark and secluded places within those lands, where the light of the sun and moon is never able to penetrate, were able to see one another, and they all exclaimed, saying, 'How is it that living beings have suddenly come into existence in this place?'

"Also the palaces of the various heavenly beings in those lands and the Brahma palaces trembled and shook in six different ways and a great light shone everywhere, completely filling the worlds and surpassing the light of the heavens. At that time in five hundred ten thousand million lands in the eastern direction the Brahma palaces shone with the brilliant light that was twice its ordinary brightness, and the Brahma kings each thought to himself. Now the brilliance of the palace is greater than ever in the past. What can be the cause of this phenomenon?

"At that time the Brahma kings visited one another to discuss this matter. Among them was a great Brahma king named Save All who, on behalf of the multitude of Brahma kings, spoke these verses, saying:

Our palaces have a brilliance
never known in the past.
What is the cause of this?
Each of us seeks an answer.
Is it because of the birth of some heavenly being of great virtue,
or because the Buddha has appeared in this world
that this great light
shines everywhere in the ten directions?

"At that time the Brahma kings of five hundred ten thousand million lands, accompanied by their palaces, each king taking his outer robe and filling it with heavenly flowers, journeyed together to the western region to observe the signs there. They saw the Great Universal Wisdom Excellence Thus Come One in the place of practice, seated on a lion seat underneath a bodhi tree, with heavenly beings, dragon kings, gandharvas, kimnaras, mahoragas, human, and nonhuman beings surrounding him and paying reverence. And they saw the sixteen princes entreating the Buddha to turn the wheel of the Law.

"At once the Brahma kings touched their heads to the ground and bowed before the Buddha, circled around him a hundred thousand times, and took the heavenly flowers and scattered them over the Buddha. The flowers they scattered piled up like Mount Sumeru. They also offered them as alms to the Buddha's bodhi tree. This bodhi tree was ten yojanas in height. When they had finished offering the flowers, each one took his place and presented it to the Buddha, speaking these words: 'We hope you will bestow comfort and benefit on us. We beg you to accept and occupy these palaces that we present.'

"At that time the Brahma kings, in the presence of the Buddha, with a single mind and joined voices recited these verses of praise:

World-Honored One, vary rarely met with,
one whom it is difficult to encounter,
endowed with immeasurable blessings,
capable of saving everyone,
great teacher of heavenly and human beings,
you bestow pity and comfort on the world.
Living beings in the ten directions
all receive benefit everywhere.
In the five hundred ten thousand million lands
from which we come,
we have put aside the joy of deep meditation
in order to offer alms to the Buddha,
Because of our good fortune in previous existences
our palaces are very richly adorned.
Now we present them to the World-Honored One,
begging that he be kind enough to accept them.

"At that time, when the Brahma kings had finished praising the Buddha in verse, they each spoke these words: 'We beg the World-Honored One to turn the wheel of the Law, save living beings, and open up the way to nirvana!'

"Then the Brahma kings with a single mind and joined voices spoke in verse form, saying:

World hero, most honored of two-legged beings,
we beg you to expound the Law,
Through the power of your great mercy and compassion,
save living beings in their suffering and anguish!

"At that time the Great Universal Wisdom Excellence Thus Come One silently agreed to do so. Now, monks, in five hundred ten thousand million lands in the southeast, the Brahma kings each observed that his palace was shining with a brilliant light such as had never been known in the past. Dancing for joy, entering a frame of mind seldom experienced, they went about visiting one another and discussing these things together.

"At that time there was among the assembly a great Brahma king named Great Compassion who on behalf of the multitude of Brahma kings, spoke in verse form, saying:

What cause is in operation
that such a sign should be manifest?
Our palaces display a brilliance
never known before.
Is it because of the birth of some heavenly being of great virtue,
or because the Buddha has appeared in the world?
We have never seen such a sign
and with a single mind we seek the reason.
Though we must travel a thousand, ten thousand a million lands,
together we will search out the cause of this light.
Likely it is because a Buddha has appeared in the world
to save living beings in their suffering.

"At that time the five hundred ten thousand million Brahma kings, accompanied by their palaces, each king taking his outer robe and filling it with heavenly flowers, journeyed together to the northwestern region to observe the signs there. They saw the Great Universal Wisdom Excellence Thus Come One in the place of practice, seated on a lion seat beneath a bodhi tree, with heavenly beings, dragon kings, gandharvas, kimnaras, mahoragas, human and nonhuman beings surrounding him and paying reverence. And they saw the sixteen princes entreating the Buddha to turn the wheel of the Law.

"At once the Brahma kings touched their heads to the ground and bowed before the Buddha, circled him a hundred thousand times, and then took the heavenly flowers and scattered them over the Buddha. The flowers they scattered piled up like Mount Sumeru. They also offered them as alms to the Buddha's bodhi tree. When they had finished offering the flowers, each one took his palace and presented it to the Buddha, speaking these words: 'We hope you will bestow comfort and benefit on us. We beg you to accept and occupy these palaces that we present.'

"At that time the Brahma kings, in the presence of the Buddha, with a single mind and joined voices recited these verses of praise:

Sage lord, heavenly being among heavenly beings,
voiced like the kalavinka bird,
you who pity and comfort living beings,
we now pay honor and reverence.
The World-Honored One is vary rarely met with,
appearing only once in many long ages.
One hundred and eighty kalpas
have passed in vain without a Buddha,
when the three evil paths were everywhere
and the multitude of heavenly beings was reduced in number.
Now the Buddha has appeared in the world
to be an eye for living beings.
The world will hurry to him
and he will save and guard one and all.
He will be a father to living beings,
comforting and benefiting them.

We through the good fortune of past existences,
now we are able to encounter the World-Honored One!

"At that time, after the Brahma kings had recited these verses in praise of the Buddha, they each spoke these words: "We beg the World-Honored One to pity and comfort one and all, to turn the wheel of the Law and cause the heavenly beings

"Then the Brahma kings with a single mind and joined voices spoke in verse form, saying:

Great sage, turn the wheel of the Law,
reveal the characteristics of teachings,
save living beings in their suffering and anguish,
allow them to attain great joy.
When living beings hear this Law
they will gain the way or be reborn in heaven;
those in the evil paths will be reduced in number
and those patient in goodness will increase.

"At that time the Great Universal Wisdom Excellence Thus Come One silently agreed to do so. Now, monks, in five hundred ten thousand million lands in the southern region the Brahma kings each observed that his palace was shining with a brilliant light such as had never been in the past. Dancing with joy, entering a frame of mind seldom experienced, they went about visiting with one another and discussing these things together, saying, 'What is the reason our palaces put forth this brilliant light?'

"Among their group there was a great Brahma king named Wonderful Law who, on behalf of the multitude of Brahma kings, spoke in verse form, saying:

Our palaces
shine with exceeding brilliance.
This cannot be without reason-
it is well we should inquire.
In the past hundred thousand kalpas
such a sign has never been seen.

It is because some heavenly being of great virtue has been born,
or because the Buddha has appeared in the world.

"At that time the five hundred ten thousand million Brahma kings, accompanied by their palaces, each king taking his outer robe and filling it with heavenly flowers, journeyed together to the northern region to observe the signs there. They saw the Great Universal Wisdom Excellence Thus Come One in the place of practice, seated on a lion seat beneath a bodhi tree, with heavenly and human beings, dragon kings, gandharvas, kimnaras, mahoragas, human and nonhuman beings surrounding him and paying reverence. And they saw the sixteen princes entreating the Buddha to turn the wheel of the Law.

"At that time the Brahma kings touched their heads to the ground and bowed before the Buddha, circled around him a hundred thousand times, and then took the heavenly flowers and scattered them over the Buddha. The flowers they scattered piled up like Mount Sumeru. They also offered them as alms to the Buddha's bodhi tree. When they had finished offering the flowers, each one took his palace and presented it to the Buddha, speaking these words: 'We hope you will bestow comfort and benefit on us. We beg you to accept and occupy these palaces that we present.'

"At that time the Brahma kings, in the presence of the Buddha, with a single mind and joined voices recited these verses of praise:

World-Honored One, most difficult to encounter,
destroyer of all earthly desires,
one hundred and thirty kalpas have pass
and now at last we can see you.
Living beings in their hunger and thirst

are made full with the rain of the Dharma.
One such as was never seen in the past,
one of immeasurable wisdom,
like the udumbara flower
today at last appears directly before us.
Our palaces because they receive your light
are wonderfully adorned.

World-Honored One, of great mercy and compassion,
we beg you to accept them.

"At that time, after the Brahma kings had recited these verses in praise of the Buddha, they each spoke these words: 'We beg the World-Honored One to turn the wheel of the Law and cause the heavenly beings, devils, Brahma kings, shramanas, and Brahmans throughout the world all to gain peace and tranquility and to attain salvation.'

At that time the Brahma kings with a single mind and joined voices recited in praise, saying;

We beg the most honored of heavenly and human beings
to turn the wheel of the unsurpassed Law.
Strike the great Dharma drum,
blow the great Dharma conch,
rain down the great Dharma rain all around
to save immeasurable living beings!
We direct all our faith and entreaties to you-
let your profound and far-reaching voice sound out!

"At that time the Great Universal Wisdom Excellence Thus Come One silently agreed to do so. In the southwestern region, and so an to the lower region, a similar succession of events occurred.

"At that time in the upper region, the Brahma Kings of five hundred ten thousand million lands all observed that the palaces where they were residing shone with a brilliant light such as had never been known in the past. Dancing with joy, entering a frame of mind seldom experienced, they went about visiting one another and discussing these things together, saying, 'What is the reason our palaces puts forth this bright light?'

"Among their group there was a Brahma king named Wonderful Law who, on behalf of the multitude of Brahma kings, spoke in verse form, saying:

Now what is the reason
that our places
glow and shine with such authority and virtue,
adorned as never before?
A wonderful sign of this kind
has never been seen or heard of in the past.
It is because some heavenly being of great virtue has been born,
or because the Buddha has appeared in the world.

"At that time the five hundred ten thousand million Brahma kings, accompanied by their palaces, each king taking his outer robe and filling it with heavenly flowers, journeyed together to the lower region to observe the signs there. They saw the Great Universal wisdom Excellence Thus Come One in the place of practice, seated on a lion seat beneath a bodhi tree, with heavenly beings, dragon kings, gandharvas, kimnaras, mahoragas, human and nonhuman beings surrounding him and paying reverence. And they saw the sixteen princes entreating the Buddha to turn the wheel of the Law.

"At that time the Brahma kings touched their heads to the ground and bowed before the Buddha, circled around him a hundred thousand times, and then took the heavenly flowers and scattered them over the

Buddha. The flowers they scattered piled up like Mount Sumeru. They also offered them as alms to the Buddha's bodhi tree. When they had finished offering the flowers, each one took his place and presented it to the Buddha, speaking these words: 'We hope you will bestow comfort and benefit on us. We beg you to accept and occupy these palaces that we present.'

"At that time the Brahma kings, in the presence of the Buddha, with a single mind and joined voices recited these verses of praise:

How fine, that we may see the Buddhas,
sage and venerable ones who save the world,
capable of rescuing and releasing living beings
from the hell of the threefold world!
Venerable among heavenly and human beings, of universal wisdom,
you pity and have mercy on the mass of burgeoning creatures,
you are capable of opening the gates of sweet dew
and broadly saving one and all.
Formerly, immeasurable kalpas
passed in vain when no Buddha was present.

The time had not yet come for the World-Honored One
to appear,
and all in the ten directions were in constant darkness.
Those in the three evil paths increased in number
and the realm of the asuras flourished;
the multitude of heavenly beings was reduced,
and many when they died fell into the evil paths.
Since no one could attend the Buddha and hear the Law,
constantly people followed ways that were not good
and their physical strength and wisdom
all diminished and declined.
Because of the sinful deeds they had done,
they lost all delight or the thought of delight.
They rested in heretical doctrines
and had no knowledge of good customs or rules.
Unable to be converted by the Buddha,
constantly they fell into the evil paths.
But now you, the Buddha, who will be the eye of the world,
after this long time have at last come forth.
In order to bring pity and comfort to living beings
you have appeared it the world.
You have transcended the world to gain correct enlightenment;
we are filled with delight and admiration.
We and all others in the assembly
rejoice, delighting in what we have never known before.
Our palaces because they receive your light
are wonderfully adorned.
Now we present them to the World-Honored One,
hoping he will have pity and accept them.
We beg that the merit gained through these gifts
may be spread far and wide to everyone,
so that we and other living beings
all together may attain the Buddha way.

"At that time, after the five hundred ten thousand million Brahma kings had recited these verses in praise of the Buddha, they each spoke to the Buddha, saying: 'We beg the World-Honored One to turn the wheel of the Law, bringing peace and tranquility to many, bringing salvation to many.' Then the Brahma kings spoke in verse form, saying:

World-Honored One, turn the wheel of the Law,
strike the Dharma drum of sweet dew,
save living beings in their suffering and anguish,
open up and show us the way to nirvana!
We beg you to accept our entreaties
and with a great, subtle and wonderful sound
to bring pity and comfort by expounding
the Law you have practiced for immeasurable kalpas.

At that time the Great Universal Wisdom Excellence Thus Come One, receiving entreaties from the Brahma kings of the ten directions and from the sixteen princes, immediately gave three turnings to the twelve-spoked wheel of the Law. Neither shramana, Brahman, heavenly being, devil, Brahma, nor any other being in the world was capable of such a turning. He said, 'Here is suffering, here is the origin of suffering, here is the annihilation of suffering, here is the path on the annihilation of suffering.'

"Then he broadly expounded the Law of the twelve-linked chain of causation: ignorance causes action, action causes consciousness, consciousness causes name and form, name and form cause the six sense organs, the six sense organs cause contact, contact causes sensation, sensation causes desire, desire causes attachment, attachment causes existence, existence causes birth, birth causes old age and death, worry and grief, suffering and anguish. If ignorance is wiped out, then action will be wiped out. If action is wiped out, then consciousness will be wiped out. If consciousness is wiped out, then name and form will be wiped out. If name and form are wiped out, then the six sense organs will be wiped out, then contact will be wiped out. If contact is wiped out, then sensation will be wiped out. If sensation is wiped out, then desire will be wiped out. If desire is wiped out, then birth will be wiped out. If birth is wiped out, then old age and death will be wiped out. If birth is wiped out, then old age and death, worry and grief, suffering and anguish will be wiped out.

"When the Buddha in the midst of the great assembly of heavenly and human beings expounded this Law, six hundred ten thousand million nayutas of persons, because they ceased to accept any of the things of the phenomenal world and because their minds were able to attain liberation from the outflows, all achieved profound and wonderful meditation practice, acquired the three understandings and the six transcendental powers, and were endowed with the eight emancipations. And when he expounded the second, third and fourth Laws, living beings equal the a thousand ten thousand millions of Ganges sands of nayutas, because they likewise ceased to accept any of the things of the phenomenal world, were able to liberate their minds from the outflows. From that time on, the multitude of voice-hearers became immeasurable, boundless, incapable of being counted.

"At that time the sixteen princes all left their families while still young boys and became shramaneras. Their faculties were penetrating and sharp, their wisdom was bright and comprehending. Already in the past they had offered alms to a hundred thousand ten thousand million Buddhas, had carried out Brahma practices in a flawless manner, and had striven to attain anuttara-samyak-sambodhi. All together they addressed the Buddha, saying: World-Honored One, these innumerable thousands, ten thousands, millions of voice-hearers of great virtue have all ready achieved success. World-Honored One, now it is fitting that you should preach the Law of anuttara-samyak-sambodhi for our sake is that, once we have heard it, we all may join in practicing and studying it. World-Honored One, we are determined to attain the insight of the Thus Come One. Deep in our minds we have this in thought, as the Buddha himself must know.'

"At that time the Buddha, responding to pleas from the shramaneras, passed a period of twenty thousand kalpas and then at last, in the midst of the four kinds of believers, preached the Great Vehicle sutra entitled the Lotus of the Wonderful Law, a Law to instruct the bodhisattvas, one that is guarded and kept in mind by the Buddhas. After he had preached the sutra, the sixteen shramaneras, for the sake of anuttara-samyak-sambodhi, all together accepted and embraced it, recited and intoned it, penetrated and understood it.

"When the Buddha preached this sutra, the sixteen bodhisattva shramaneras all took faith in it and accepted it, and among the multitude of voice-hearers there were also those who believed in it and understood it. But the other thousand ten thousand million types of living beings all gave way to doubt and perplexity.

"The Buddha preached this sutra for a period of eight thousand kalpas, never once stopping to rest. After he had preached this sutra, he entered a quiet room and dwelled in meditation for a period of eighty-four thousand kalpas.

"At this time the sixteen bodhisattva shramaneras, knowing that ascended a Dharma seat and likewise for a period of eighty-four thousand kalpas for the sake of the four kinds of believers broadly preached the distinctions put forth in the Lotus Sutra of the Wonderful Law. In this way each of them one by one saved living beings equal in number to six hundred ten thousand million nayutas of Ganges sands, instructing them, bringing them benefit and joy, and causing them to set their minds upon anuttara-samyak-sambodhi.

"The Great Universal Wisdom Excellence Buddha, after passing eighty-four thousand kalpas, arose from his samadhi and approached the Dharma seat. Seating himself calmly, he addressed the whole of the great assembly, saying: these sixteen bodhisattva shramaneras are of a kind very rarely to be found, their faculties penetrating and sharp, their wisdom bright and company of those Buddhas they have constantly carried Brahma practices, received and embraced the Buddha wisdom, and expounded it to living beings, causing them to enter therein. Now all of you should from time to time associate closely with them and offer them alms. Why? Because if any of you, voice-hearers or pratyekabuddhas or bodhisattvas, are able to take faith in the sutra teachings preached by these sixteen bodhisattvas, and will accept and embrace them and never disparage them, then such persons will all be able to attain anuttara-samyak-sambodhi, the wisdom of the Thus Come One.'"

The Buddha, addressing the monks, said: "These sixteen bodhisattvas have constantly desired to expound this Sutra of the Lotus of the Wonderful Law. The living beings converted by each one of these bodhisattvas are equal in number to six hundred ten thousand million nayutas of Ganges sands. Existence after existence these living beings are reborn in company with that Bodhisattva, hear the Law from him, and all have faith in and understand it. For this reason they have been able to encounter forty thousand million Buddhas, World-Honored Ones, and have never ceased to do so down to the present.

"You monks, I will now tell you this. These disciples of the Buddha, these sixteen shramaneras, have now all attained anuttara-samyak-sambodhi. In the lands in the ten directions they are at present preaching the Law, with immeasurable hundreds, thousands, ten thousands, millions of bodhisattvas and voice-hearers for their retinue. Two of these shramaneras have become Buddhas in the eastern region. One is named Akshobhya and lives in the Land of Joy. The other is named Sumeru Peak. Two are Buddhas in the southeastern region, one named Lion Voice, the other named Lion Appearance. Two are Buddhas in the southern region, one named Void-Dwelling, the other named Ever Extinguished. Two are Buddhas in the south-western region, one named Emperor Appearance, the other named Brahma Appearance. Two are Buddhas in the western region, one named Amitayus, the other named Saving All from Worldly Suffering. Two are Buddhas in the northwestern region, one named Tamalapatra Sandalwood Fragrance Transcendental Power, the other named Sumeru Appearance. Two are Buddhas in the northern region, one named Cloud Freedom, the other named Cloud Freedom King. Of the Buddhas of the northeastern region, one is named Destroying all Worldly Fears, The sixteenth is I, Shakyamuni Buddha, who in this saha land gave attained anuttara-samyak-sambodhi.

"Monks, when I and these others were shramaneras, each one of us taught and converted living beings equal in number in immeasurable hundreds, thousands, ten thousands, millions of Ganges sands. They heard the Law from us and attained anuttara-samyak-sambodhi. Some of these living beings are now dwelling in the ranks of voice-hearers. But we have constantly instructed them in anuttara-samyak-sambodhi, and these persons should be able, through this Law, to enter into the Buddha Way, albeit gradually. Why do I say this? Because the wisdom of the Thus Come One is difficult to believe and difficult to understand. Those living beings equal in number to immeasurable Ganges sands who converted at that time are you who are now monks, and those who, after I have entered extinction, in ages to come will be voice-hearer disciples.

"After I have entered extinction, there will be other disciples who will not hear this sutra and will not understand or be aware of the practices carried out by the Bodhisattvas, but who, through the blessings they have been able to attain, will conceive an idea of extinction and enter into what they believe to be nirvana. At that time I will be a Buddha in another land and will be known by a different name. Those disciples, though they have conceived an idea of extinction and entered into what they take to be nirvana, will in that other land seek the Buddha wisdom and will be able to hear this sutra. For it is only through the Buddha vehicle that one can attain extinction. There is no other vehicle, if one excepts the various doctrines that the Thus Come Ones preach as an expedient means.

"Monks, if a Thus Come One knows that the time has come to enter nirvana, and knows that the members of the assembly are pure and clean, firm in faith and understanding, thorough in their comprehension of the Law of emptiness and deeply entered into meditation practice, then he will call together the assembly of bodhisattvas and voice-hearers and will preach this sutra for them. In the world there are not two vehicles whereby one may attain extinction. There is only the one Buddha vehicle for attaining extinction and one alone.

"Monks, you must understand this. The Thus Come One in his use of expedient means penetrates deeply into the nature of living beings. He knows how their minds delight in petty doctrines and how deeply they are attached to the five desires. And because they are like this, when he expounds nirvana, he does so in such a way that these persons, hearing it, can readily believe and accept it.

"Let us suppose there is a stretch of bad road five hundred yojanas long, steep and difficult, wild and deserted, with no inhabitants around, a truly fearful place. And suppose there are a number of people who want to pass over this road so they can reach a place where there are rare treasures. They have a leader, of comprehensive wisdom and keen understanding, who is thoroughly acquainted with this steep road, knows the layout of its passes and defiles, and is prepared to guide the group of people and go with them over this difficult terrain. The group he is leading, after going part way on the road, become disheartened and say to the leader, "We are utterly exhausted and fearful as well. We cannot go any farther. Since there is still such a long distance ahead, we would like now to turn around and go back.'

"The leader, a man of many expedients, thinks to himself, What a pity that they should abandon the many rare treasures they are seeking and want to turn and go back! Having had this thought, he resorts to the power of expedient means and, when they have gone three hundred yojanas along the steep road, conjures up a city. He says to the group, 'Don't be afraid! You must not turn back, for now here is a great city where you can stop, rest, and do just as you please. If you enter this city you will be completely at ease and tranquil. Then later, if you feel you can go on to the place where the treasure is, you can leave the city.'

"At that time the members of the group, being utterly exhausted, are overjoyed in mind, exclaiming over such an unprecedented event, 'Now we can escape from this dreadful road and find ease and tranquility!' The people in the group thereupon press forward and enter the city where, feeling that they have been saved from their difficulties, they have a sense of complete ease and tranquility.

"At that time the leader, knowing that the people have become rested and are no longer fearful or weary, wipes out the phantom city and says to the group, 'You must go now. The place where the treasure is, is close by. That great city of a while ago was a mere phantom that I conjured up so that you could rest.'

"Monks, the Thus Come One is in a similar position. He is now acting as a great leader for you. He knows that the bad road of birth and death and earthly desires is steep, difficult, long and far-stretching, but that it must be traveled, it must be passed over. If living beings hear only of the one Buddha vehicle, then they will not want to see the Buddha, will now want to draw near him, but will immediately think to themselves, The Buddha road is long and far reaching and one must labor diligently and undergo difficulties over a long period before he can ever attain success!

"The Buddha knows that the minds of the living beings are timid, weak and lowly, and so, using the power of expedient means, he preaches two nirvanas in order to provide a resting place along the road. If living beings choose to remain in these two stages, then the Thus Come One will say to them, 'You have not yet understood that is to be done. This stage where you have chosen to remain is close to the Buddha wisdom. But you should observe and ponder further. This nirvana that you have attained is not the true one. It is simply that the Thus Come One, using the power of expedient means, has taken the one Buddha vehicle and, making distinctions, has preached it as three.'

"The Buddha is like that leader who, in order to provide a place to rest, conjured up a great city and then, when he knew that the travelers were already rested, said to them, 'The place where the treasure is, is nearby. This city is not real. It is merely something I conjured up.'"

At that time the World-Honored One, wishing to state his meaning once more, spoke in verse form, saying:

The Great Universal Wisdom Excellence Buddha
sat in the place of practice for ten kalpas,
but the Law of the Buddha did not appear before him
and he could not attain the Buddha way.
The assembly of heavenly gods, dragon kings,
asuras and others
constantly rained down heavenly flowers
as alms offered to that Buddha.
The heavenly beings beat on heavenly drums
and made many kinds of music.
A fragrant wind blew away the withered flowers,
whereupon fresh and beautiful ones rained down.
When ten small kalpas had passed,
then at last he was able to attain the Buddha way.
The heavenly beings and people of the world
in their hearts all felt like dancing.
That Buddha's sixteen sons
all, in company with their followers,
a thousand ten thousand million of them gathered around,
all came to the place of the Buddha,
touching heads to the ground, bowing at the Buddha's feet
and entreating him to turn the wheel of the Law, saying,
"Saintly Lion, let the Dharma rain
fall in full upon us and all others!"
The World-Honored One is very difficult to encounter;
only once in a long time does he appear.
In order to bring enlightenment to the many beings
he shakes and moves the regions all around.
In the worlds in the eastern direction
in five hundred ten thousand million lands
the palaces of the Brahma kings glowed with a light
they had never known in the past.
When the Brahma kings saw this sign
they came in search of the Buddha's place
scattering flowers as a form of offering,
at the same time presenting their palaces,
entreating the Buddha to turn the wheel of the Law
and praising him in verses.
The Buddha knew that the time had not yet come,
and though they entreated, he sat in silence.
In the other three directions and the four directions in between
and in the upper and lower regions, the same occurred,
the Brahma kings scattering flowers, presenting their palaces,
entreating the Buddha to turn the wheel of the Law, saying,
"The World-Honored One is very difficult to encounter.

We beg you in your great mercy and compassion
to open wide the gates of sweet dew
and turn the wheel of the unsurpassed Law."
The World-Honored One, immeasurable in wisdom,
accepted the entreaties of the assembly
and for their sake proclaimed various doctrines,
the four noble truths, the twelve-linked chain of causation,
describing how, from ignorance to old age and death,
all are produced through the cause of birth, saying,
"With regard to these many faults and vexations,
you should understand this about them."
When he expounded this Law,
six hundred ten thousand million trillion beings
were able to exhaust the limits of sufferings,
all attaining the status of arhat.
The second time he preached the Law
a multitude like a thousand Ganges sands
ceased to accept the things of the phenomenal world
and they too were able to become arhats.
Thereafter those who attained the way
were immeasurable in number-
one might calculate for ten thousand million kalpas
and never be able to reckon their extent.
At that time the sixteen princes
left their families and became shramaneras.
All together they entreated that Buddha
to expound the Law of the Great Vehicle, saying,
"We and our attendants
are all certain to attain the Buddha way.
We desire the wisdom eye of foremost purity
such as the World-Honored One possesses."
The Buddha understood their boyish minds
and the actions they had carried out in past existences,
and employing immeasurable causes and conditions
and various similes and parables,
he preached the six paramitas
and matters concerning transcendental powers,
distinguishing the true Law,
the way practiced by bodhisattvas,
preaching this Lotus Sutra
in verses as numerous as the Ganges sands.
When the Buddha had finished preaching the sutra
he entered into meditation in a quiet room,
with a single mind sitting in a single place
for eighty-four thousand kalpas.
The shramaneras knew
the Buddha would not yet emerge from meditation
and so for the assembly of immeasurable millions
they preached the unsurpassed wisdom of the Buddha,
each one sitting in a Dharma seat,
preaching this Great Vehicle sutra.
And after the Buddha had entered peaceful tranquility,
they continued to proclaim, helping to convert others to
the Law.
The living beings saved
by each one of those shramaneras

were equal in number
to six hundred ten thousand million Ganges sands.
After that Buddha had passed into extinction,
those persons who had heard the Law
dwelled here and there in various Buddha lands,
constantly reborn in company with their teachers.
And these sixteen shramaneras,
having fully carried out the Buddha way,
at present are dwelling in the ten directions,
where each has attained correct enlightenment.
The persons who heard the Law at that time
are each in a place where there is one of these Buddhas,
and those who remain at the stage of voice-hearer
are gradually being instructed in the Buddha way.
I myself was numbered among the sixteen
and in the past preached for you.
For this reason I will employ an expedient means
to lead you in the pursuit of Buddha wisdom;
because of these earlier causes and conditions
I now preach the Lotus Sutra.
I will cause you to enter the Buddha way-
be atteÃive and harbor no fear!
Suppose there was a stretch of steep bad road,
in a remote wasteland with many harmful beasts,
a place moreover without water or grass,
one dreaded by people.
A group of countless thousands and ten thousands
wanted to pass over this steep road,
but the road was very long and far-stretching,
extended five hundred yojanas.
At this time there was a leader,
well informed, possessing wisdom,
of clear understanding and determined mind,
capable of saving endangered persons from manifold difficulties.
The members of the group were all weary and disheartened
and said to their leader,
"We are now exhausted with fatigue
and wish at this point to turn around and go back."

The leader thought to himself,
These people are truly pitiful!
Why do the wish to turn back
and miss the many rare treasures ahead?
At that time he thought of an expedient means,
deciding to exercise his transcendental powers.
He conjured up a great walled city
and adorned its mansions,
surrounding them with gardens and groves,
channels of flowing water, ponds and lakes,
with double gates and tall towers and pavilions,
all filled with men and women.
As soon as he had created this illusion,
he comforted the group, saying, "Have no fear-
you can enter this city
and each amuse himself as he pleases."
When the people had entered the city,

they were all overjoyed in heart.
All had a feeling of ease and tranquility,
telling themselves that they had been saved.
When the leader knew they were rested,
he called them together and announced,
"Now you must push forward--
this is nothing more than a phantom city.
I saw that you were weary and exhausted
and wanted to turn back in mid-journey.
Therefore I used the power of expedient means
to conjure up this city for the moment.
Now you must press forward diligently
so that together you may reach the place where the treasure is."
I too do likewise,
acting as a leader to all beings.
I see the seekers of the way
growing disheartened in mid-journey,
unable to pass over the steep road
of birth and death and earthly desires,
and therefore I see the power of expedient means
and preach nirvana to provide them with rest,
saying, "Your sufferings are extinguished,
you have carried out all there is to be done."
When I know they have reached nirvana
and all have attained the stage of arhat,
thin I can call the great assembly together
and preach the true Law for them.
The Buddhas through the power of expedient means
make distinctions and preach three vehicles,
but there is only the single Buddha vehicle--
the other two nirvanas are preached to provide a resting place.
Now I expound the truth for you-
what you have attained is not extinction.
For the sake of the comprehensive wisdom of the Buddha
you must expend great effort and diligence.
If you gain enlightenment in the Law of the Buddha
with its comprehensive wisdom and ten powers
and are endowed with the thirty-two features,
then this will be true extinction.
The Buddhas in their capacity as leaders
preach nirvana to provide a rest.
But when they know you have become rested,
they lead you onward to the Buddha wisdom.

Chapter Eight: Prophecy of Enlightenment
for Five Hundred Disciples

At that time Purna Maitrayaniputra, hearing from the Buddha this Law as it was expounded through wisdom and expedient means and in accordance with what was appropriate, and also hearing the prophecy that the major disciples would attain anuttara-samyak-sambodhi, hearing matters relating to causes and conditions of previous existences, and hearing how the Buddha possesses great freedom and transcendental powers, obtained what he had never before, and his mind was purified and felt like dancing. Immediately he rose from his seat, advanced to a position in front of the Buddha, touched his head to the ground and bowed to the Buddha's feet. Then he withdrew to one side, gazed up in reverence at the face of the Honored One, his eyes never leaving it for an instant, and thought to himself: the World-Honored One is very extraordinary, very special, his actions rarely to be encountered! Adapting himself to the various natures of the people of this world and employing expedient means and insight, he preaches the Law for them, drawing living beings away from their greed and attachment to this or that. The Buddha's blessings are such that we cannot set them forth in words. Only the Buddha, the World-Honored One, is capable of knowing the wish that we have had deep in our hearts from the start.

At that time the Buddha said to the monks: "Do you see this Purna Maitrayaniputra? I have always commended him as being foremost among those who preach the Law. And I have always praised his various blessings, his diligence in protecting, upholding, aiding and proclaiming my Law, his ability in teaching, benefiting and delighting the four kinds of believers, the thoroughness with which he understands the correct Law of the Buddha, the great degree to which he enriches those who carry out its Brahma practices. If one excepts the Thus Come One, there is no other who can so thoroughly exemplify the eloquence of its theories.

"You should not suppose that Purna is capable of protecting, upholding, aiding and proclaiming my Law only. In the presence of ninety million Buddhas of the past too he protected, upheld, aided and proclaimed the correct Law of the Buddhas. Among all those who at that time preached the Law, he was likewise foremost.

"In addition, concerning the Law of emptiness preached by the Buddhas he has clear and thorough understanding, he has gained the four unlimited kinds of knowledge, and is at all times capable of preaching the Law in a lucid and pure manner, free of doubts and perplexities. He is fully endowed with the transcendental powers of a bodhisattva. Throughout his allotted life span he constantly carries out Brahma practices, so that the other people living in the era of that particular Buddha all think, 'Here is a true voice-hearer!'

"And Purna by employing this expedient means has brought benefit to immeasurable hundreds and thousands of living beings, and has converted immeasurable asamkhayas of persons, causing them to turn toward anuttara-samyak-sambodhi. In order to purify the Buddha lands he constantly devotes himself to the Buddha's work, teaching and converting living beings.

"Monks, Purna was foremost among those who preached the Law in the time of the seven Buddhas. He is also foremost among those who preach the Law in my presence now. And he will likewise be foremost among those who preach the Law in the time of the future Buddhas who appear in the present Wise Kalpa, in all cases protecting, upholding, aiding and proclaiming the Law of the Buddha. In the future too he will protect, uphold, aid and proclaim the Law of immeasurable, boundless Buddhas, teaching, converting and enriching immeasurable living beings and causing them to turn toward anuttara-samyak-sambodhi. In order to purify the Buddha lands he will constantly apply himself with diligence, teaching and converting living beings.

Little by little he will become fully endowed with the way of the bodhisattva, and when immeasurable asamkhya kalpas have passed, here in the land where he is dwelling he will attain anuttara-samyak-sambodhi. He will be called Law Bright Thus Come One, worthy of offerings, of right and universal knowledge, perfect clarity and conduct, well gone, understanding the world, unexcelled worthy, trainer of people, teacher of heavenly and human beings, Buddha, World-Honored One.

"This Buddha will have thousand-million fold worlds equal in number to Ganges sands as his Buddha land. The ground will be made of the seven treasures and level as the palm of a hand, without hills or ridges, ravines or gullies. The land will be filled with terraces and towers made of the seven treasures, and the heavenly palaces will be situated close by in the sky, so that human and heavenly beings can communicate and be within sight of each other. There will be no evil paths of existence there, nor will there be any women. All living beings will be born through transformation and will be without lewd desires. They will gain great transcendental powers, their bodies will emit a bright glow, and they will be able to fly at will. They will be firm in intent and thought, diligent and wise, and all alike will be adorned with golden color and the thirty-two features. All the living beings in that land will regularly take two kinds of food, one being the food of Dharma joy, the other the food of meditation delight. There will be immeasurable asamkhya, thousands, ten thousands, millions of nayutas of bodhisattvas there, who will gain great transcendental powers and the four unlimited kinds of knowledge, and will be skilled and capable in teaching and converting the different varieties of living beings. The number of voice-hearers will be beyond the power of calculation or reckoning to determine. All will be fully endowed with the six transcendental powers, the three understandings, and the eight emancipations.

"This Buddha land will thus possess measureless blessings of this kind that will adorn and complete it. The kalpa will be named Treasure Bright and the land named Good and Pure. The Buddha's life span will be immeasurable asamkhya kalpas, his Law will endure for a very long time, and after the Buddha has passed into extinction, towers adorned with the seven treasures will be erected to him throughout the entire land."

At that time the World-Honored One, wishing to state his meaning once more, spake in verse form, saying:

You monks, listen carefully!
The way followed by the sons of the Buddha,
because they are well learned in expedient means,
is wonderful beyond conception.
They know how most beings delight in a little Law
and are fearful of great wisdom.
Therefore the bodhisattvas
pose as voice-hearers or pratyekabuddhas,
employing countless expedient means
to convert the different kinds of living beings.
They proclaim themselves to be voice-hearers
and say they are far removed from the Buddha way,
and so bring emancipation to immeasurable multitudes,
allowing them all to achieve success.
Limited in aspiration, lazy and indolent though the
multitudes are,
bit by bit they are led to the attainment of Buddhahood.
Inwardly, in secret, the sons act as bodhisattvas,
but outwardly the show themselves as voice-hearers.
They seem to be lessening desires out of hatred for birth
and death,
but in truth they are purifying the Buddha lands.
Before the multitude they seem possessed of the three poisons
or manifest the signs of heretical views.
My disciples in this manner
use expedient means to save living beings.
If I were to describe all the different ways,
the many manifestations they display in converting others,
the living beings who heard me
would be doubtful and perplexed in mind.

Now this Purna in the past
diligently practiced the way
under a thousand million Buddhas,
proclaiming and guarding the Law of those Buddhas.
In order to seek out unsurpassed wisdom
he went to where the Buddhas were,
became a leader among their disciples,
one of wide knowledge and wisdom.
He showed no fear in what he expounded
and was able to delight the assembly.
Never was he weary or disheartened
in assisting the work of the Buddhas.
Already he had passed over into great transcendental powers
and possessed the four unlimited kinds of knowledge.
He knew whether the capacities of the multitude were keen or dull
and constantly preached the pure Law.
He expounded such principles as these,
teaching a multitude of thousands of millions,
causing them to reside in the Great Vehicle Law
and himself purifying the Buddha lands.
And in the future to will offer alms
to immeasurable, countless Buddhas,
protecting, aiding and proclaiming their correct Law
and himself purifying the Buddha lands,
constantly employing various expedient means,
preaching the Law without fear,
saving multitudes beyond calculation,
causing them to realize comprehensive wisdom.
He will offer alms to the Thus Come Ones,
guarding and upholding the treasure storehouse of the Law.

And later he will become a Buddha
known by the name Law Bright.
His land will be called Good and Pure
and will be composed of the seven treasures.
The kalpa will be named Treasure Bright.
The Multitude of bodhisattvas will be very numerous,
numbering immeasurable millions,
all having passed over into great transcendental powers,
endowed with dignity, virtue, strength,
filling the entire land.
Voice-hearers too will be numberless,
with the three understandings and eight emancipations,
having attained the four unlimited kinds of knowledge--
such as these will be monks of the Order. The living beings of that land
will all be divorced from lewd desires.
They will be born in a pure manner by the process
of transformation,
with all the features adorning their bodies.
With Dharma joy and meditation delight to feed upon,
they will have no thought of other food.
There will be no women there
and non of the evil paths of existence.
The monk Purna
has won all these blessings to the fullest
and will acquire a pure land such as this,

with its great multitude of worthies and sages.
Of the countless matters pertaining to it
I have now spoken only in brief.

At that time the twelve hundred arhats, being free in mind, thought to themselves, We rejoice at gaining that we have never had before. If the World-Honored One should give each of us a prophecy of enlightenment such as he has given to this other major disciples, would that be a cause for delight?

The Buddha, knowing that this thought was in their minds, said to Mahakashyapa: on these twelve hundred arhats who are now before me I will one by one bestow a prophecy that they will attain anuttara-samyak-sambodhi. Among this assembly is a major disciple of mine, the monk Kaundinya he will offer alms to sixty-two thousand million Buddhas, and after that will become a Buddha. He will be designated Universal knowledge, perfect clarity and conduct, well gone, understanding the world, unexcelled worthy, trainer of people, teacher of heavenly and human beings, Buddha, World-Honored One. Five-hundred arhats, including Uruvilvakashyapa, Gayakashyapa, Nadikashyapa, Kalodayin, Udayin, Aniruddha, Revata, Kapphina, Bakkula, Chunda, Svagata, and others, will attain anuttara-samyak-sambodhi. All will have the same designation, being called Universal Brightness."

The World-Honored One, wishing to state his meaning once more, spoke in verse form, saying:

The monk Kaundinya
will see immeasurable Buddhas
and after asamkhya kalpas have passed
will at last achieve impartial and correct enlightenment.
Constantly he will emit a great bright light,
will be endowed with transcendental powers,
and his name will be known in all ten quarters,
respected by one and all.
Constantly he will preach the unsurpassed way;
therefore he will be named Universal Brightness.
His realm will be pure and clean,
his bodhisattvas brave and spirited.
All will ascend the wonderful towers,
travel to the lands in the ten directions,
in order to offer unsurpassed articles
as gifts to the various Buddhas.
After they have offered these alms
their minds will be filled with great joy
and they will speedily return to their native lands--
such will be their supernatural powers.
The life span of this Buddha will be sixty thousand kalpas,
his Correct Law will endure twice that time,
his Counterfeit Law twice that time again,
and when his Law is extinguished, heavenly and human beings will grieve.
The five hundred monks
will one by one become Buddhas,
all with the same name, Universal Brightness.
Each will bestow a prophecy on his successor, saying,
"After I have entered extinction,
you, so-and-so, will become a Buddha.
The world in which you carry out conversions
will be like mine today."
The adornment and purity of their lands,
their various transcendental powers,
their bodhisattvas and voice-hearers,
their Correct Law and Counterfeit Law,

the number of kalpas in their life span--
all will be as I have described above.
Kashyapa, now you know the future
of these five hundred who are free in mind.
The remainder of the multitude of voice-hearers
will also be like this.
As for those not in this gathering,
you must expound and preach to them.

At that time the five hundred arhats in the presence of the Buddha, having received a prophecy of enlightenment, danced for joy. Immediately they rose from their seats, advanced to a position in front of the Buddha, touched their heads to the ground and bowed to the Buddha's feet. They bewailed their error, reproving themselves and saying, "World-Honored One, we always used to think to ourselves, We have already attained the ultimate extinction. But now we know that we were like persons of no wisdom. Why? Because, although we were capable of attaining the wisdom of the Thus Come One, we were willing to content ourselves with petty wisdom.

"World-Honored One, it was like the case of a man who went to the house of a close friend and, having become drunk on wine, lay down to sleep. At that time the friend had to go out on official business. He took a priceless jewel, sewed it in the lining of the man's robe, and left it with him when he went out. The man was asleep drunk and knew nothing about it. When he got up, he set out on a journey to other countries. In order to provide himself with food and clothing he had to search with all his energy and diligence, encountering very great hardship and making do with what little he could come by.

"Later, the close friend happened to meet him by chance. The friend said, 'How absurd, old fellow! Why should you have to do all this for the sake of food and clothing? In the past I wanted to make certain you would be able to live in ease and satisfy the five desires, and so on such-and-such a day and month and year I took a priceless jewel and sewed it in the lining of your robe. It must still be there now. But you did not know about it, and fretted and wore yourself out trying to provide a living for yourself. What nonsense! Now you must take the jewel and exchange it for goods. Then you can have whatever you wish at all times and never experience poverty or want.'

"The Buddha is like this friend. When he was still a bodhisattva, he taught and converted us, inspiring in us the determination to seek comprehensive wisdom. But in time we forget all that, became unaware, unknowing. Having attained the way of the arhat, we supposed we had gained extinction. Finding it difficult to provide for our livelihood, as it were, we made do with what little we could come by. However, we not yet lost the desire for comprehensive wisdom. And now the World-Honored One awakens us and makes us aware, speaking these words: 'Monks, what you have acquired is not the ultimate extinction. For a long time I caused you to cultivate the good roots of Buddhahood, and as on expedient means I showed you the outward signs of nirvana, but you supposed that you had in truth attained nirvana.'

"World-Honored One, now we understand. In fact we are bodhisattvas and have received a prophecy that we will attain anuttara-samyak-sambodhi. Fro this reason we are filled with great joy, having gained what we never had before."

At that time Ajnata Kaundinya and the others, wishing to state their meaning once more, spoke in verse form, saying:

We have heard the sound of this prophecy
assuring us of unsurpassed ease and tranquility;
we rejoice in gaining what we never had before
and make obeisance to the Buddha of measureless wisdom.
Now in the presence of the World-Honored One
we bewail our faults and errors.
Of the Buddha's immeasurable treasure
we have gained only a small portion of nirvana,

and like ignorant and foolish persons
have taken that to be sufficient.
We are like the poor and impoverished man
who went to the house of a close friend.
The house was a very prosperous one
and he served many trays of delicacies.
The friend took a priceless jewel,
sewed it in the lining of the poor man's robe,
gave it without a word and then went away,
and the man, being asleep, knew nothing of it.
After the man had gotten up,
he journeyed here and there to other countries,
seeking food and clothing to keep himself alive,
finding it very difficult to provide for his livelihood
He made do with what little he could get
and never hoped for anything finer,
unaware that in the lining of his robe
he had a priceless jewel.
Later the close friend who had given him the jewel
happened to meet the poor man
and after sharply rebuking him,
showed him the jewel sewed in the robe.
When the poor man saw the jewel
his heart was filled with great joy,
for he was rich, possessed of wealth and goods
sufficient to satisfy the five desires.
We are like that man.
Through the long night the World-Honored One
constantly in his pity teaches and converts us,
causing us to plant the seeds of an unsurpassed aspiration.
But because we are without wisdom,
we are unaware of this, unknowing.
Having gained a small portion of nirvana,
we are satisfied and seek nothing more.
But now the Buddha awakens us,
saying 'This is not really extinction,
when you have gained the Buddha's unsurpassed wisdom,
then that will be true extinction!'
Now we have heard from the Buddha
these prophecies and descriptions of adornment,
and how each in turn will bestow a prophecy on his successor,
and in body and mind we are filled with joy.

Chapter Nine: Prophecies Conferred
on Learners and Adepts

At that time Ananda and Rahula thought to themselves, whenever we reflect, we consider how delightful it would be if we should receive a prophecy of enlightenment! Immediately they rose from their seats, advanced to a position in front of the Buddha, touched their heads to the ground and bowed to the Buddha's feet. Together they spoke to the Buddha, saying:

"World-Honored One, we too should have a share of this! We have put all our trust in the Thus Come One alone, and we are well known to the heavenly and human beings and asuras of all the world. Ananda constantly attends the Buddha and guards and upholds the Dharma storehouse, and Rahula is the Buddha's son. If the Buddha should bestow on us a prophecy that we will attain anuttara-samyak-sambodhi, then our wishes will be fulfilled and the longings of the multitude will likewise be satisfied."

At that time two thousand of the voice-hearers disciples, both learners and adepts who had nothing who had nothing more to learn, all rose from their seats, bared their right shoulders, advanced to a position in front of the Buddha, pressed their palms together with a single mind and, gazing up in reverence at the World-Honored One, repeated the wish expressed by Ananda and Rahula and then stood to one side.

At that time the Buddha said to Ananda: "In a future existence you will become a Buddha with the name Mountain Sea Wisdom Unrestricted Power King Thus Come One, worthy of offerings, of right universal knowledge, perfect clarity and conduct, well gone, understanding the world, unexcelled worthy, and trainer of people, teacher of heavenly and human beings, Buddha, World-Honored One. You will offer alms to sixty-two million Buddhas and will guard and uphold their Dharma storehouses, and after that you will attain anuttara-samyak-sambodhi. You will teach and convert bodhisattvas as numerous as twenty thousand ten thousand million Ganges sands and will cause them to attain anuttara-samyak-sambodhi. Your land will be named Ever Standing Victory Banner, its soil will be clean and pure and made of lapis lazuli. The kalpa will be named Wonderful Sound Filling Everywhere. The life span of that Buddha will be immeasurable thousands, ten thousands millions of asamkhayas of kalpas-though men should calculate and reckon thousands, ten thousands, millions of immeasurable asamkhayas of kalpas, they could never ascertain the life span of the Buddha and the Counterfeit Law will endure in the world for twice the time of the correct law. Ananda, this Mountain Sea Wisdom Unrestricted Power King Buddha will be praised alike by Thus Come Ones of the ten directions who are equal in number to immeasurable thousands, ten thousands, millions of Ganges sands, and they will extol his blessings."

At that time the World-Honored One, wishing to state his meaning once more, spoke in verse form, saying:

I now say to the monks that
Ananda, upholder of the Law,
will give alms to the Buddhas
and after will achieve correct enlightenment.
His name will be Mountain Sea Wisdom
Unrestricted Power King Buddha,
His land will be clean and pure,
named ever Standing Victory Banner.
He will teach and convert bodhisattvas
in numbers like Ganges sands.
This Buddha will possess great dignity and virtue,
his renown will fill the ten directions.
His life span will be immeasurable
because he takes pity on living beings.
His Correct Law, twice that again.
His Counterfeit Law, twice again.
As numerous as Ganges sands

will be the countless living beings
who in the midst of the Buddha's Law
will plant causes and conditions leading to the Buddha way.

At that time in the assembly eight thousand bodhisattvas who had newly conceived the determination to attain enlightenment all thought to themselves, We have never heard of even a great bodhisattva receiving a prophecy such as this. For what reason should these voice-hearers receive such a prediction?

At that time the World-Honored One, knowing the thought that was in the mind of these bodhisattvas, said to them: "Good men, when Ananda and I were at the place of Void King Buddha, we both at the same time conceived the determination to attain anuttara-samyak-sambodhi. Ananda constantly delighted in wide knowledge [of the Law], I constantly put forth diligent effort. Therefore I have already succeeded in attaining anuttara-samyak-sambodhi, while Ananda guards and upholds my Law. And he will likewise guard the Dharma storehouses of the Buddha of future existences and will teach, convert and bring success to the multitude of bodhisattvas. Such was his original vow, and therefore he has received this prophecy."

When Ananda in the presence of the Buddha heard this prophecy delivered to him and heard of the land and adornments he was to receive, all that he had vowed to achieve was realized and his mind was filled with great joy, for he had gained what he had never had before. Immediately he recalled to mind the Dharma storehouses of immeasurable thousands, ten thousands, millions of Buddhas of the past, and he could fully comprehend them without hindrance, as though he had just now heard them. He also recalled his original vow.

At that time Ananda spoke in verse form, saying:

The World-Honored One, very rarely met with,
has caused me to recall the past,
the Law of immeasurable Buddhas,
as though I had heard it today.
Now I have no more doubts
but dwell securely in the Buddha way.
As an expedient means I act as attendant,
guarding and upholding the Law of the Buddhas.

At that time the Buddha said to Rahula: In a future existence you will become a Buddha with the name Stepping on Seven Treasure Flowers Thus Come One, worthy of offerings, of right and universal knowledge, perfect clarity and conduct, well gone, understanding the world, unexcelled worthy, trainer of people, teacher of heavenly and human beings, Buddha, World-Honored One. You will offer alms to Buddhas and Thus Come Ones as numerous as the dust particles of ten worlds. In all cases you will be the eldest son of those Buddhas, just as you are my son now. The adornments of the land of Stepping on Seven Treasure Flowers Buddha, the number of kalpas in his life span, the disciples he converts, his Correct Law and Counterfeit Law will not differ from those of the Thus Come One Mountain Sea Wisdom Unrestricted Power King. You will be the eldest son of that Buddha, and after that you will attain anuttara-samyak-sambodhi."

At that time the World-Honored One, wishing to state his meaning once more, spoke in verse form, saying:

When I was crown prince
Rahula was my eldest son.
Now that I have gained the Buddha way
he receives the Dharma and is my Dharma son.
In existences to come
he will see immeasurable millions of Buddhas.

As eldest son to all of them,
with a single mind he will seek the Buddha way.
The covert actions of Rahula

I alone am capable of knowing.
He manifests himself as my eldest son,
showing himself to living beings.
With immeasurable millions, thousands, ten thousands
of blessings beyond count,
he dwells securely in the Buddha's Law
and thereby seeks the unsurpassed way.

At that time the World-Honored One observed the two thousand learners and adepts, mild and gentle in will, serenely clean and pure, gazing at the Buddha with a single mind. The Buddha said to Ananda, "Do you see these two thousand learners and adepts?"

"Yes, I see them."

"Ananda, these persons will offer alms to Buddhas and Thus Come Ones equal in number to the dust particles of fifty worlds, paying honor and reverence to them, guarding and upholding their Dharma storehouses. In their final existence they will all at the same time succeed in becoming Buddhas in lands in the ten directions. All will have the identical designation, being called Jewel Sign Thus Come One, worthy of offerings, of right and universal knowledge, perfect clarity and conduct, well gone, understanding the world, unexcelled worthy, trainer of people, teacher of heavenly and human beings, Buddha, World-Honored One. Their life span will be one kalpa, and the adornment of their lands, their voice-hearers and bodhisattvas, Correct Law and Counterfeit Law will be all cases the same."

At that time the World-Honored One, wishing to state his meaning in verse form, saying:

These two thousand voice-hearers
who now stand in my presence-
on all of them I bestow a prophecy
that in a future existence they will become Buddhas.
The Buddhas to whom they offer alms
will be numerous as the dust particles described above.
They will guard and uphold the Dharma storehouses
and after that will gain correct enlightenment.
Each will have a land in one of the ten directions
and all will share the same name and designation.
All at the same time will sit in the place of practice
and thereby will gain proof of unsurpassed wisdom.
All will be named Jewel Sign
and their lands and disciples,
their Correct Law and Counterfeit Law
will all be identical and without difference.
All will employ transcendental powers
to save living beings in the ten directions.
Their renown will spread everywhere around
and in due time they will enter nirvana.

At that time, when the two thousand learners and adepts heard the Buddha bestow this prophecy, they danced for joy ad spoke in verse form, saying:

World-Honored One, bright lamp of wisdom,
we hear your voice bestowing this prophecy
and our hearts are filled with joy
as though we were bathed in sweet dew!

Chapter Ten: The Teacher of the Law

At that time the World-Honored One addressed Bodhisattva Medicine King. And through him the eighty thousand great men, saying: "Medicine King, do you see in this great assembly the immeasurable number of heavenly beings, dragons kings, yakshas, gandharvas, asuras, garudas, kimnaras, mahoragas, human and nonhuman beings, as well as monks, nuns, laymen and laywomen, those who seek to become voice-hearers, who seek to become pratyekabuddhas, or those seek the Buddha way? Upon these various kinds of beings who in the presence of the Buddha listen to one verse or one phrase of the Lotus Sutra of the Wonderful Law and for a moment think of it with joy I will bestow on all of them a prophecy that they will attain anuttara-samyak-sambodhi.

The Buddha said to Medicine King: "In addition, if after the Thus Come One has passed into extinction there should be someone who listens to the Lotus Sutra of the Wonderful Law, even one verse or one phrase, and for a moment thinks of it with joy, I will likewise bestow on him a prophesy that he will attain anuttara-samyak-sambodhi. Again if there are persons who embrace, read, recite, expound and copy the Lotus Sutra of the Wonderful Law, even only one verse, and look upon this sutra with the same reverence as they would the Buddha, presenting various offerings of flowers, incense, necklaces, powdered incense, paste incense, incense for burning, silken canopies, streamers and banners, clothing and music, and pressing their palms together in reverence, then, Medicine King, you should understand million Buddhas that such person have already offered alms to a hundred thousand million Buddhas and in the place of the Buddhas have fulfilled their great vow, and because they take pity on living beings they have been born in this human world

"Medicine King, if someone should ask what living beings will be able to attain Buddhahood in a latter-day existence, then you should show him all these people in a latter-day existence are certain to attain Buddhahood. Why? Because if good men and good women embrace, read, recite, expound and copy the Lotus Sutra, even one phrase of it, offer various kinds of alms to the sutra, flowers, incense, necklaces, powdered incense, paste incense, incense for burning, silken canopies, streamers and banners, clothing and music, and press their hands together in reverence, then these persons will be looked up to and honored by all the world. Alms will be offered to them such as would be offered to the Thus Come One. You should understand that these persons are great bodhisattvas who have succeeded in attaining anuttara-samyak-sambodhi. Pitying living beings, they have vowed to be born among them where they may broadly expound and make distinctions regarding the Lotus Sutra of the Wonderful Law. How much more so is this true, then, of those who embrace the entire sutra and offer various types of alms to it!

"Medicine King, you should understand that these persons voluntarily relinquish the reward due for their pure deeds and, in the time after I have passed into extinction, because they pity living beings, they are born in this evil world so they may broadly expound this sutra. If one of these good men or good women in the time after I have passed into extinction is able to secretly expound the Lotus Sutra to one person, even one phrase of it, then you should know that de or she is the envoy of the Thus Come One. He has been dispatched bf the Thus Come One and carries out the Thus Come One's work. And how much more so those who in the midst of the great assembly broadly expound the sutra for others!

"Medicine King, if there should be an evil person who, his mind destitute of goodness, should for the space of a kalpa appear in the presence of the Buddha and constantly curse and revile the Buddha, that person's offense would still be rather light. But if there were a person who spoke only one evil word to curse or defame the lay persons or monks or nuns who read and recite the Lotus Sutra, then his offense would be very grave.

"Medicine King, these persons who read and recite the Lotus Sutra-you should understand that these persons adorn themselves with the adornments of the Buddhas they are borne upon the shoulders of the Thus Come One. Wherever they may go, one should greet them with bows, with palms pressed single-mindedly together, with reverence and alms, with respect and praise, flowers, incense, necklaces, powdered incense, paste incense, incense for burning, silken canopies, streamers and banners, clothing, delicacies and the making of music. The finest alms that can be offered to a person should be offered to them. Heavenly treasures should be scattered over them, the treasure hoards of heaven should be given them as gifts. Why do I say this?

Because these persons delight in expounding the Law. And if one listens to them for even a moment, he will immediately attain the ultimate anuttara-samyak-sambodhi.

An that time the World-Honored One, wishing to state his meaning once more, spoke in verse form, saying:

If you wish to abide in the Buddha way
and successfully gain the wisdom that comes of itself,
you should be constantly diligent in offering alms
to those who embrace the Lotus Sutra.
If you have a wish to quickly obtain
wisdom regarding all species of things,
you should embrace this sutra
and at the same time give alms to those who do so.
If one is capable of embracing
the Lotus Sutra of the Wonderful Law,
know that such a person is an envoy of the Buddha
who thinks wit pity of living beings.
Those who are capable of embracing
the Lotus of the Wonderful Law
relinquish their claim to the pure land
and out of pity for living beings are born here.
Know that persons such as these
freely choose where they will be born,
and choose to be born in this evil world
so they may broadly expound the unsurpassed Law.
You should offer heavenly flowers and incense,
robes decked with heavenly treasures,
the wonderful treasure hoards of heaven
as alms to those who preach the Law.
In the evil world following my extinction
if there are those who can embrace this sutra,
you should press your palms together in reverence
and offer alms to them as you would to the
World-Honored One.
The choicest delicacies, all that is sweet and tasty,
along with various types of clothing
you should offer as alms to these Buddha sons
in hopes you may hear a moment of their preaching.
If there are those in a later age
who can accept and embrace this sutra,
they are my envoys sent out among the people
to perform the Thus Come One's work.
If for the space of a kalpa
one should constantly harbor a mind destitute of good
and with angry looks should revile the Buddha,
he will be committing an offense of immeasurable gravity.
But if toward those who read, recite and embrace
this Lotus Sutra
one should even for a moment direct evil words,
his offense will be even greater.
If there is someone who seeks the Buddha way
and during a certain kalpa
presses palms together in my presence
and recites numberless verses of praise,
because of these praises of the Buddha
he will gain immeasurable blessings.

And if one lauds and extols those who uphold this sutra,
his good fortune will be even greater.
For the space of eighty million kalpas,
with the most wonderful shapes and sounds,
with that which is pleasing to smell, taste and touch,
offer alms to the upholders of this sutra!
If you have offered alms in this manner
and have heard the teachings for even a moment,
then you will experience joy and good fortune,
saying, "I have gained great benefit!"
Medicine King, now I say to you,
I have preached various sutras,
and among those sutras
the Lotus is foremost!

At that time the Buddha spoke once more to the bodhisattva and mahasattva Medicine King, saying: "The sutras I have preached number immeasurable thousands, ten thousands millions, among the sutras I have preached, now preach, and will preach, this Lotus Sutra is the most difficult to believe and the most difficult to understand. Medicine King, this sutra is the storehouse of the secret crux of the Buddhas, it must not be distributed recklessly transmitted to others. It has been guarded by the Buddhas, the World-Honored Ones, and from times past until now has never been openly expounded, and since hatred and jealousy toward this sutra abound even when the Thus Come One is in the world, how much more will this be so after his passing?

"Medicine King, you should know that after the Thus Come One has entered extinction, if there are those who can copy, uphold, read and recite this sutra, offer alms to it and expound it for others, then the Thus Come One will cover them with his robe, and they will also be protected and kept in mind by the Buddhas who are now present in other regions. Such persons possess the power of great faith, the power of aspiration, the power of good roots, you should know that such persons lodge in the same place as the Thus Come One, and the Thus Come One pats them on the head with his hand.

"Medicine King, in any place whatsoever where this sutra is preached, where it is read, where it is recited, where it is copied, or where a roll of it exists, in all such places there should be erected towers made of the seven kinds of gems, and they should be made very high and broad and well adorned. There is no need to enshrine the relics of the Buddha there. Why? Because in such towers the entire body of the Thus Come One is already present. All kinds of flowers, incense, necklaces, silken canopies. Streamers and banners, music and hymns should be offered as alms to these towers. And they should be accorded reverence, honor and praise. If when people see these towers they bow in obeisance and offer alms, then you should know that such persons have all drawn near to anuttara-samyak-sambodhi.

"Medicine King, suppose there is a man who is parched with thirst and in need of water. On an upland plateau he begins digging a hole in search of water, but he sees that the soil is dry and knows that water is still far away. He does not cease his efforts, however, and bit by bit he sees the soil becoming damper, until gradually he has worked his way into mud. Now he is determined in his mind to go on, for he knows that he is bound to be nearing water.

"The way of the bodhisattva is the same as this. As long as a person has not yet heard. Not yet understood. And not yet been able to practice this Lotus Sutra, then you should know that person is still far away from anuttara-samyak-sambodhi. Why? Because all bodhisattvas who attain anuttara-samyak-sambodhi in all cases do so through this sutra. This sutra opens the gate of expedient means and shows the form of true reality. This storehouse of the Lotus Sutra is hidden deep and far away where no person can reach it. But the Buddha, teaching, converting and leading to success the bodhisattvas, opens it up for them.

"Medicine King, if there are bodhisattvas who, on hearing this Lotus Sutra, respond with surprise, doubt and fear, then you should know that they are bodhisattvas who have only newly embarked on their course. And if there are voice-hearers who, on hearing this sutra, respond with surprise, doubt, and fear, then you should know that they are persons of overbearing arrogance.

"Medicine King, if there are good men and good women who, after the Thus Come One has entered extinction, wish to expound this Lotus Sutra for the four kinds of believers, how should they expound it? These good men and good women should enter the Thus Come One's room put on the Thus Come One's robe, sit in the Thus Come One's seat, and then for the sake of the four kinds of believers broadly expound this sutra.

"The 'Thus Come One's room' is the state of mind that shows great pity and compassion toward all living beings. The Thus Come One's robe is the mind that is gentle and forbearing. The 'Thus Come One's seat is the emptiness of all phenomena. One should seat oneself comfortably therein and after that, with a mind never lazy or remiss, should for the sake of the bodhisattvas and the four kinds of believers broadly expound this Lotus Sutra.

"Medicine King, I will send persons conjured up by magic to other lands to gather together assemblies to listen to the Law, and I will also send monks, nuns, laymen and laywomen conjured up by magic to listen to the preaching of the Law, believe and accept it, and abide by it without violation. If the preachers of the Law are in an empty and silent place, I will at that time send large numbers of heavenly beings, dragons, spirits, gandharvas, asuras, and others to listen to their preaching of the law. Though I should be in another land, from time to time I will make it possible for the preachers of the Law to see my body. If they should forget a phrase of this sutra, I will appear and prompt them so that they are able to recite the text correctly and in full."

At that time the World-Honored One, wishing to state his meaning once more, spoke in verse form, saying:

If you wish to put aside all sloth and remissness,
you must listen to this sutra,
It is hard to get a chance to hear this sutra,
and believing and accepting it too is hard.
If a person is thirsty and wants water
he may dig a hole in the high plateau,
but as long as he sees the soil dry
he knows the water is still far away.
But bit by bit he sees the soil grow damp and muddy
and then he knows for certain he is nearing water.
Medicine King, you should understand
that people are like this-
if they do not hear the Lotus Sutra,
they will be far removed from the Buddha's wisdom,
But if they hear this profound sutra
which defines the Law of the voice-hearer,
if they hear this king of the sutras
and afterward carefully ponder it,
then you should know such persons
are close to the wisdom of the Buddha.
If a person expounds this sutra,
he should enter the Thus Come One's room,
put on the Thus Come One's robe,
sit in the Thus Come One's seat,
confront the assembly without fear
and broadly expand it for them, making distinctions.
Great pity and compassion are the room.
Gentleness and patience are the robe.
The emptiness of all phenomena is the seat,
and from that the position one should expound the Law for them.

If when a person expounds this sutra
there is someone who speaks ill and reviles him
or attacks him with swords and staves, tiles and stones,
he should think of the Buddha and for that reason be patient.
In a thousand, ten thousand, million lands
I will manifest my pure and durable body
and for immeasurable millions of kalpas
will expound the Law for living beings,
If after I have entered extinction
there are those who can expound this sutra,
I will send the four kinds of believers, magically conjured,
monks and nuns
and men and women of pure faith,
to offer alms and cause them to listen to the Law;
they will lead and guide living beings,
assemble them and cause them to listen to the Law.
If someone thinks to do evil to the preachers
with swords and staves or with tiles and stones,
I will dispatch persons magically conjured
who will act to guard and protect them.
If those who expound the Law
are alone in an empty and silent place,
and in that stillness where no human voice sounds
they read and recite this sutra
at that time I will manifest
my pure and radiant body for them.
If they forget a passage or a phrase
I will prompt them so they will be thorough and effective,
If persons endowed with these virtues
should expound to the four kinds of believers
and read and recite the sutra in an empty place,
I will enable all of them to see my body.
And if the expounders are in an empty and silent place
I will send heavenly beings, dragon kings,
yakshas, spirits and others
to be an assembly and listen to the Law.
Persons such as this will delight in expounding the Law,
making distinctions and encountering no hindrance.

Because the Buddhas guard and keep them in mind.
They will be able to bring joy to the great assembly.
If one stays close to the teachers of the Law
he will speedily gain the bodhisattva way.
By following and learning from these teachers
he will see Buddhas as numerous as the Ganges sands.

Chapter Eleven: The Emergence of the Treasure Tower

At that time in the Buddha's presence there was a tower adorned with the seven treasures, five hundred yojanas in height and two hundred and fifty yojanas in width and depth, that rose up out of the earth and stood suspended in the air. Various kinds of precious objects adorned it. It had five thousand railings, a thousand, ten thousand rooms, and numberless streamers and banners decorated it. Festoons of jewels hung down and ten thousand million jeweled bells were suspended from it. All four sides emitted a fragrance of tamalapatra and sandalwood that pervaded the whole world. Its banners and canopies were made of the seven treasures, namely, gold, silver, lapis Lazuli, seashell, agate, pearl, and carnelian, and it as so high it reached to the heavenly places of the Four Heavenly Kings. The gods of the Trayastrimsha heaven rained down heavenly mandarava flowers as an offering to the treasure tower, and the other heavenly beings and the dragons, yakshas, gandharvas, asuras, garudas, kimnaras, mahoragas, human and nonhuman beings, an assembly of thousands, ten thousands, millions, offered all kinds of flowers, incense, necklaces, streamers, canopies and music as alms to the treasure tower, paying it reverence, honor and praise.

At that time a loud voice issued from the treasure tower, speaking words of praise: "Excellent, excellent! Shakyamuni, World-Honored One, that you can take a great wisdom of equality, a Law to instruct the bodhisattvas, guarded and kept in mind by the Buddhas, the Lotus Sutra of the Wonderful law, and preach it for the sake of the great assembly! It is as you say, as you say. Shakyamuni, World-Honored One, all that you have expounded is the truth!"

At that time the four kinds of believers saw the great treasure tower suspended in the air, and they heard the voice that issued from the tower. All experienced the joy of the Law, marveling at this thing they had never known before. They rose from their seats, pressed their palms together in reverence, and then retired to one side.

At that time there was a bodhisattva and mahasattva named Great Joy of Preaching, who understood the doubts that were in the minds of the heavenly and human beings, asuras and other beings of all the world. He said to the Buddha: "World-Honored One, for what reason has this treasure tower risen up out of the earth? And why does this voice issue from its midst?"

At that time the Buddha said: "Bodhisattva Great Joy of Preaching, in the treasure tower is the complete body of a Thus Come One. Long ago, an immeasurable thousand, ten thousand million of asamkhayas of worlds to the east, in a land called Treasure Purity, there was a Buddha named Many Treasures. When this Buddha was originally carrying out the bodhisattva way, he made a great vow, saying, "If after I have become a Buddha and entered extinction, in the lands in the ten directions there is any place where the Lotus Sutra is preached, then my funerary tower, in order that I may listen to the sutra, will come forth and appear in that spot to testify to the sutra and praise its excellence.'

"When that Buddha had finished carrying out the Buddha way and was on the point of passing into extinction, in the midst of the great assembly of heavenly and human beings he said to the monks, 'After I have passed into extinction, if there are those who wish to offer alms to my complete body, then they should erect a great tower.' That Buddha, through his transcendental powers and the power of his vow, insures that, throughout the worlds in the ten directions, no matter in what place, if there are those who preach the Lotus Sutra, this treasure tower will in all cases come forth and appear in their presence, and his complete body will be in the tower, speaking words of praise and saying, Excellent, excellent!

"Great Joy of Preaching, now this tower of the Thus Come One Many Treasures, because it heard the preaching of the Lotus Sutra, has come forth out of the ground and speaks words of praise, saying, Excellent, Excellent!"

At this time Bodhisattva Great Joy of Preaching, knowing the supernatural powers of the Thus Come One, spoke to the Buddha, saying, "World-Honored One, we wish to see the body of this Buddha."

The Buddha said to the bodhisattva and mahasattva Great Joy of Preaching, "This Many Treasures Buddha has taken a profound vow, saying, 'When my treasure tower, in order to listen to the Lotus Sutra comes forth into the presence of one of the Buddhas, if there should be those who wish me to show my body to the four kinds of believers, then let the various Buddhas who are emanations of that Buddha and who are preaching the Law in the worlds in the ten directions all return and gather around that Buddha in a single spot. Only when that has been done will my body become visible.' Great Joy Preaching, I will now gather together the various Buddhas that are emanations of my body and that are preaching the Law in the worlds in the ten directions."

Great Joy of Preaching said to the Buddha, "World-Honored One, I and the others also wish to see these Buddhas that are emanations of the World-Honored One, and to make obeisance to them and offer alms."

At that time the Buddha emitted a ray of light from the tuft of white hair [between his eyebrows], immediately making visible the Buddhas in the eastern region in lands as numerous as five hundred ten thousand million nayutas of Ganges sands. The earth in all these lands was made of crystal, and the lands were adorned with jeweled trees and jeweled robes. Countless thousands, ten thousands, millions of bodhisattvas filled them, and everywhere were hung jeweled curtains, with jeweled nets covering them over. The Buddhas in these lands preached the various doctrines of the Law with great and wonderful voices, and one could see immeasurable thousands, ten thousands, millions of bodhisattvas filling all these lands and preaching the Law for the assembly. In the southern, western and northern regions as well, and in the four intermediate quarters and up and down, wherever the beam from the tuft of white hair, a characteristic feature of the Buddha, shone, the same was true.

At that time the Buddhas of the ten directions each spoke to his multitude of bodhisattvas, saying, "Good men, now I must go to the saha world, to the place where Shakyamuni Buddha is, and also offer alms to the treasure tower of Many Treasures Thus Come One."

The saha world thereupon immediately changed into a place of cleanness and purity. The ground was made of lapis lazuli, jeweled trees adorned it, and ropes of gold marked off the eight highways. There were no villages, towns or cities, great seas of rivers, mountains, streams or forests; great jeweled incense was burning there and mandarava flowers covered the ground all over. Jeweled nets and curtains were spread above, hung with jeweled bells, and the members of this assembly alone were gathered there, all other heavenly and human beings having been moved to another region.

At that time the Buddhas, each with a great bodhisattva to act as his attendant, arrived in the saha world and proceeded to a position beneath one of the jeweled trees. Each of these jeweled trees was five hundred yojanas high and adorned with branches, leaves, flowers and fruit in due proportion. Under all the jeweled trees were lion seats five yojanas in height, and these too were decorated with large jewels. At that time each of the Buddhas took one of these seats, seating himself in cross-legged position. In this way the seats were filled throughout the thousand-million-fold world, but still there was no end even to the emanations of Shakyamuni Buddha arriving from merely one direction.

At that time Shakyamuni Buddha, wishing to provide space for all the Buddhas that were emanations of his body, in addition transformed two hundred ten thousand million nayutas of lands in each of the eight directions, making them all clean and pure and without hells, hungry spirits, beasts or asuras. He also moved all their heavenly and human beings to another region. The ground in these lands that he had transformed was also made of lapis lazuli, Jeweled trees adorned them, each tree five hundred yojanas high and adorned with branches, leaves, flowers and flowers and fruit in due proportion. There were jeweled lion seats under all the trees, five yojanas in height and ornamented with various kinds of treasures, these lands too were without great seas or rivers, or any kingly ranges of mountains such as the Muchilinda Mountains, Mahamuchilinda Mountains, Iron Encircling Mountains, Great Iron Encircling mountains, or Mount Sumeru. The whole area comprised a single Buddha land, a jeweled region level and smooth. Curtains crisscrossed with festoons of jewels were spread everywhere, banners and canopies hung down, great jeweled incense burned, and heavenly jeweled flowers covered the ground all around.

Shakyamuni Buddha, in order to provide seats for all the Buddhas that were arriving, once more transformed two hundred ten thousand million nayutas of lands in each of the eight directions, making them all clean and pure and without hells, hungry spirits, beasts or asuras. He also moved all the heavenly and human beings to another region. The ground in these lands that he had transformed was likewise made of lapis lazuli. Jeweled trees adorned the lands, each tree five hundred yojanas in height and adorned with branches, leaves, flowers and fruit in due proportion. There were jeweled lion seats under all the trees, five yojanas in height and ornamented with great jewels, these lands too were without great seas or rivers, or any kingly ranges such as the Muchilinda Mountains, Great Mahamuchilinda Mountains, iron Encircling Mountains, Great Iron Encircling Mountains, or Mount Sumeru, the whole area comprising a single Buddha land, a jeweled region level and smooth. Curtains crisscrossed with festoons of jewels were spread everywhere, banners and canopies hung down, great jeweled incense burned, and heavenly jeweled flowers covered the ground all around.

At that time the emanations of Shakyamuni Buddha from the eastern region, Buddhas in lands equal in number to hundreds, thousands, ten thousands, millions of nayutas of Ganges sands, each preaching the Law, had assembled there. And bit by bit the Buddhas from the ten directions all came and assembled in this way and were seated in the eight directions. At this time each of the directions was filled with Buddhas, Thus Come Ones, in four hundred ten thousand million nayutas of lands.

At that time the Buddhas, each seated on a lion seat under one of the jeweled trees, all dispatched their attendants to go and greet Shakyamuni Buddha. Each Buddha presented his attendant with a handful of jeweled flowers and said, "Good man, you must go to Mount Gridhrakuta to the place where Shakyamuni Buddha is and speak to him as I instruct you. Say, 'Are your illnesses few, and your worries few? In spirit and vigor are you well and happy? And are the bodhisattvas and voice-hearers all well and at peace?' Then take these jeweled flowers and scatter them over the Buddha as an offering, and say, 'The Buddha So-and-so would like to participate in the opening of this treasure tower.'

All the Buddhas dispatched their attendants to speak in this manner. At that time Shakyamuni Buddha saw the Buddhas that were his emanations all assembled, each sitting on a lion seat, and heard all these Buddhas say that they wished to participate in the opening of the treasure tower. Immediately he rose from his seat and stationed himself in midair. All the four kinds of believers likewise stood up, pressed their palms together and gazed at the Buddha with a single mind.

Shakyamuni Buddha with the fingers of his right hand then opened the door of the tower of seven treasures. A loud sound issued from it, like the sound of a lock and crossbar being removed from a great city gate, and at once all the members of the assembly caught sight of Many Treasures Thus Come One seated on a lion seat inside the treasure tower, his body whole and unimpaired, sitting as thought engaged in meditation. And they heard him say, "excellent, excellent, Shakyamuni Buddha! You have preached this Lotus Sutra in a spirited manner. I have come here in order that I may hear this sutra."

At that time the four kinds of believers, observing this Buddha who had passed into extinction immeasurable thousands, ten thousands, millions of kalpas in the past speaking in this way, marveled at what they had never known before and took the masses of heavenly jeweled flowers and scattered them over Many Treasures Buddha and Shakyamuni Buddha.

At that time Many Treasures Buddha offered half of his seat in the treasure tower to Shakyamuni Buddha, saying, "Shakyamuni Buddha, sit here!" Shakyamuni Buddha at once entered the tower and took half of the seat, seating himself in cross-legged position.

At that time the members of the great assembly, seeing the two Thus Come Ones seated cross-legged on the lion seat in the tower of seven treasures, all thought to themselves, These Buddhas are seated high up and far away! If only the Thus Come Ones would employ their transcendental powers to enable all of us to join them there in the air!

Immediately Shakyamuni Buddha used his transcendental powers to lift the members of the great assembly up into the air. And in a loud voice he addressed all the four kinds of believers, saying, "Who is capable of broadly preaching the Lotus Sutra of the Wonderful Law in this saha world? Now is the time to do so, for before long the Thus Come One will enter nirvana. the Buddha wishes to entrust this Lotus Sutra of the Wonderful Law to someone so that it may be preserved."

At that time the World-Honored One, wishing to state his meaning once more, spoke in verse form, saying:

This holy lord, this World-Honored One,
though he passed into extinction long ago,
still seats himself in the treasure tower,
coming here for the sake of the Law.
You people, why then do you not also
strive for the sake of the Law?
This Buddha passed into extinction
an endless number of kalpas ago,
but in many places he comes to listen to the Law
because such opportunities are hard to encounter.
This Buddha originally made a vow, saying,
"After I have passed into extinction,
wherever I may go, in whatever place,
my constant aim will be to hear the Law!"
In addition, these emanations of my body,
Buddhas in immeasurable numbers
like Ganges sands,
have come, desiring to hear the Law,
and so they may see Many Treasures Thus Come One
who has passed into extinction.

Each has abandoned his wonderful land,
as well as his host disciples,
the heavenly and human beings, dragons and spirits,
and all the offerings they give him,
and has come to this place on purpose
to make certain the Law will long endure.
In order to seat these Buddhas
I have employed transcendental powers,
moving immeasurable multitudes,
causing lands to be clean and pure,
leading each of these Buddhas
to the foot of a jeweled tree,
adorned as lotus blossoms
adorn a clear cool pond.
Beneath these jeweled trees
are lion seats,
and the Buddhas seat themselves on them,
adorning them with their brilliance
like a huge torch burning
in the darkness of the night.
A wonderful incense exudes from their bodies,
pervading the lands in the ten directions.
Living beings are wrapped in the aroma,
unable to restrain their joy,
as though a great wind
were tossing the branches of small trees.
Through this expedient means
they make certain that the Law will long endure.
So I say to the great assembly:

After I have passed into extinction,
who can guard and uphold,
read and recite this sutra?
Now in the presence of the Buddha
let him come forward and speak his vow!
This Many Treasures Buddha,
though he passed into extinction long ago,
because of his great vow
roars the lion's roar.

Many Treasures Thus Come One, I myself,
and these emanation Buddhas who have gathered there,
surely know this is our aim.
You sons of the Buddha,
who can guard the Law?
Let him make a great vow
to ensure that it will long endure!
He who is capable of guarding
the Law of this sutra
will thereby have offered alms
to me and to Many Treasures.
This Many Treasures Buddha
dwelling in his treasure tower
journeys constantly throughout the ten directions
for the sake of this sutra.
One who guards this sutra will also have offered alms
to the emanation Buddhas who have come here
adorning and making brilliant
all the various worlds.
If one preaches this sutra,
he will be able to see me
and Many treasures Thus Come One
and these emanation Buddhas.
All you good men,
each of you must consider carefully!
This is a difficult matter-
it is proper you should make a great vow.
The other sutras
number as many as Ganges sands,
but though you expound those sutras,
that is not worth regarding as difficult.
If you were to seize Mount Sumeru
and fling it far off
to the measureless Buddha lands,
that too would not be difficult.
If you used the toe of your foot
to move a thousand-million-fold world,
booting it far away to other lands,
that too would not be difficult.
If you stood in the Summit of Being heaven
and for the sake of the assembly
preached countless other sutras,
that too would not be difficult.
But if after the Buddha has entered extinction ,
in the time of evil,
you can preach this sutra,

that will be difficult indeed!
If there were a person
who took the empty sky in his hand
and walked all around with it,
that would not be difficult.
But if after I have passed into extinction
one can write out and embrace this sutra
and cause others to write it out,
that will be difficult indeed!
If one took the great earth,
placed it on his toenail,
and ascended with it to the Brahma heaven,
that would not be difficult.
But if after the Buddha has passed into extinction,
in the time of evil,
one can even for a little while read this sutra,
that will be difficult indeed!
If , when the fires come at the end of the kalpa,
one can load dry grass on his back
and enter the fire without being burned,
that would not be difficult.
But after I have passed into extinction
if one can embrace this sutra
and expound it to even one person,
that will be difficult indeed!
If one were to embrace this storehouse
of eighty-four thousand doctrines,
the twelve divisions of the sutras,
and expound it to others,
causing listeners
to acquire the six transcendental powers-
though one could do that,
that would not be difficult.
But after I have entered extinction
if one can listen to and accept this sutra
and ask about its meaning,
that will be difficult indeed!
If a person expounds the Law,
allowing thousands, ten thousands, millions,
immeasurable number of living beings
equal to Ganges sands
to become arhats
endowed with the six transcendental powers,
though one might confer such benefits
that would not be difficult.
But after I have entered extinction
if one can honor and embrace
a sutra such as this one,
that will be difficult indeed!
For the sake of the Buddha way
in immeasurable numbers of lands
from the beginning until now
I have widely preached many sutras,
and among them
this sutra is foremost.
If one can uphold this,

he will be upholding the Buddha's body.
All you good men,
after I have entered extinction
who can accept and uphold,
read and recite this sutra?
Now in the presence of the Buddha
let him come forward and speak his vow!
This sutra is hard to uphold;
if one can uphold it even for a short while
I will surely rejoice
and so will the other Buddhas.
A person who can do this
wins the admiration of the Buddhas.
This is what is meant by valor,
this is what is meant by diligence.
This is what is called observing the precepts
and practicing dhuta.
This way one will quickly attain
the unsurpassed Buddha way.
And if in future existences
one can read and uphold this sutra,
he will be a true son of the Buddha,
dwelling in a land spotless and good.
If after the Buddha has passed into extinction
one can understand the meaning of this sutra,
he will be the eyes of the world
for heavenly and human beings.
If in that fearful age
one can preach this sutra for even a moment,
he will deserve to receive alms
from all heavenly and human beings.

Chapter Twelve: Devadatta

At that time the Buddha addressed the bodhisattvas, the heavenly and human beings, and the four kinds of believers saying: "Immeasurable kalpas in the past, I sought the Lotus Sutra without ever flagging. During those many kalpas, I constantly appeared as the ruler of a kingdom who made a vow to seek the unsurpassed bodhi. His mind never wavered or turned aside, and in his desire to fulfill the six paramitas he diligently distributed alms, never stinting in heart, whether the gift was elephants or horses, the seven rare articles, countries, cities, wife, children, maidservants, or his own head, eyes, marrow and brain, his own flesh and limbs. He did not begrudge even his own being and life. At that period the human life span was immeasurably long. But for the sake of the Law this king abandoned his kingdom and throne, delegated the government to the crown prince, sounded drums and sent out proclamations, seeking the Law in four directions and saying, 'Who can expound the Great Vehicle for me? To the end of my life I will be his provider and servant!'

"At that time there was a seer who came to the king and said, "I have a Great Vehicle text called the Sutra of the Wonderful Law. If you will never disobey me, I will expound it for you.'

"When the king heard these words of the seer, he danced for joy. At once he accompanied the seer, providing him with whatever he needed, picking fruit, drawing water, gathering firewood, setting out meals, even offering his own body as a couch and seat, never stinting in body or mind. He served the seer in this manner for a thousand years, all for the sake of the Law, working diligently acting as a provider and seeing to it that the seer lacked for nothing."

At that time the World-Honored One, wishing to state his meaning once more, spoke in verse form, saying:

I recall those departed kalpas of the past
when in order to seek the great Law,
though I was the ruler of a worldly kingdom,
I was not greedy to satisfy the five desires
but instead struck the bell, crying in four quarters,
"Who possesses the great Law?
If he will explain and preach it for me
I will be his slave and servant!"
At that time there was a seer named Asita
who came and announced to this great King,
"I have a subtle and wonderful Law,
rarely known in this world.
If you will undertake religious practice
I will expound it for you."
When the king heard the seer's words
his heart was filled with great joy.
Immediately he accompanied the seer,
providing him with whatever he needed,
gathering firewood, fruit and wild rice,
presenting them at appropriate times with respect and
reverence.
Because the wonderful Law was then his thoughts
he never flagged in body or mind.
For the sake of living beings everywhere
he diligently sought the great Law,
taking no heed for himself
or for the gratification of the five desires.
Therefore the ruler of a great kingdom
through diligent seeking was able to acquire this Law
and eventually to attain Buddhahood,
as I will now explain to you.

The Buddha said to his monks: "The king at that time was I myself, and this seer was the man who is now Devadatta. All because Devadatta was a good friend to me, I was able to become fully endowed with this six paramitas, pity, compassion, joy, and indifference, with the thirty-two features, the eighty characteristics, the purple-tinged golden color, the ten powers, the four kinds of fearlessness, the four methods of winning people, the eighteen unshared properties, and the transcendental powers and the power of the way. The fact that I have attained impartial and correct enlightenment and can save living beings on a broad scale is all due to Devadatta who was a good friend."

Then the Buddha said to the four kinds of believers: "Devadatta, after immeasurable kalpas have past, will attain Buddhahood. He will be called Heavenly King Thus Come One, worthy of offerings of right and universal knowledge, perfect parity and conduct, well gone, understanding the world, on itself worthy, trainer of people, teacher of heavenly and human beings, Buddha, World-Honored One. This world will be called Heavenly Way, and at the same time Heavenly King Buddha will abide in the world for twenty medium kalpas, broadly preaching the Wonderful Law for the sake of living beings. Living beings numerous as Ganges sands will attain the fruit of arhatship. Immeasurable numbers of living beings will conceive that desire to become pratyekabuddhas, living beings numerous as Ganges sands will conceive a desire for the unsurpassed way, will gain that truth of birthless-ness, and will never regress. After Heavenly King Buddha enters parinirvana, his Correct Law will endure in the world for twenty medium kalpas. The relics from his whole body will be housed in a tower built of the seven treasures, sixty yojanas in height and forty yojanas in width and depth. All the heavenly and human beings will take assorted flowers, powdered incense, incense for burning, paste incense, clothing, necklaces, steamers and banners, jeweled canopies, music and songs of praise that offer them with obeisance to the wonderful seven- jeweled tower. Immeasurable numbers of living beings will attain the fruits of arhatship, numerous living beings will become enlightened as pratyekabuddhas, and unimaginable numbers of living beings will conceive a desire for bodhi and will in reach the level of no regression."

The Buddha said to the monks: "In future ages if there are good men or good women who, on hearing the Devadatta Chapter of the Lotus Sutra of the Wonderful Law, believe and revere it with pure hearts harbor no doubts are perplexities, they will never fall into hell or the realm of hungry spirits or of beasts, but will be born in the presence of the Buddhas of the ten directions, and in the place where they are born they will constantly hear this sutra. If they are born among human or heavenly beings, they will enjoy exceedingly wonderful delights, and if they are born in the presence of the Buddha, they will be born by transformation from lotus flowers."

At that time there was a bodhisattva who was among the followers of Many Treasures World-Honored One from the lower region and whose name was Wisdom Accumulated. He said to Many Treasures Buddha, "Shall return to our homeland?"

Shakyamuni Buddha said to Wisdom Accumulated, 'good man, wait a little while. There is a bodhisattva named Manjushri here whom you should see. Debate and discuss the wonderful Law with him, and then you may return to your homeland."

At that time Manjushri was seated on a thousand-pedaled lotus blossom big as a carriage wheel, and the bodhisattvas who had come with them were also seated on jeweled lotus blossoms. Manjushri had emerged in a natural manner from the palace of the dragon king Sagara in the great ocean and was suspended in the air. Proceeding to Holy Eagle Peak, he descended from the lotus blossom and, having entered the presence of the Buddhas, bowed his head and paid obeisance to the feet of the two World-Honored Ones. When he had concluded these gestures of respect, he went to where Wisdom Accumulated was and exchanged greetings with him, and retired then retired and sat at one side.

Bodhisattva Wisdom Accumulated questioned Manjushri, saying, "When you went to the palace of the dragon king, how many living beings did you convert?"

Manjushri replied, "The number is immeasurable, incapable of calculation. The mouth cannot express it, the mind cannot have fathom it. Wait a moment and there will be proof."

Before he had finished speaking, countless bodhisattvas seated on jeweled lotus blossoms emerged from the Ocean proceeded to Holy Eagle Peak, where they remained suspended in the air. These bodhisattvas all had been converted and saved by Manjushri. They had carried out all the bodhisattva practices and discussed and expounded the six paramitas with one another. Those who had originally been voice-hearers expounded the practices of the voice-hearer when they were in the air, but now all were practicing the Great Vehicle principle of emptiness.

Manjushri said to Wisdom Accumulated, "The work of teaching and converting carried out that in the ocean was as you can see."

At that time Bodhisattva Wisdom Accumulated recited these verses of praise:

Of great wisdom and virtue, brave and stalwart, you have converted and saved immeasurable beings.
Now those in this great assembly,
as well as I myself, have all seen them.
You expound the principle of the true entity,
open up the Law of the single vehicle,
broadly guiding the many beings,
causing them quickly to attain bodhi.

Manjushri said, "When I was in the ocean I constantly expounded the Lotus Sutra of the Wonderful Law alone."

Bodhisattva Wisdom Accumulated questioned Manjushri, saying, "This sutra is a profound, subtle and wonderful, a treasure among sutras, a rarity in the world. Are there perhaps any living beings who, by earnestly and diligently practicing this sutra, have been able to attain Buddhahood quickly?"

Manjushri replied, "There is the daughter of the dragon king Sagara, who was just turned eight. Her wisdom has keen roots and she is good at the understanding the root activities and of living beings. She has mastered the dharanis, has been able to accept and embrace all the store house of profound secrets preached by the Buddhas, has entered deep into meditation, thoroughly grasping the doctrines, and in the space of an instant conceived the desire for bodhi and reached the level of no regression. Her eloquence knows no hindrance, and she thinks of living beings with compassion as though they were her own children. She is fully endowed with blessings, and when it comes to conceiving in mind and expounding by mouth, she is subtle, wonderful, comprehensive and great. Kind, compassionate, benevolent, yielding, she is gentle and refined in will, capable of attaining bodhi."

Bodhisattva Wisdom Accumulated said, "When I observe Shakyamuni Thus Come One, I see that for immeasurable kalpas he carried out harsh and difficult practices, accumulated merit, piling up virtue, seeking the way to the bodhisattva without ever resting. I observe that throughout the thousand-million fold world there is not a single spot tiny as a mustard seed where this bodhisattva failed to sacrifice body and life the sake of living beings. Only after he had done that was he able to complete the bodhi way. I cannot believe that this girl in the space of the instant could actually achieve correct enlightenment."

Before his words had come to an end, the dragon king's daughter suddenly appeared before the Buddha, bowed her head in obeisance, and then retired to one side, reciting these verses of praise:

He profoundly understands the signs of guilt and good fortune
and illuminates the ten directions everywhere.
His subtle, wonderful pure Dharma body
is endowed with the thirty-two features;
the eighty characteristics
adorn his Dharma body.
Heavenly and human beings gaze up in awe,
dragons and spirits all pay honor and respect;

among all living beings,
none who do not hold him in reverence.
And having heard his teachings, I have attained bodhi -
the Buddha alone can bear witness to this.
I unfold the doctrines of the Great Vehicle
to rescue living beings from suffering.

At that time Shariputra said to the dragon girl, "You suppose that in this short time you have been able to attain the unsurpassed way. But this is difficult to believe. Why? Because a woman's body is soiled and defiled, not a vessel for the Law. How could you attain the unsurpassed bodhi? The road to Buddhahood is long and far-reaching. Only after one has spent immeasurable kalpas pursuing austerities, accumulating deeds, practicing all kinds of paramitas, can one finally achieve success. Moreover, a woman is subject to the five obstacles. First, she cannot become a Brahma heavenly king. Second, she cannot become the king Shakra. Third, she cannot become a devil king. Fourth, she cannot become a wheel-turning sage king. Fifth, she cannot become a Buddha. How then could a woman like you be able to attain Buddhahood so quickly?"

At that time the dragon girl had a precious jewel worth as much as the thousand-million-fold world which she presented to the Buddha. The Buddha immediately excepted it. The dragon girl said to Bodhisattva Wisdom Accumulated to the venerable one, Shariputra, "I presented the precious jewel and the World-Honored One accepted it - was that not quickly done?"

They replied, "Very quickly!"

The girls said, "employ your supernatural powers and watch me attain Buddhahood. It shall be even quicker than that!"

At that time the members of the assembly all saw the dragon girl in the space of an instant change into a man and carry out all the practices of a bodhisattva, immediately proceeding to the Spotless World of the south, taking a seat on a jeweled lotus, and attaining impartial and correct enlightenment. With the thirty-two features and the eighty characteristics, he expounded the wonderful Law for all living beings everywhere in the ten directions.

At that time in the saha world to a the bodhisattvas, voice-hearers, gods, dragons and others of the eight kinds of guardians, human and non-human beings all from a distance saw the dragon girl become a Buddha and preach the law to all the human and heavenly beings in the assembly at that time. Their hearts were filled with great joy and all from a distance paid reverent obeisance. Immeasurable living beings, hearing the Law, understood it and were able to reach the level of no regression. Immeasurable living beings received prophecies that they would gain the away. The Spotless World quaked and trembled in six different ways. Three thousand living beings of the saha world remained on the level of no regression. Three thousand living beings conceived a desire for bodhi and received prophecies of enlightenment. Bodhisattva Wisdom Accumulated, Shariputra and all the other members of the assembly silently believed an accepted these things.

Chapter Thirteen: Admonition to Embrace the Sutra

At that time the Bodhisattva and mahasattva Medicine King, along with the bodhisattva and mahasattva Great Joy of Preaching and twenty thousand bodhisattva followers who were accompanying them, all in the presence of the Buddha took this vow, saying: "We beg the World-Honored One to have no further worry. After the Buddha has entered extinction we will honor, embrace, read, recite and preach this sutra. Living beings in the evil age to come will have fewer and fewer good roots. Many will be overbearingly arrogant and greedy for offerings and other forms of gain, increasing the roots that are not good and moving farther away than ever from emancipation. But although it will be difficult to teach and convert them, we will summon up the power of great patience and will read and recite this sutra, embrace, preach, and copy it, offering it many kinds of alms and never begrudging our bodies or lives.

At that time in the assembly there were five hundred arhats who received a prophecy of enlightenment. They said to the Buddha, "World-Honored One, we too make a vow. In lands other than this one we will broadly preach this sutra."

Also there were eight thousand persons, some still learning, others with nothing more to learn, who received a prophecy of enlightenment. They rose from their seats, pressed their palms together and, turning toward the Buddha, made this vow: "World-Honored One, we too in other lands will broadly preach this sutra. Why? Because in this saha world the people are given to corruption and evil, beset by overbearing arrogance, shallow in blessings, irascible, muddled, fawning and devious, and their hearts are not sincere."

At that time the Buddha maternal aunt, the nun Mahaprajapati, and the six thousand nuns who accompanied her, some still learning, others with nothing more to learn, rose from their seats, pressed their palms together with a single mind and gazed up at the face of the honored one, their eyes never leaving him for instance.

At that time the World-Honored One said to Gautami , "Why do you look at the Thus Come One in that perplexed manner? In your heart are you perhaps worrying that I have failed to mention your name among those of received a prophecy of the attainment of anuttara-samyak-sambodhi? But Gautami, I earlier made a general statement saying that all the voice-hearers had received such a prophecy. Now if you would like to know the prophecy for you, I will say that in ages to come, amid the Law of sixty-eight thousands of millions of Buddhas, you will be a great teacher of Law, and the six thousand nuns, some still learning, some already sufficiently learned, will accompany you as teachers of the Law. In this manner you will bit by bit fulfill the way of the bodhisattva until you are able to become a Buddha with the name Gladly Seen by All Living Beings Thus Come One, worthy of offerings, of right and universal knowledge, perfect clarity and conduct, well gone, understanding the world, unexcelled worthy, trainer of people, teacher of heavenly and human beings, Buddha, World-Honored One. Gautami, this Gladly Seen by All Living Beings Buddha will confer a prophecy upon the six thousand bodhisattvas, to be passed from one to another, that they will attain anuttara-samyak-sambodhi."

At that time the mother of Rahula, the nun Yashodhara, thought to herself, the World-Honored One in his bestowal of prophecies has failed to mention my name alone!

The Buddha said to Yashodhara, "In future ages, amid the Law of hundreds, thousands, ten thousands, millions of Buddhas, you will practice the deeds of a bodhisattva, will be a great teacher of the Law, and will gradually fulfill the Buddha way. Then in a good land you will become a Buddha named Endowed with a Thousand Ten Thousand Glowing Marks Thus Come One, worthy of offerings, of right and universal knowledge, perfect clarity and conduct, well gone, understanding the world, unexcelled worthy, trainer of people, teacher of heavenly and human beings, Buddha, World-Honored One. The life span of this Buddha will be immeasurable asamkhya kalpas."

At that time the nun Mahaprajapati, the nun Yashodhara, and their followers were all filled with great joy, having gained what they had never had before. Immediately in the presence of the Buddha they spoke in verse form, saying:

World-Honored One, leader and teacher,
you bring tranquility to heavenly and human beings.
We have heard these prophecies
and our minds are peaceful and satisfied.

The nuns, having recited these verses, said to the Buddha, "World-Honored One, we too will be able to go to lands in other regions and broadly propagate this sutra.

At that time the World-Honored One looked at the eight hundred thousand million nayutas of bodhisattvas and mahasattvas. These bodhisattvas had all reached the level of avivartika, turned the unregressing wheel of the Law, and had gained dharanis. They rose from their seats, advanced before the Buddha and, pressing their palms together with a single mind, thought to themselves, if the World-Honored One should order us to embrace and preach this sutra, we would do as the Buddha instructed and broadly propagate this Law. And then they thought to themselves, But the Buddha now is silent and gives us no such order. What shall we do?

At that time the bodhisattvas, respectfully complying with the Buddha's will and at the same time wishing to fulfill their own original vows, proceeded in the presence of the Buddha to roar the Lion's roar and to make a vow, saying: "World-Honored One, after the Thus Come One has entered extinction we will travel here and there, back and forth through the worlds in the ten directions so as to enable living beings to copy this sutra, receive, embrace, read and recite it, understand and preach its principles, practice it in accordance with the Law, and properly keep it in their thoughts. All this will be done through the Buddha's power and authority. We beg that the World-Honored One, though in another region, will look on from afar and guard and protect us.

At that time the bodhisattvas joined their voices together and spoke in verse form, saying:

We beg you not to worry.
After the Buddha has passed into extinction,
in an age of fear and evil
we will preach far and wide.
There will be many ignorant people
who will curse and speak ill of us
and will attack us with swords and staves,
but we will endure all these things.
In that evil age there will be monks
with perverse wisdom and hearts that are fawning and crooked
who will suppose they have attained what they have not attained,
being proud and boastful in heart.
Or there will be forest-dwelling monks
wearing clothing of patched rags and living in retirement,
who will claim they are practicing the true way,
despising and looking down on all humankind.
Greedy for profit and support,
they will preach the law to white-robed laymen
and will be respected and revered by the world
as though they were arhats who possess the six
transcendental powers.
These men with evil in their hearts,
constantly thinking of worldly affairs,
will borrow the name of forest-dwelling monks
and take delight in proclaiming our faults,
saying things like this:
"These monks are greedy
for profit and support
and therefore they preach non-Buddhist doctrines
and fabricate their own scriptures

to delude the people of the world.
Because they hope to gain fame and renown thereby
they make distinctions when preaching this sutra."
Because in the midst of the great assembly
they constantly try to defame us,
they will address the rulers, high ministers,
Brahmans and householders,
as well as other monks,
slandering and speaking evil of us,
saying, "These are men of perverted views
who preach non-Buddhist doctrines!"
But because we revere the Buddha
we will bear all these evils.
Though they treat us with contempt, saying,
"You are all no doubt Buddhas!"
All such words of arrogance and contempt
we will endure and accept.
In a muddied kalpa, in an evil age
there will be many things to fear.
Evil demons will take possession of others
and through them curse, revile and heap shame on us.
But we, reverently trusting in the Buddha,
will put on the armor of perseverance.
In order to preach this sutra
we will bear these difficult things.
We care nothing for our bodies or lives
but are anxious only for the unsurpassed way.
In ages to come we will protect and uphold
what the Buddha has entrusted to us.
This the World-Honored One must know.
The evil monks of that muddied age,
failing to understand the Buddha's expedient means,
how he preaches the Law in accordance with what is appropriate,
will confront us with foul language and angry frowns;
again and again we will be banished
to a place far removed from towers and temples.
All these various evils,
because they keep in mind the Buddha's orders,
we will endure.
If in the settlements and towns
of those who seek the Law,
we will go to wherever they are
and preach the Law entrusted by the Buddha.
We will be envoys of the World-Honored One,
facing the assembly without fear.
We will preach the law with skill,
for we desire the Buddha to rest in tranquility.
In the presence of the World-Honored One
and of the Buddhas who have gathered from the ten directions
to proclaim this vow.
The Buddha must know what is in our hearts.

Chapter Fourteen: Peaceful Practices

At that time Manjushri, Dharma prince, bodhisattva and mahasattva, said to the Buddha: "World-Honored One, these bodhisattvas undertake something that is very difficult. Because they revere and obey the Buddha, they have taken a great vow that in the evil age hereafter they will guard, uphold, read, recite and preach this Lotus Sutra. World-Honored One, in the evil age hereafter, how should these bodhisattvas, mahasattvas go about preaching this sutra?"

The Buddha said to Manjushri: "If these bodhisattvas and mahasattvas in the evil age hereafter wish to preach this sutra they should abide by four rules. First they should abide by the practices and associations proper for bodhisattvas so that they can expound this sutra for the sake of living beings. Manjushri, what do I mean by the practices of a bodhisattva or mahasattva? If a bodhisattva or mahasattva takes his stand on perseverance, is gentle and compliant, never violent, and never alarmed in mind; and if with regard to phenomena he takes no action but observes the true entity of phenomena without acting or making any distinction, then this one might call the practices of a bodhisattva and mahasattva.

"As for the associations proper for them, bodhisattvas and mahasattvas should not associate closely with rulers, princes, high ministers or heads of offices. They should not associate closely with non-Buddhists, Brahmans or Jains, or with those who compose works of secular literature or books extolling the heretics, nor should they be closely associated with Lokayatas or anti-Lokayatas. They should not be closely associated with hazardous amusement, boxing or wrestling, or with actors or others engaging in various kinds of illusionary entertainment, or with the chandalas, persons engaging in raising pigs, engaged in raising pigs, sheep, chickens or dogs, or those who engage in hunting or fishing or other evil activities. If such persons at times come to one, then one may preach the Law for them, but one should expect nothing from it. Again one should not associate with monks, nuns, laymen or laywomen who seek to become voice-hearers, nor should one question or visit them. One should not stay with them in the same room, or in the place where one exercises, or in the lecture hall. One should not join them in their activities. If at times they come to one, one should preach the Law in accordance with what is appropriate, but should expect nothing from it.

"Manjushri, the bodhisattva or mahasattva should not, when preaching the Law to women, do so in a manner that could arouse thoughts of desire in them, nor should he delight in seeing them. If he enters the house of another person, he should not engage in talk with the young girls, unmarried women or widows. Nor should he go near the five types of unmanly men or have any close dealings with them 5. He should not enter another person's house alone. If for some reason it is imperative to enter alone, he should concentrate his full mind on thoughts of the Buddha. If he should preach the Law for a woman, he should not bear his teeth in laughter or let his chest become exposed. He should not have any intimate dealings with her even for the sake of the Law, much less for any other purpose.

"He should not delight in nurturing underage disciples, shramaneras or children, and should not delight in sharing the same teacher with them. He should constantly take pleasure in sitting in meditation, being in quiet surroundings and learning to still his mind. Manjushri, these are what I call the things he should first of all associate himself with.

"Next, the bodhisattva or mahasattva should view all phenomena as empty, that being their true entity. They do not turn upside down, do not move, do not regress, do not revolve. They are like empty space, without innate nature, beyond the reach of all words. They are not born, do not emerge, do not arise. They are without name, without form, without true being. They are without volume, without limits, without hindrance, without barriers. It is only through causes and conditions that they exist, and come to be taken upside down, to be born. Therefore I say that one should constantly delight in viewing the form of phenomena as this. This is what I call the second thing that the bodhisattva or mahasattva should associate himself with."

At that time the World-Honored One, wishing to state his meaning once more, spoke in verse form, saying:

If there are bodhisattvas
who in the evil age hereafter
wish with fearless hearts
to preach this sutra,
these are the places they should enter
and the persons they should closely associate with.
At all times shun rulers
and the princes of kingdoms,
high ministers, heads of offices,
those engaged in hazardous amusements
as well as chandalas,
non-Buddhists and Brahmans.
One should not associate
with persons of overbearing arrogance
or those who stubbornly adhere to the Lesser Vehicle
and are learned in its three storehouses.
Monks who violate the precepts,
arhats who are so in name only,
nuns who are fond
of jesting and laughter,
or women lay believers
who are profoundly attached to the five desires
or who seek immediate entry into extinction -
all these one should not associate with.
If there are persons
who come with good hearts
to the place of the bodhisattva
in order to hear the Buddha way,
then the bodhisattva
with a fearless heart
but without harboring expectations
should preach the Law for them.
But widows and unmarried women
and the different kinds of unmanly men -
all these he should not associate with
or treat with intimacy.
Also he must not associate with
slaughterers or flesh-carvers,
those who hunt animals or catch fish,
or kill to do harm for profit.
Those who peddle meat for a living
or display women and sell their favors -
all persons such as this
one should never associate with.
Those engaged in hazardous sports,
wrestling, or other kinds of amusements,
women of lascivious nature -
never associate with any of these.
Never go alone into an enclosed place
to preach the Law to a woman.
When you preach the Law,
let there be no jesting or laughter.
When you enter a village to beg for food,
take another monk with you;
if there is no other monk around,
with a single mind concentrate on the Buddha.

These are what I call
proper practices and associations.
By being careful about these two,
one can preach in a peaceful manner.
One should not speak in terms of
superior medial or inferior doctrines,
of doctrines of the conditioned or unconditioned,
or the real or the not real.
Again one should not make distinctions
by saying "This is a man," "This is a woman."
Do not try to apprehend phenomena,
to understand or to see them.
These are what I call
the practices of the bodhisattva.
All phenomena
are empty, without being,
without any constant abiding,
without arising or extinction.
This I call the position
the wise person associates himself with.
From upside-down-ness come distinctions,
that phenomena exist, do not exist,
are real, or not real,
are born, are not born.
Place yourself in quiet surroundings,
learn to still your mind,
remain tranquil, and moving,
like Mount Sumeru.
Look upon all phenomena
as having no existence,
like empty space,
as without firmness or hardness,
not born, not emerging,
not moving, and regressing,
constantly abiding in a single form -
this I call the place to draw near to.
If after I have entered extinction
there are monks
who take up these practices
and these associations,
then when they preach this sutra
they will be free of quailing and timidity.
If a bodhisattva will at times
enter a quiet room
and with the correct mental attitude
will view phenomena according to the doctrine,
and then, rising from his meditation,
will for the sake of the ruler,
the princes, ministers and people,
the Brahmans and others,
unfold, propagate, expound
and preach this sutra,
then his mind will be tranquil,
free of quailing and timidity.
Manjushri,
these I call the first set of rules

for the bodhisattva to abide by
to enable him in later ages
to preach the Lotus Sutra.

"Furthermore, Manjushri, after the Thus Come One has passed into extinction, in the Latter Day of the Law, if one wishes to preach this sutra, you should abide by these peaceful practices. When he opens his mouth to expound or when he reads the sutra, he should not delight in speaking of the faults of other people or scriptures. He should not display contempt for other teachers of the Law or speak of other people's tastes or shortcomings. With regard to the voice-hearers he should not refer to them by name and describe their faults, or name them and praise their good points. Also he should not allow his mind to become filled with resentment or hatred. Because he is good at cultivating this kind of peaceful mind, his listeners will not oppose his ideas. If he is asked difficult questions, he should not reply in terms of the Law of a Lesser Vehicle. He should explain things solely in terms of the Great Vehicle so that people will be able to acquire wisdom embracing all species."

At that time the World-Honored One, wishing to state his meaning once more, spoke in verse form, saying:

The bodhisattva should at all times delight
in preaching the Law in a tranquil manner.
On pure and clean ground
he should spread his sitting mat,
anoint his body with oil,
wash away dust and impurities,
put on a new clean robe
and make himself both inwardly and outwardly pure.
Seating himself comfortably in the Dharma seat,
he should preach the Law in accordance with questions.
If there are monks
or nuns,
men lay believers,
women lay believers,
rulers and princes,
officials, gentlemen and common people,
with a mild expression he should preach for them
the subtle and wonderful doctrines.
If there are difficult questions
he should answer them in accordance with the doctrines,
employing causes and conditions, similes and parables
to expound and make distinctions,
and through these expedient means
cause all listeners to aspire to enlightenment,
to increase their benefits little by little
and enter the Buddha way.
He should put aside all ideas of laziness,
all thought of negligence or ease,
remove himself from cares and worries
and with a compassionate mind preach the Law.
Day and night constantly he should expound
the teachings of the unsurpassed way,
employing causes and conditions,
immeasurable similes and parables
to instruct living beings
and cause them all to be joyful.
Clothing and bedding,
food, drink, medicine -
with regard to such things

he should have no expectations
but with a single mind concentrate
upon the reasons for preaching the Law,
desiring to complete the Buddha away
and to cause those in the assembly to do likewise.
That will bring great gain to them,
an offering of peace.
After I have passed into extinction
if there are monks
who are able to expound
this Lotus Sutra of the Wonderful Law
their minds will be free of the jealousy and anger,
of all worry and hindrance.
No one will trouble them,
curse or revile them.
They will know no fear,
no attacks by sword or staff,
nor will they ever be banished,
because they abide in patience.
Wise persons will be good
at cultivating their minds like this
and be able to abide in peace
as I have described above.
The blessings of such persons
are beyond calculation, simile or parable;
thousands, ten thousands, millions of kalpas
would not suffice to describe them.

"Also, Manjushri, if a bodhisattva or mahasattva in the latter age hereafter, when the Law is about to parish, should accept and embrace, read and recite this sutra, he must not harbor a mind marked by jealousy, fawning or deceit. And he must not be contemptuous of or revile those who study the Buddha away or seek out their shortcomings.

"If there are monks, nuns, laymen, or laywomen who seek to become voice-hearers, seek to become pratyekabuddhas, or seek the bodhisattva way, one must not trouble them by causing them to have doubts or regrets, by saying to them, 'You are far removed from the way and in the end will never be able to attain wisdom embracing all species. Why? Because you are self-indulgent and willful people who are negligent of the way!'

"Also one should never engage in frivolous debate over the various doctrines or dispute or wrangle over them. With regard to all living beings one should think of them with great compassion. With regard to the Thus Come Ones, think of them as kindly fathers; with regard to the bodhisattvas, think of them as great teachers. Toward the great bodhisattvas of the ten directions at all times maintain a serious mind, paying them due reverence and obeisance. To all living beings preach the Law and in an equitable manner. Because a person is heedful of the Law, that does not mean one should vary the amount of preaching. Even to those who show a profound love for the Law one should not on that account preach at greater length.

"Manjushri, if among these bodhisattvas and mahasattvas there are those who in the latter age hereafter, when the Law is about to perish, succeed in carrying out this third set of peaceful practices, then when they preach this Law they will be free from anxiety and confusion, and will find good fellow students to read and recite this sutra with. They will attract a large assembly of persons who come to listen and assent. After they have listened, they will embrace; after they have embraced, they will recite; after they have recited, they will preach; and after they have preached, they will copy, or will cause others to copy, and will present offerings to the sutra rolls, treating them with reverence, respect and praise."

At that time the World-Honored One, wishing to state his meaning once more, spoke in verse form, saying:

If you wish to preach this sutra,
you must set aside jealousy, hatred, arrogance,
a mind that is fawning, deceitful, false,
and constantly practice honest and upright conduct.
Do not look with contempt on others
or hold frivolous debates on the doctrine.
Do not cause others to have doubts or regrets
by saying, "You will never become a Buddha!"
When a son of the Buddha preaches the Law
he is at all times gentle and full of forbearance,
having pity and compassion on all,
never giving way to a negligent or a slothful mind.
The great bodhisattvas of the ten directions
out of pity for the multitude carry out the way.
One should strive to respect and read and revere them,
saying, "These are great teachers!"
Regarding the Buddhas, the World-Honored Ones,
learn to think of them as unsurpassed fathers.
Wipe out the mind of pride and arrogance
and preach the Law without hindrance.
Such is the third set of rules;
wise persons should guard and obey them.
If with a single mind they observe these peaceful practices,
they will be respected by immeasurable multitudes.

"Manjushri, if among these bodhisattvas and mahasattvas there are those who in the age hereafter, when the Law is about to perish, accept and embrace the Lotus Sutra, toward the believers who are still in the household or those who have left the household they should cultivate a mind of great compassion, and toward those who are not bodhisattvas they should also cultivate a mind of great compassion, and should think to themselves: These persons have made a great error. Though the Thus Come One as an expedient means preaches the Law in accordance with what is appropriate, they do not listen, do not know, do not realize, do not inquire, do not believe, do not understand. But although these persons do not inquire about, do not believe and do not understand this sutra, when I have attained anuttara-samyak-sambodhi, wherever I happen to be, I will employ my transcendental powers and the power of wisdom to draw them to me to cause them to abide in this Law.

"Manjushri after the Thus Come One has entered extinction, if among these bodhisattvas and mahasattvas there are those who will succeed in carrying out this fourth set of rules, then when they preach the Law they will commit no error. Monks, nuns, laymen, laywomen, and rulers, princes, great ministers, common people, Brahmans and householders will constantly offer them alms and will revere, respect and praise them. The heavenly beings in the sky, in order to listen to the Law, will constantly follow and attend them. If they are in a settlement or town or in a quiet and deserted place or a forest and people come and want to ask them difficult questions, the heavenly beings day and night will for the sake of the Law constantly guard and protect them and will cause all the listeners to rejoice. Why? Because this sutra is protected by the supernatural powers of all the Buddhas of the past, future, and present.

"Manjushri, as for this Lotus Sutra, throughout immeasurable numbers of lands one cannot even hear its name, much less be able to see it, accept and embrace, read and recite it. Manjushri, suppose, for example, that there is a powerful wheel-turning sage king who wants to use his might to subdue other countries, but the petty rulers will not heed his commands. At that time the wheel-turning king calls up his various troops and sets out to attack. If the king sees any of his fighting forces who have won distinction in battle, he is greatly delighted and immediately rewards the persons in accordance with their merits, handing out fields, houses, settlements and towns, or robes and personal adornments, or perhaps giving out various precious objects such as gold, silver, lapis lazuli, seashell, agate, coral or amber, or elephants, horses, carriages, men and women servants, and people. Only the bright jewel that is in his topknot he does not give away. Why?

Because this one jewel exists only on the top of the King's head, and if he were to give it away, his followers would be certain to express great consternation and alarm.

"Manjushri, the Thus Come One is like this. He uses the power of meditation and wisdom to win Dharma lands and become king of the threefold world. But the devil kings are unwilling to obey and submit. The worthy and sage military leaders of the Thus Come One engage them in battle, and when any of the Buddha's soldiers achieve distinction, the Buddha is delighted in heart and in the midst of the four kinds of believers he preaches various sutras, causing their hearts to be joyful. He presents them with meditations, emancipations, roots and powers that are free of outflows, and other treasures of the Law. He also presents them with the city of nirvana, telling them that they have attained extinction, guiding their minds and causing them all to rejoice. But he does not preach the Lotus Sutra to them.

"Manjushri, when the wheel-turning king sees someone among his soldiers who has gained truly great distinction, he is so delighted in heart that he takes the unbelievably fine jewel that has been in his topknot for so long and has never been recklessly given away, and now gives it to this man. And the Thus Come One does the same. In the threefold world he acts as the great Dharma king. He uses the Law to teach and convert all living beings, watches his worthy and sage armies as they battle with the devils of the five components, the devils of earthly desires, and the death devil. And when they have won great distinction and merit, wiping out the three poisons, emerging from the threefold world, and destroying the nets of the devils, at that time the Thus Come One is filled with great joy. This Lotus Sutra is capable of causing all living beings to attain comprehensive wisdom. It will face much hostility in the world and be difficult to believe. It has not been practiced before, but now I preach it.

"Manjushri, this Lotus Sutra is foremost among all that is preached by the Thus Come One. Among all that is preached it is the most profound. And it is given at the very last, the way that profound ruler did when he took the bright jewel he had guarded for so long and finally gave it away.

"Manjushri this Lotus Sutra is the secret storehouse of the Buddhas, the Thus Come Ones. Among the sutras, it holds the highest place. Through the long night I have guarded and protected it and have never recklessly propagated it. But today for the first time I expound it for your sake."

At that time the World-Honored One, wishing to state his meaning once more, spoken in verse form, saying:

Constantly practice perseverance,
have pity on all beings,
and do your best to expound and preach
the sutra praised by the Buddha.
In the latter age hereafter
those who embrace this sutra should,
without regard to persons in the household, persons who have
left it,
or persons who are not bodhisattvas,
cultivate pity and compassion,
saying, "If they do not listen to
and do not believe this sutra
they will be committing a great error.
If I gain the bodhisattva away
I will employ expedient means
and preach this Law for them,
causing them to abide in it.
Suppose there is a powerful
wheel-turning king.
His soldiers have won merit in battle
and he rewards them with various articles,
elephants, horses, carriages,
adornments for their person,

fields and houses,
settlements and towns,
or gives them clothing,
various kinds of precious objects,
men and women servants, wealth and goods,
delightedly bestowing all these.
But if there is someone brave and stalwart
who can carry out difficult deeds,
the king will remove the bright jewel from his topknot
and present it to the man.
The Thus Come One is like this.
He acts as king of the doctrines,
possessing the great power of perseverance
and the precious storehouse of wisdom,
and with his great pity and compassion
he converts the age in accordance with the Law.
He sees all persons
as they undergo suffering and anxiety,
seeking to gain emancipation
battling with the devils,
and for the sake of the living beings
he preaches various doctrines,
employing great expedient means
and preaching these sutras.
And when he knows that living beings
have gained powers through them,
then at the very last for their sake
he preaches this Lotus Sutra,
like the king who unbinds his topknot
and gives away his bright jewel.
This sutra is to be honored
as highest among all sutras.
Constantly I guard and protect it,
and do not purposely reveal it.
But now the time is right
for me to preach it to you.
After I have entered extinction
if someone seeks the Buddha away
and hopes to be able in tranquility
to expound this sutra,
then he should associate himself closely
with the four rules described.
Anyone who reads this sutra
will at all times be free of worry and anxiety;
likewise he will be without illness or pain,
his expression fresh and bright.
He will not be born in poverty or want,
in humble or ugly circumstances.
Living beings will delight to see him
and look up to him as a worthy sage.
The young sons of heavenly beings
will wait on him and serve him.
Swords and staves will not touch him
and poison will have no power to harm him.
If people speak ill and revile him,
their mouths will be closed and stopped up.

He will stroll about without fear
like the lion king.
The brilliance of his wisdom
will be like the shining of the sun;
even in his dreams
he will see only wonderful things.
He will see the Thus Come Ones
seated in their lion seats
surrounded by multitudes of monks
and preaching the Law.
And he will see dragons, spirits,
asuras and others,
numerous as Ganges sands,
reverently pressing their palms together.
He will see himself there
and will preach the Law for them.
Again he will see Buddhas,
their bodies marked by a golden hue,
emitting immeasurable rays
that light up all things,
employing Brahma sounds
to expound the doctrines.
For the four kinds of believers
the Buddha will preach the unsurpassed Law,
and he will see himself among them
pressing his palms together and praising the Buddha.
He will hear the Law and delight
and will offer alms.
He will obtain dharanis
and proof of the wisdom without regression.
And when the Buddha knows that his mind
has entered deep into the Buddha way,
then he will give him a prophecy
that he will attain the highest, the correct enlightenment.
"You, good man,
in an age to come
will attain immeasurable wisdom,
the great way of the Buddha.
Your land will be adorned and pure,
incomparably broad and great,
with the four kinds of believers
who press their palms together and listen to the Law.
Again he will see himself
in the midst of mountains and forests
practicing the good Law,
understanding the true nature of all phenomena,
deeply entering meditation
and seeing the Buddhas of the ten directions.
Of Buddhas, their bodies of golden hue,
adorned with the marks of a hundred kinds of good fortune,
of listening to the Law and preaching it to the people -
such will be the good dreams he constantly dreams.
Again he will dream he is king of a country
but casts aside palaces and attendants
and the superb and wonderful objects of the five desires,
repairs to the place of practice

and under the bodhi tree
seats himself in a lion seat,
seeking the way, and after seven days
gains the wisdom of the Buddhas.
Having succeeded in the unsurpassed way,
he rises and turns the wheel of the Law,
preaching the Law for the four kinds of believers,
for thousands, ten thousands, millions of kalpas
preaching the wonderful Law free of outflows,
saving immeasurable living beings.
And afterward he will enter nirvana
like smoke coming to an end when a lamp goes out.
If in that evil age hereafter
someone preaches this foremost Law,
that person will gain great benefits,
blessings such as have been described above.

Chapter Fifteen: Emerging from the Earth

At that time the bodhisattvas and mahasattvas who had gathered from the lands of the other directions, greater in number than sands of eight Ganges, stood up in the midst of the great assembly, pressed their palms together, bowed in obeisance and said to the Buddha: "World-Honored One, if you will permit us in the age after the Buddha has entered extinction to diligently and earnestly protect, read, recite, copy and offer alms to this sutra in the saha world, we will preach it widely throughout this land!"

At that time the Buddha said to the bodhisattvas and mahasattvas: Leave off, good men! There is no need for you to protect this sutra. Why? Because in this saha world of mine there are bodhisattvas and mahasattvas who are as numerous as the sands of sixty thousand Ganges, and each of these bodhisattvas has a retinue equal to the sands of sixty thousand Ganges. After I have entered extinction these persons will be able to protect, read, recite and widely preach this sutra.

When the Buddha spoke these words, the earth of the thousand million fold countries of the saha world all trembled and split open, and out of it emerged at the same instant immeasurable thousands, ten thousands, millions of bodhisattvas and mahasattvas. The bodies of these bodhisattvas were all golden in hue, with the thirty-two features and an immeasurable brightness. Previously they all had been dwelling in the world of empty space beneath the saha world. But when these bodhisattvas heard the voice of the Shakyamuni Buddha speaking, they came up from below.

Each one of these bodhisattvas was the leader of his own great assembly, and each brought with him a retinue equal in number to the sands of sixty thousand Ganges. To say nothing of those who brought retinues equal to the sands of fifty thousand, forty thousand, thirty thousand, twenty thousand, or ten thousand Ganges. Or a retinue equal to as little as the sands of one Ganges, half a Ganges, one fourth of a Ganges, or as little as one part in a thousand, ten thousand, a million nayutas of Ganges. Or those whose retinue was only one thousand ten thousand million nayutas. Or only a million ten thousand. Or only a thousand ten thousand, a hundred ten thousand, or just ten thousand. Or only one thousand, one hundred, or ten. Or who brought with them only five, four, three, two or one disciple. Or those who came alone, preferring to carry out solitary practices. Such were they, then, immeasurable, boundless, beyond anything that can be known through calculation, simile or parable.

After these bodhisattvas that emerged from the earth, they each one proceeded to the wonderful tower of seven treasures suspended in the sky where Many Treasures Thus Come One and Shakyamuni Buddha were. On reaching it, they turned to the two World-Honored Ones, bowed their heads and made obeisance at their feet. They also all performed obeisance to the Buddhas seated on lion thrones underneath the jeweled trees. Then they circled around to the right three times, pressed their palms together in a gesture of respect, utilizing the bodhisattvas' various methods of praising to deliver praises, and then took up a position to one side, gazing up in joy at the two World-Honored Ones. While these bodhisattvas and mahasattvas who had emerged from the earth were employing the bodhisattva's various methods of praising to praise the Buddhas, an interval of fifty small kalpas passed by.

At that time Shakyamuni Buddha sat silent, and the four kinds of believers likewise all remained silent for fifty small kalpas, but because of the supernatural powers of the Buddha, it was made to seem to the members of the great assembly like only half a day.

At that time the four kinds of believers, also because of the supernatural powers of the Buddha, saw these bodhisattvas filling the sky over immeasurable hundreds, thousands, ten thousands, and millions of lands. Among these bodhisattvas were four leaders. The first was called Superior Practices, the second was called Boundless Practices, the third was called Pure Practices, and the fourth was called Firmly Established Practices. These four bodhisattvas were the foremost leaders and guiding teachers among all the group. In the presence of the great assembly, each one of these pressed his palms together, gazed at Shakyamuni Buddha and inquired: "World-Honored One, are your illnesses few, are your worries few, are your practices proceeding comfortably? Do those whom you propose to save readily receive instruction? Does the effort not cause the World-Honored One to become weary and spent?

At that time the four great bodhisattvas spoke in verse form saying:

Is the World Honored One comfortable,
with few illnesses, few worries?
In teaching and converting living beings,
can you do so without fatigue and weariness?
And do living beings
receive instruction readily or not?
Does it not cause the World-Honored One
to become weary and spent?

At that time in the midst of the great assembly of bodhisattvas the World-Honored One spoke these words: "Just so, just so, good men! The Thus Come One is well and happy, with few ills and few worries.

The living beings are readily converted and saved and I am not weary and spent. Why? Because for age after age in the past the living beings have constantly received my instruction. And also they have offered alms and paid reverence to the Buddhas of the past and have planted various good roots. So when these living beings see me for the first time and listen to my preaching, they all immediately believe and accept it, entering into the wisdom of the Thus Come One, with the exception of those who earlier practiced and studied the Lesser Vehicle. And now I will make it possible for these persons to listen to this sutra and enter the wisdom of the Buddha."

At that time the [four] great bodhisattvas spoke in verse form, saying:

Excellent, excellent,
Great hero, World-Honored One!
The living beings
are readily converted and saved.
They know how to inquire about
the most profound wisdom of the Buddha,
and having heard, they believe and understand it.
We are accordingly overjoyed.

At that time the World-Honored One praised the great bodhisattvas who led the group, saying: "Excellent, excellent, good men! You know how to rejoice in your hearts for the Thus Come One."

At that time the bodhisattva Maitreya and the multitude of bodhisattvas equal in number to the sands of eight thousand Ganges all thought to themselves: Never in the past have we seen or heard of such a great multitude of bodhisattvas and mahasattvas as these who have emerged from the earth and now stand before the World-Honored One pressing their palms together, offering alms, and inquiring about the Thus Come One!

At that time the bodhisattva and mahasattvas Maitreya, knowing the thought that was in the minds of the bodhisattvas as numerous as the sands of eight thousand Ganges, and wishing also to resolve his own doubts, pressed his palms together, turned to the Buddha and made this inquiry in verse form:

Immeasurable thousands, ten thousands, millions,
a great host of bodhisattvas
such as was never seen in the past -
I beg the most honored of two-legged beings to explain
where they have come from,
what causes and conditions bring them together!
Huge in body, with great transcendental powers,
unfathomable in wisdom,
firm in their intent and thought,

with the power of great perseverance,
the kind living beings delight to see -
where have they come from?
Each one of these bodhisattvas
brings with them a retinue
immeasurable in number
like the sands of the Ganges.
Some of these great bodhisattvas
bring numbers equal to sixty thousand Ganges sands.
And this great multitude
with a single mind seek the Buddha way.
These great teachers
equal in number to sixty thousand Ganges sands
together come to offer alms to the Buddha
and to guard and uphold this sutra.
More numerous are those with followers
like the sands of fifty thousand Ganges,
those with followers like the sands of forty thousand,
thirty thousand,
twenty thousand, ten thousand,
one thousand, one hundred,
or the sands of the single Ganges,
half a Ganges, one-third, one-fourth,
or only one part in a million ten thousand;
those with one thousand, ten thousand nayutas,
ten thousand, a million disciples,
or half a million-
they are more numerous still.
Those with a million or ten thousand followers,
a thousand or a hundred,
fifty or ten,
three, two or one,
or those who come alone without followers,
delighting in solitude,
all coming to where the Buddha is-
they are even more numerous than those described above.
If one should try to use an abacus
to calculate the number of this great multitude,
though he spent as many kalpas as Ganges sands
he could never know the full sum.
This host of bodhisattvas
with their great dignity, virtue and diligence -
who preached the Law for them,
who taught and converted them and brought them to this?
Under whom did they first set their minds on enlightenment,
what Buddha's Law do they praise and proclaim?
What sutra do they embrace and carry out,
what Buddha way do they practice?
These bodhisattvas
possess transcendental powers and the power of great wisdom.
The earth in four directions trembles and splits
and they all emerged from out of it.
World-Honored One, from times past
I have seen nothing like this!
I beg you to tell me where they come from,
the name of the land.

I have constantly journeyed from land to land
but never have I seen such a thing!
In this whole multitude
there is not one person that I know.
Suddenly they have come up from the earth -
I beg you to explain the cause.
The members of this great assembly now,
the immeasurable hundreds, thousands, millions
of bodhisattvas,
all want to know these things.
Regarding the causes that govern the beginning and end
of this multitude of bodhisattvas,
possessor of immeasurable virtue, World-Honored One,
we beg you to dispel the doubts of the assembly!

At that time the Buddhas who were emanations of Shakyamuni Buddha and had arrived from immeasurable
thousands, ten thousands, millions of lands in other directions, were seated cross-legged on lion seats under
the jeweled trees in the eight directions. The attendants of these Buddhas all saw the great multitude of
bodhisattvas who had emerged from the earth in the four directions of the thousand-million-fold world and
were suspended in the air, and each one said to his respective Buddha: "World-Honored One, this great
multitude of immeasurable, boundless asamkhayas of bodhisattvas - were did they come from?"

At the time each of the Buddhas spoke to his attendants, saying: "Good men, wait a moment. There is a
bodhisattva and mahasattva named Maitreya who has received a prophecy from Shakyamuni Buddha that he
will be the next thereafter to become a Buddha. He has already inquired about this matter and the Buddha is
now about to answer him. You should take this opportunity to listen to what he says."

At that time Shakyamuni Buddha said to the bodhisattva Maitreya: "Excellent, excellent, Ajita that you should
question the Buddha about this great affair. All of you with a single mind should don the armor of diligence
and determine to be firm in intent. The Thus Come One wishes now to summon forth and declare the
wisdom of the Buddhas, the freely exercised transcendental power of the Buddhas, the power of the Buddhas
that has the lion's ferocity, the fierce and greatly forceful power of the Buddhas.

At the time the World-Honored One, wishing to state his meaning once more, spoke in verse form, saying:

Be diligent and of a single mind,
for I wish to explain this affair.
Have no doubts or regrets -
the Buddha wisdom is hard to fathom.
Now you must put forth the power of faith,
abiding in patience in goodness.

A Law which in the past was never heard
you will now be able to hear.
Now I will bring you ease and consolation -
do not harbor doubts or fears.
The Buddha has nothing but truthful words,
his wisdom cannot be measured.
This foremost Law that he has gained
is very profound, incapable of analysis.
He will now expound it -
you must listen with a single mind.

At that time the World-Honored One, having spoken these verses, said to the bodhisattva Maitreya: "With
regard to this great multitude I now say to you. Ajita, these bodhisattvas and mahasattvas who in
immeasurable and countless asamkhayas have emerged from the earth and whom you have never seen before

in the past - when I had attained anuttara-samyak-sambodhi in this saha world, I converted and guided these bodhisattvas, trained their minds and caused them to develop a longing for the way. These bodhisattvas all have been dwelling in the world of empty space underneath the saha world. They read, recite, understand the various scriptures, ponder them, make distinctions and keep them correctly in mind.

Ajita, these good men take no delight in being in the assembly and indulging in much talk. Their delight is constantly to be in a quiet place, exerting themselves diligently and never resting. Nor do they linger among human or heavenly beings, but constantly delight in profound wisdom, being free from all hindrances. And they constantly delight in the law of the Buddhas, diligently and with a single mind pursuing unsurpassed wisdom."

At that time the World-Honored One, wishing to state his meaning once more, spoke in verse form, saying:

Ajita, you should understand this.
These great bodhisattvas
for countless kalpas
have practice the Buddha wisdom.
All have been converted by me;
I caused them to set their minds on the great way.

These are my sons,
they dwell in this world,
constantly carrying out dhuta practices,
preferring a quiet place,
rejecting the fret and confusion of the great assembly,
taking no delight in much talk.
In this manner these sons
study and practice my way and Law.
And in order that day and night with constant diligence
they may seek the Buddha way,
in this saha world
they dwell in the empty space in its lower part.
Firm in the power of will and concentration,
with constant diligence seeking wisdom,
they expound various wonderful doctrines
and their minds are without fear.
When I was in the city of Gaya,
seated beneath the bodhi tree,
I attained the highest, the correct enlightenment
and turned the wheel of the unsurpassed Law.
Therefore I taught and converted them,
caused them for the first time to set their minds on the way.
Now all of them dwell in the stage of no regression,
and all in time will be able to become Buddhas.
What I speak now are true words -
with a single mind you must believe them!
Ever since the long distant past
I have been teaching and converting this multitude.

At that time the bodhisattva and mahasattva Maitreya, as well as the countless other bodhisattvas, found doubts and perplexities rising in their minds. They were puzzled at this thing that had never happened before and thought to themselves: How could the World-Honored One in such a short space of time have taught and converted an immeasurable, boundless asamkhya number of great bodhisattvas of this sort enabled them to dwell in anuttara-samyak-sambodhi?

Thereupon Maitreya said to the Buddha: "World-Honored One, when the Thus Come One was crown prince, you left the palace of the Shakyas and sat in the place of practice not far from the city of Gaya, and there attained anuttara-samyak-sambodhi. Barely forty years or more have passed since then. World-Honored One, how in that short time could you have accomplished so much work as a Buddha? Was it through the authoritative powers of the Buddha, or through the blessings of the Buddha, that you were able to teach and convert such an immeasurable number of great bodhisattvas and enable them to achieve anuttara-samyak-sambodhi? World-Honored One, a multitude of great bodhisattvas such as this - a person might spend a thousand, ten thousand, a million kalpas counting them and never be able to reach the end or discover the limit! Since the far distant past, in the dwelling place of immeasurable, boundless numbers of Buddhas, they must have planted good roots, carried out the bodhisattva way, and engaged, constantly in Brahma practices. World-Honored One, it is hard for the world to believe such thing!

Suppose, for example, that a young man of twenty-five, with ruddy complexion and hair still black, should point to someone who was a hundred years old and say, 'This is my son!' or that the hundred year old man should point to the youth and say, 'This is my father who sired and raised me!' This would be hard to believe, and so too is what the Buddha says.

"It has in fact not been long since you attained the way. But this great multitude of bodhisattvas have already for immeasurable thousands, ten thousands, millions of kalpas applied themselves diligently and earnestly for the sake of the Buddha way. They have learned to enter into, emerge from and dwell in immeasurable hundreds, thousands, ten thousands, millions of samadhis, have acquired great transcendental powers, have over a long period carried out Brahma practices, and have been able step by step to practice various good doctrines, becoming skilled in questions and answers, a treasure among persons, something seldom known in all the worlds. And today, World-Honored One, you tell us that, in the time since you attained the Buddha way, you have caused these persons for the first time to aspire to enlightenment, have taught, converted and led them, and directed them toward anuttara-samyak-sambodhi!

"World-Honored One, it is not long since you attained Buddhahood, and yet you have been able to carry out this great meritorious undertaking! We ourselves have faith in the Buddha, believing that he preaches in accordance with what is appropriate, that the words spoken by the Buddha are never false, and that the Buddha's knowledge is in all cases penetrating and comprehensive. Nevertheless, in the period after the Buddha has entered extinction, if bodhisattvas who have just begun to aspire to enlightenment should hear these words, they will perhaps not believe or accept them but will be led to commit the crime of rejecting the Law. Therefore, World-Honored One, we beg you to explain so we may put aside our doubts, and so that, in future ages when good men hear this matter, they will not entertain doubts!

At that time the bodhisattva Maitreya, wishing to state his meaning once more, spoke in verse form, saying:

In the past the Buddha departed from the Shakya clan,
left his household, and near Gaya
set under the bodhi tree.
Little time has passed since then,
yet these sons of the Buddha
are immeasurable in number!
Already for a long time they have practiced the Buddha way,
dwelling in transcendental powers and the power of wisdom,
skillfully learning the bodhisattva way,
unsoiled by worldly things
like the lotus flower in the water.
Emerging from the earth,
all display a reverent and respectful mind,
standing in the presence of the World-Honored One.
This is difficult to fathom -
How can one believe it?
The Buddha attained the way very recently,
yet those he has helped to gain success are so many!

We beg you to dispel the doubts of the assembly,
to make distinctions and explain the truth of the matter.
It is though a young man
just turned twenty-five
were to point to a hundred year old man
with gray hair and wrinkled face
and say, I sired him!'
And the old man were to say, 'This is my father!'

The father youthful, the son old -
no one in the world could believe this!
World-Honored One, your case is similar.
Only very recently you attained the way.
These bodhisattvas
are firm in will, in no way timid or immature.
For measurable kalpas
they have been practicing the bodhisattva way.
They are clever at difficult questions and answers,
their minds know no fear.
They have firmly cultivated a persevering mind,
upright in dignity and virtue.
They are praised by the Buddhas of the ten directions
as able and adept at preaching distinctions.
They have no wish to remain among the crowd
but constantly favor a state of meditation,
and in order to seek the Buddha way
they have been dwelling in the space under the earth.
This we have heard from the Buddha
and have no doubts in the matter.
But for the sake of future ages we beg the Buddha
to explain and bring about understanding.
If with regard to this sutra
one should harbor doubt and fail to believe,
he will fall at once into the evil paths.
So we beg you now to explain.
These immeasurable bodhisattvas -
how in such a short time
did you teach them, cause them to have aspiring minds,
and to dwell in the stage of no regression?

Chapter Sixteen: The Life Span of the Tathagata

At that time the Buddha spoke to the Bodhisattvas and all the great assembly: "Good men, you must believe and understand the truthful words of the Thus Come One." And again he said to the great assembly: You must believe and understand the truthful words of the Thus Come One." And once more he said to the great assembly: "You must believe and understand the truthful words of the Thus Come One."

At that time the bodhisattvas and the great assembly, with Maitreya as their leader, pressed their palms together and addressed the Buddha, saying: "World-Honored One, we beg you to explain. We will believe and accept the Buddha's words." They spoke in this manner three times, and then said once more: "We beg you to explain it. We will believe and accept the Buddha's words."

At that time the World-Honored One, seeing that the bodhisattvas repeated their request three times and more, spoke to them, saying: "You must listen carefully and hear of the Thus Come One's secret and his transcendental powers. In all the worlds the heavenly and human beings and asuras all believe that the present Shakyamuni Buddha, after leaving the palace of the Shakyas, seated himself in the place of practice not far from the city of Gaya and there attained anuttara-samyak-sambodhi. But good men, it has been immeasurable, boundless hundreds, thousands, ten thousands, millions of nayutas of kalpas since I in fact attained Buddhahood.

"Suppose a person were to take five hundred, a thousand, ten thousand, a million nayuta asamkhya thousand-million-fold worlds and grind them to dust. Then, moving eastward, each time he passes five hundred, a thousand, ten thousand, a million nayuta asamkhya worlds he drops a particle of dust. He continues eastward in this way until he has finished dropping all the particles. Good men, what is your opinion? Can the total number of all these worlds be imagined or calculated?"

The bodhisattva Maitreya and the others said to the Buddha: "World-Honored One, these worlds are immeasurable, boundless--one cannot calculate their number, nor does the mind have the power to encompass them. Even all the voice-hearers and pratyekabuddhas with their wisdom free of outflows could not imagine or understand how many there are. Although we abide in the stage of avivartika, we cannot comprehend such a matter. World-Honored One, these worlds are immeasurable and boundless."

At that time the Buddha said to the multitude of great bodhisattvas: "Good men, now I will state this to you clearly. Suppose all these worlds, whether they received a particle of dust or not, are once more reduced to dust. Let one particle represent one kalpa. The time that has passed since I attained Buddhahood surpasses this by a hundred, a thousand, ten thousand, a million nayuta asamkhya kalpas.

"Ever since then I have been constantly in this saha world, preaching the Law, teaching and converting, and elsewhere I have led and benefited living beings in hundreds, thousands, ten thousands, millions of nayutas and asamkhayas of lands.

"Good men, during that time I have spoken about the Buddha Burning Torch and others, and described how they entered nirvana. All this I employed as an expedient means to make distinctions.

"Good men, if there are living beings who come to me, I employ my Buddha eye to observe their faith and to see if their other faculties are keen or dull, and then depending upon how receptive they are to salvation, I appear in different places and preach to them under different names, and describe the length of time during which my teachings will be effective. Sometimes when I make my appearance I say that I am about to enter nirvana, and also employ different expedient means to preach the subtle and wonderful Law, thus causing living beings to awaken joyful minds.

"Good men, the Thus Come One observes how among living beings there are those who delight in a little Law, meager in virtue and heavy with defilement. For such persons I describe how in my youth I left my household and attained anuttara-samyak-sambodhi. But in truth the time since I attained Buddhahood is extremely long, as I have told you. It is simply that I use this expedient means to teach and convert living beings and cause them to enter the Buddha way. That is why I speak in this manner.

"Good men, the scriptures expounded by the Thus Come One are all for the purpose of saving and emancipating living beings. Sometimes I speak of myself, sometimes of others: sometimes I present myself, sometimes others; sometimes I show my own actions, sometimes those of others. All that I preach is true and not false.

Why do I do this? The Thus Come One perceives the true aspect of the threefold world exactly as it is. There is no ebb or flow of birth and death, and there is no existing in this world and later entering extinction. It is neither substantial nor empty, neither consistent nor diverse. Nor is it what those who dwell in the threefold world perceive it to be. All such things the Thus Come One sees clearly and without error.

"Because living beings have different natures, different desires, different actions, and different ways of thinking and making distinctions, and because I want to enable them to put down good roots, I employ a variety of causes and conditions, similes, parables, and phrases and preach different doctrines. This, the Buddha's work, I have never for a moment neglected.

"Thus, since I attained Buddhahood, an extremely long period of time has passed. My life span is an immeasurable number of asamkhya kalpas, and during that time I have constantly abided here without ever entering extinction. Good men, originally I practiced the bodhisattva way, and the life span that I acquired then has yet to come to an end but will last twice the number of years that have already passed. Now, however, although in fact I do not actually enter extinction, I announce that I am going to adopt the course of extinction. This is an expedient means which the Thus Come One uses to teach and convert living beings.

"Why do I do this? Because if the Buddha remains in the world for a long time, those persons with shallow virtue will fail to plant good roots but, living in poverty and lowliness, will become attached to the five desires and be caught in the net of deluded thoughts and imaginings. If they see that the Thus Come One is constantly in the world and never enters extinction, they will grow arrogant and selfish, or become discouraged and neglectful. They will fail to realize how difficult it is to encounter the Buddha and will not approach him with a respectful and reverent mind.

"Therefore as an expedient means the Thus Come One says: 'Monks, you should know that it is a rare thing to live at a time when one of the Buddhas appears in the world.' Why does he do this? Because persons of shallow virtue may pass immeasurable hundreds, thousands, ten thousands, millions of kalpas with some of them chancing to see a Buddha and others never seeing one at all. For this reason I say to them: 'Monks, the Thus Come One is hard to get to see.' When living beings hear these words, they are certain to realize how difficult it is to encounter the Buddha. In their minds they will harbor a longing and will thirst to gaze upon the Buddha, and then they will work to plant good roots. Therefore the Thus Come One, though in truth he does not enter extinction, speaks of passing into extinction.

"Good men, the Buddhas and Thus Come Ones all preach a Law such as this. They act in order to save all living beings, so what they do is true and not false.

"Suppose, for example, that there is a skilled physician who is wise and understanding and knows how to compound medicines to effectively cure all kinds of diseases. He has many sons, perhaps ten, twenty, or even a hundred. He goes off to some other land far away to see about a certain affair. After he has gone, the children drink some kind of poison that make them distraught with pain and they fall writhing to the ground.

"At that time the father returns to his home and finds that his children have drunk poison. Some are completely out of their minds, while others are not. Seeing their father from far off, all are overjoyed and kneel down and entreat him, saying: 'How fine that you have returned safely. We were stupid and by mistake drank some poison. We beg you to cure us and let us live out our lives!'

"The father, seeing his children suffering like this, follows various prescriptions. Gathering fine medicinal herbs that meet all the requirements of color, fragrance and flavor, he grinds, sifts and mixes them together.

Giving a dose of these to his children, he tells them: 'This is a highly effective medicine, meeting all the requirements of color, fragrance and flavor. Take it and you will quickly be relieved of your sufferings and will be free of all illness.'

"Those children who have not lost their senses can see that this is good medicine, outstanding in both color and fragrance, so they take it immediately and are completely cured of their sickness. Those who are out of their minds are equally delighted to see their father return and beg him to cure their sickness, but when they are given the medicine, they refuse to take it. Why? Because the poison has penetrated deeply and their minds no longer function as before. So although the medicine is of excellent color and fragrance, they do not perceive it as good.

"The father thinks to himself: My poor children! Because of the poison in them, their minds are completely befuddled. Although they are happy to see me and ask me to cure them, they refuse to take this excellent medicine. I must now resort to some expedient means to induce them to take the medicine. So he says to them: 'You should know that I am now old and worn out, and the time of my death has come. I will leave this good medicine here. You should take it and not worry that it will not cure you.' Having given these instructions, he then goes off to another land where he sends a messenger home to announce, 'Your father is dead.'

"At that time the children, hearing that their father has deserted them and died, are filled with great grief and consternation and think to themselves: If our father were alive he would have pity on us and see that we are protected. But now he has abandoned us and died in some other country far away. We are shelter-less orphans with no one to rely on!

"Constantly harboring such feelings of grief, they at last come to their senses and realize that the medicine is in fact excellent in color and fragrance and flavor, and so they take it and are healed of all the effects of the poison. The father, hearing that his children are all cured, immediately returns home and appears to them all once more.

"Good men, what is your opinion? Can anyone say that this skilled physician is guilty of lying?"

"No, World-Honored One."

The Buddha said: "It is the same with me. It has been immeasurable, boundless hundreds, thousands, ten thousands, millions of nayuta and asamkhya kalpas since I attained Buddhahood. But for the sake of living beings I employ the power of expedient means and say that I am about to pass into extinction. In view of the circumstances, however, no one can say that I have been guilty of lies or falsehoods."

At that time the World-Honored One, wishing to state his meaning once more, spoke in verse form, saying:

Since I attained Buddhahood
the number of kalpas that have passed
is an immeasurable hundreds, thousands, ten thousands,
millions, trillions, asamkhayas.
Constantly I have preached the Law, teaching, converting
countless millions of living beings,
causing them to enter the Buddha way,
all this for immeasurable kalpas.
In order to save living beings,
as an expedient means I appear to enter nirvana
but in truth I do not pass into extinction.
I am always here preaching the Law.
I am always here,
but through my transcendental powers
I make it so that living beings in their befuddlement
do not see me even when close by.

When the multitude see that I have passed into extinction,
far and wide they offer alms to my relics.

All harbor thoughts of yearning
and in their minds thirst to gaze at me.
When living beings have become truly faithful,
honest and upright, gentle in intent,
single-mindedly desiring to see the Buddha
not hesitating even if it costs them their lives,
then I and the assembly of monks
appear together on Holy Eagle Peak.
At that time I tell the living beings
that I am always here, never entering extinction,
but that because of the power of an expedient means
at times I appear to be extinct, at other times not,
and that if there are living beings in other lands
who are reverent and sincere in their wish to believe,
then among them too
I will preach the unsurpassed Law.
But you have not heard of this,
so you suppose that I enter extinction.
When I look at living beings
I see them drowned in a sea of suffering;
therefore I do not show myself,
causing them to thirst for me.
Then when their minds are filled with yearning,
at last I appear and preach the Law for them.
Such are my transcendental powers.
For asamkhya kalpas
constantly I have dwelled on Holy Eagle Peak
and in various other places.
When living beings witness the end of a kalpa
and all is consumed in a great fire,
this, my land, remains safe and tranquil,
constantly filled with heavenly and human beings.
The halls and pavilions in its gardens and groves
are adorned with various kinds of gems.
Jeweled trees abound in flowers and fruit
where living beings enjoy themselves at ease.
The gods strike heavenly drums,
constantly making many kinds of music.

Mandarava blossoms rain down,
scattering over the Buddha and the great assembly.
My pure land is not destroyed,
yet the multitude see it as consumed in fire,
with anxiety, fear and other sufferings
filling it everywhere.
These living beings with their various offenses,
through causes arising from their evil actions,
spend asamkhya kalpas
without hearing the name of the Three Treasures.
But those who practice meritorious ways,
who are gentle, peaceful, honest and upright,
all of them will see me
here in person, preaching the Law.

At times for this multitude
I describe the Buddha's life span as immeasurable,
and to those who see the Buddha only after a long time
I explain how difficult it is to meet the Buddha.
Such is the power of my wisdom
that its sagacious beams shine without measure.
This life span of countless kalpas
I gained as the result of lengthy practice.
You who are possessed of wisdom,
entertain no doubts on this point!
Cast them off, end them forever,
for the Buddha's words are true, not false.
He is like a skilled physician
who uses an expedient means to cure his deranged sons.
Though in fact alive, he gives out word he is dead,
yet no one can say he speaks falsely.
I am the father of this world,
saving those who suffer and are afflicted.
Because of the befuddlement of ordinary people,
though I live, I give out word I have entered extinction.
For if they see me constantly,
arrogance and selfishness arise in their minds.
Abandoning restraint, they give themselves up to the
five desires
and fall into the evil paths of existence.
Always I am aware of which living beings
practice the way, and which do not,
and in response to their needs for salvation
I preach various doctrines for them.
At all times I think to myself:
How can I cause living beings
to gain entry into the unsurpassed way
and quickly acquire the body of a Buddha?

Chapter Seventeen: Distinction of Benefits

At that time, when the great assembly heard the Buddha describe how his life span lasted such a very long number of kalpas, immeasurable, boundless asamkhayas of living beings gained a great many rich benefits.

At that time the World-Honored One said to the bodhisattva and mahasattva Maitreya: "Ajita, when I described how the life span of the Thus Come One lasts for such an exceedingly long time, living beings numerous as the sands of six hundred and eighty ten thousands, millions, nayutas of Ganges attained the truth of birthlessness. And bodhisattvas and mahasattvas a thousand times more in number gained the dharani teaching that allows them to retain all that they hear. And bodhisattvas and mahasattvas numerous as the dust particles of entire world gained the eloquence that allows them to speak pleasingly and without hindrance. And bodhisattvas and mahasattvas numerous as the dust particles of entire world gained dharanis that allow them to retain hundreds, thousands, then thousands, millions, immeasurable repetitions of the teachings. And bodhisattvas and mahasattvas numerous as the dust particles of a thousand-million fold world were able to turn the unregressing wheel of a Law. And bodhisattvas and mahasattvas numerous as dust particles of two thousand middle sized lands were able to turn the pure wheel of a Law. And bodhisattvas and mahasattvas numerous as the dust particles of a thousand small lands gained assurance that they would attain anuttara-samyak-sambodhi after eight rebirths. And bodhisattvas and mahasattvas numerous as a dust particles of four four-continent worlds gained assurance that they would attain anuttara-samyak-sambodhi after four rebirths. And bodhisattvas and mahasattvas numerous as the dust particles of three four-continent worlds gained assurance that they would attain anuttara-samyak-sambodhi after two rebirths. And bodhisattvas and mahasattvas numerous as the dust particles of two four-continent worlds gained assurance that they will attain anuttara-samyak-sambodhi after two rebirths. And bodhisattvas and mahasattvas numerous as the dust particles of one four-continent world gained assurance that they would attain anuttara-samyak-sambodhi after one rebirth. And living beings numerous as the dust particles of eight worlds were all moved to set their minds upon anuttara-samyak-sambodhi.

When the Buddha announced that these bodhisattvas and mahasattvas had gained the great benefits of the Law, from the midst of the air mandarava flowers and great mandarava flowers rained down, scattering over the immeasurable hundreds, thousands, ten thousands, millions of Buddhas who were seated on lion seats under jeweled trees, and also scattering over Shakyamuni Buddha, and over Many Treasures Thus Come One who long ago entered extinction, both of whom were seated on lion seats in the tower of seven treasures. They also scattered over all the great bodhisattvas and the four kinds of believers. In addition, finely powdered sandalwood and aloes rained down, and in the midst of the air heavenly drums sounded of their own accord, wonderful notes deep and far-reaching. And a thousand varieties of heavenly robes rained down, draped with various necklaces, pearl necklaces, mani jewel necklaces, necklaces of wish-granting jewels, spreading everywhere in nine directions. In jewel-encrusted censers priceless incenses burned, their fragrance of their own accord permeating everywhere as an offering to the great assembly. Above each one of the Buddhas there appeared bodhisattvas holding banners and canopies, in rows reaching up to the Brahma heaven. These bodhisattvas employed their wonderful voices in singing immeasurable hymns of praise to the Buddhas.

At that time the bodhisattva Maitreya rose from his seat, bared his right shoulder and, pressing his palms together and facing the Buddha, spoke in verse form, saying:

The Buddha preaches a rarely encountered Law,
one never heard from past times.
The World-Honored One possesses great powers
and his life span cannot be measured.
The countless sons of the Buddha,
hearing the World-Honored One make distinctions
and describe the benefits of the Law they will gain,
find their whole bodies filled with joy.
Some abide in this stage of no regression,
some have acquired dharanis,

some can speak pleasingly and without hindrance
or retain ten thousand, a million repetitions of the teachings.
Some bodhisattvas numerous as the dust particles
of a thousand major worlds
are all able to turn
the unregressing wheel of the Law.
Some Bodhisattvas numerous as the dust particles
of a thousand intermediate worlds
are all able to turn
the pure wheel of the Law.
And some bodhisattvas numerous as the dust particles
of a thousand minor worlds
are assured that after eight more rebirths
they will be able to complete the Buddha way.
Some bodhisattvas numerous as the dust particles
of four, three, two times
the four continents
after a corresponding number of rebirths will become Buddhas;
some bodhisattvas numerous as the dust particles
of one set of the four continents
after one more rebirth
will attain comprehensive wisdom.
Thus when living beings
hear of the great length of the Buddha's life,
they gain pure fruits and rewards
that are immeasurable and free of outflows.
Again living beings numerous as the dust particles
of eight worlds,
hearing the Buddha describe his life span,
all set their minds on the unsurpassed way.
The World-Honored One preaches a Law
that is immeasurable and cannot be fathomed,
and those who benefit from it are many,
as boundless as the open air.
Heavenly mandarava flowers
and great mandarava flowers rain down;
Shakyas and Brahmas like Ganges sands.
Arrive from countless Buddha lands.
Sandalwood and aloes
in the jumble of fine powder rain down;
like birds flying down from the sky
they scatter as an offering over the Buddhas.
In the midst of the air heavenly drums
of their own accord emit wonderful sounds;
heavenly robes by the thousand, ten thousand, million
come whirling and fluttering down;
wonderful jewel-encrusted censers
burn priceless incense
which of his own accord permeates everywhere,
an offering to all the World-Honored Ones.
The multitude of great bodhisattvas
hold banners and canopies adorned with the seven treasures,
ten thousand, a million in kind, lofty, wonderful,
in rows reaching up to the Brahma heaven.
Before each one of the Buddhas
hang jeweled streamers and superlative banners,

while in thousands, ten thousands of verses
the praises of the Thus Come One are sung.
All these many things
have never been known in the past.
Hearing that the Buddha's life is immeasurable,
all beings are filled with joy.
The Buddha's name is heard in ten directions,
widely benefiting living beings,
and all are endowed with good roots
to help them set their minds on the unsurpassed way.

At that time the Buddha said to the bodhisattva in mahasattva Maitreya: "Ajita, if there are living beings who, on hearing that the life span of the Buddha is of such long duration, are able to believe and understand it even for a moment, the benefits they gain thereby will be without limit or measure. Suppose there are good men or good women who, for the sake of anuttara-samyak-sambodhi, over a period of eight hundred thousand million nayutas of kalpas practice the five paramitas - the paramitas of dana (almsgiving), shila (keeping of the precepts), kshanti (forbearance), virya (assiduousness) and dhyana (meditation), the paramita of prajna being omitted - the benefits they obtain will now measure up to even a hundred part, the thousandth part, a hundred, thousand, ten thousand, millionth part of the benefits mentioned previously. Indeed, it is beyond the power of calculation, simile or parable to convey the comparison. For good men who have gained such benefits as those [mentioned previously] to fall back without reaching the goal of anuttara-samyak-sambodhi is utterly unimaginable."

At that time the World-Honored One, wishing to state his meaning once more, spoke in verse form, saying:

If someone seeking the Buddha wisdom
for a period of eight hundred thousand million
nayutas of kalpas
should practice the five paramitas,
during all those kalpas
distributing alms to the Buddhas
and to the pratyekabuddhas and disciples
and the multitude of bodhisattvas,
rare delicacies of food and drink,
fine garments and articles of bedding,
or building religious retreats of sandalwood
adorned with gardens and grows
if he should distribute alms
of many varieties, all refined and wonderful,
and do this for the entire number of kalpas
to express his devotion to the Buddha away;
and if moreover he should keep the precepts,
in purity and without omission or outflow,
seeking the unsurpassed way,
praised by the Buddhas;
and if he should practice forbearance,
remaining in a posture of submission and gentleness,
even when various evils are visited on him,
not allowing his mind to be roused or swayed;
when others, convinced they have gained the Law,
harbor thoughts of overbearing arrogance
and he is treated with contempt and vexed by them,
if he can still endure it with patience;
and if he is diligent and assiduous,
ever firm in intent and thought,
for immeasurable millions of kalpas

single-minded, and never lax or neglectful,
for countless kalpas
dwelling in a deserted and quiet place;
and if he practices sitting and walking exercises,
banishing drowsiness, constantly regulating his mind,
and as a result of such actions
is able to produce states of meditation,
for eighty million ten thousand kalpas
remaining calm, his mind never deranged;
and if he holds to the blessings of this single-mindedness
and with it seeks the unsurpassed way,
saying, "I will gain comprehensive wisdom
and exhaust all the states of meditation!"
If this person for a hundred, a thousand,
ten thousand, a million kalpas
should carry out these meritorious practices
as I have described above,
still those good men and women
who hear me describe my life span
and believe it for even a moment
win blessings that surpass those of such a person.
If a person is completely free
of all doubt and regret,
if in the depths of this mind he believes for one instant,
his blessings will be such as this.
These bodhisattvas
who have practiced the way for immeasurable kalpas
when they hear me describe my life span
are able to believe and accept what I say.
These persons will
gratefully accept this sutra, saying,
"Our wish is that in future ages
we may use our long lives to save living beings.
Just as today the World-Honored One,
king of the Shakyas,
roars like a lion in the place of practice,
preaching the Law without fear,
so may we too in ages to come,
honored and revered by all,
when we sit in the place of practice
describe our life span in the same manner."
If there are those profound in mind,
pure, honest and upright,
who, hearing much, can retain it all,
who follow principle in understanding the Buddha's words,
then persons such as this
will have no doubts [about my lives span].

"Furthermore, Ajita, if there is someone who, hearing of the long duration of the Buddha's life span, can understand the import of such words, the benefits that such a person acquires will be without limit or measure, able to awaken in him unsurpassed wisdom of the Thus Come One. How much more so, then, if far and wide a person listens to this sutra or cause others to listen to it, embraces it himself or causes others to embrace it, copies it himself or cause others to copy it, or presents flowers, incense, necklaces, streamers, banners, silken canopies, fragrant oil or lamps of butter oil as offerings to the sutra rolls. The benefits of such a person will be immeasurable, boundless, able to inspire in him to wisdom that embraces all species.

"Ajita, if good men and good women, hearing me describe the great length of my life span, in the depths of their mind believe and understand, then they will see the Buddha constantly abiding on Mount Gridhrakuta, with the great bodhisattvas and multitude of voice-hearers surrounding him, preaching the Law. They will also see this saha world, its ground of lapis lazuli level and well ordered, the Jambunada gold bordering its eight highways, the rows of Jeweled trees, the terraces, towers and observatories all made of jewels, and all the multitude of bodhisattvas who live in their midst. If there are those who are able to see such things, you should known that it is a mark of their deep faith and understanding.

"Again, if after the Thus Come One has entered extinction there are those who hear this sutra and do not slander or speak ill of it but have already shown deep faith and understanding. How much more in the case of persons who read, recite and embrace this sutra! Such persons are in effect receiving the Thus Come One on the crown of their heads.

"Ajita, these good men and good women need not for my sake erect towers and temples or build monks quarters or make the four kinds of offerings to the community of monks. Why? Because these good men and good women, in receiving, embracing, reading and reciting this sutra, have already erected towers, constructed monks quarters, and given alms to the community of monks. It should be considered that they have erected towers adorned with the seven treasures for the relics of the Buddha, broad at the base and tapering at the top, reaching to the Brahma heaven, hung with banners, canopies, and a multitude of jeweled bells, with flowers, incense, necklaces, powdered incense, paste incense, incense for burning, many kinds of drums, musical instruments, pipes, harps, and various types of dances and diversions, and with wonderful voices that sing and intone hymns of praise. It is as though they have already offered alms for immeasurable thousands, ten thousands, millions of kalpas.

"Ajita, if after I have entered extinction there are those who hear this sutra and can accept and uphold it, copy it themselves or cause others to copy it, then it may be considered that they have already erected monks quarters, or used red sandalwood to construct thirty-two halls, as tall as eight tala trees, lofty, spacious and beautifully adorned to accommodate hundreds and thousands of monks. Gardens, groves, pools, lakes, exercise grounds, caves for meditation, clothing, food, drink, beds, matting, medicines, and all kinds of utensils for comfort fill them, and these monks quarters and halls number in the hundreds, thousands, ten thousands, millions, and indeed are immeasurable in number. All these are presented before me as alms for me in the community of monks.

"So I say, if after the Thus Come One enters extinction there are those who accept, uphold, read and recite the sutra or preach it to others, who copy it themselves or cause others to copy it, or who offer alms to the sutra rolls, then they need not erect towers or temples or build monks quarters or offer alms to the community of monks. And how much more is this true for those who are able to embrace this sutra and at the same time dispense alms, keep the precepts, practice forbearance, and display diligence, single-mindedness and wisdom! Their virtue will be uppermost, immeasurable and boundless, as the open sky, east, west, north and south, in the four intermediate directions and up and down, is immeasurable and boundless. The blessings of such persons will be as immeasurable and boundless as this, and such persons will quickly attain the wisdom embraces all species.

"If a person reads, recites, accepts and upholds this sutra or preaches it to others; if he copies it himself or causes others to copy it; and if he can erect towers, build monks quarters, offer alms and praise to the community of voice-hearers; if he can employ hundreds, thousands, ten thousands, millions of modes of praise to praise the merits of the bodhisattvas; and if for the sake of others he employs various causes and conditions and accords with principle in explaining and preaching this Lotus Sutra; and if he can observe the precepts with purity, keep company with those who are gentle and peaceful, be forbearing and without anger, firm in intent and thoughts, constantly prizing the practice of sitting and meditation, attaining various states of profound meditation, diligent and courageous, mastering all the good doctrines, keen in faculties and wisdom, good at answering difficult questions - Ajita, if after I have entered extinction there are good men and good women who accept, uphold, read and recite this sutra and have good merits such as these, you should know that they have already proceeded to the place of practice and are drawing near to anuttara-samyak-sambodhi as they sit beneath the tree of the way. Ajita, wherever these good men and good women sit or stand or circle in exercise, there one should erect a tower, and all heavenly and human beings should offer alms to it as they would to the tower of the Buddha."

At that time the World-Honored One, wishing to state his meaning once more, spoke in verse form, saying:

If after I have entered extinction
a person who can honor and uphold this sutra,
his blessings will be immeasurable,
as I have described above.
It is as though he had supplied
all manner of alms,
erecting a tower for the Buddha's relics
adorned with the seven treasures
and with a central pole very tall and wide
that tapers gradually as it reaches the Brahma heaven.
Jeweled bells by the thousands, ten thousand, million,
move in the wind, emitting a wonderful sound.
And for immeasurable kalpas
he offers alms to this tower,
flowers, incense, various kinds of necklaces,
heavenly robes and assorted musical instruments,
and burns fragrant oil and lamps of butter oil
that constantly light up the area around.
In the evil age of the Latter Day of the Law
if there is someone who can uphold this sutra,
it will be as though he supplied all alms
ascribed above.
If someone can uphold this sutra,
it will be as though in the presence of the Buddha
he should use ox-head sandalwood
to build monks quarters as an offering,
or thirty-two halls
as high as eight tala trees,
or supply all kinds
of superior foods and wonderful clothes and bedding,
residences for assemblies of hundreds, thousands,
gardens, groves, pools and lakes,
exercise grounds and caves for meditation,
all with various kinds of fine adornments.
If someone with a believing and understanding mind
accepts, upholds, reads, recites and copies this sutra
or causes others to copy it
or offers alms to the sutra rolls,
scattering flowers, and incense and powdered incense
or constantly burning fragrant oil
extracted from sumana, champaka
or atimuktaka flowers,
if he offers alms such as these
he will gain immeasurable merits,
boundless as the open air,
and his blessings will also be like this.
How much more so if one upholds this sutra
and at the same time dispense alms, keeps the precepts,
is forbearing, delights in meditation,
and never gives way to anger or evil speaking.
If one displays reverence toward memorial towers,

humbles himself before monks,
gives a wide berth to an arrogant mind,
constantly ponders upon wisdom
and is never angry when asked difficult questions
but responds compliantly with an explanation -
if one can carry out such practices,
his merits will be beyond measure.

If you see a teacher of the Law
who has cultivated virtues such as these,
you should scatter heavenly flowers over him,
clothe his body in heavenly robes,
bow your head before his feet in salutation,
and in your mind imagine you see the Buddha.
You should also think to yourself:
before long he will proceed to the place of practice
and attain a state of no outflows and no action,
bringing wide benefits to heavenly and human beings!
In the place where such a person resides,
where he walks, sits or lies down,
or recites even one verse of scripture,
there you should erect a tower
adorned in a fitting and wonderful manner
and offer alms of various kinds to it.
When a son of the Buddha dwells in such places
the Buddha will accept and utilize them,
and constantly in their midst
will walk, sit or lie down.

Chapter Eighteen: The Benefits of Joyful Acceptance

At that time the bodhisattva and mahasattva Maitreya said to the Buddha: World-Honored One, if there are good men or good women who, hearing this Lotus Sutra, respond with joy, what amount of blessings do they acquire?"

Then he spoke in verse, saying:

After the World-Honored One has passed into extinction,
if those who hear this sutra
are able to respond with joy,
what a mount of blessings will they acquire?

At that time the Buddha said to the bodhisattva Maitreya: "Ajita, after the Thus Come One has entered extinction, suppose there are monks, nuns, laymen, laywomen, or other persons of wisdom, whether old or young, who, hearing the sutra, respond with joy and, leaving the Dharma assembly, go to some other place, perhaps a monks quarters, a spot that is deserted and quiet, a city, a community, the settlement or a village, and there in accordance with what they have heard they put forth effort and preaching in expounding for the sake of their parents and relatives, their good friends and acquaintances. These persons, after hearing, respond with joy and they too set about spreading the teachings. One person, having heard, responds with joy and spreads the teachings, and the teachings in this way continue to be handed along from one to another until they reach a fiftieth person.

"Ajita, the benefits received by this fiftieth good man or good woman who responds with joy I will now describe to you - he must listen carefully. Imagine all the beings in the six paths of existence of four hundred ten thousand million asamkhya worlds, all the four kinds of living beings, those born from the egg, those born from the womb, those born from dampness, and those born by transformation, those with form, those without form, those with thought, those without thought, those who are not with thought, those who are not without thought, those without legs, those with two legs, four legs or many legs. And imagine that, among all of this vast number of living beings, a person should come who is seeking blessings and, responding to their various desires, dispenses objects of amazement and playthings to all these living beings. Each one of these living beings is given gold, silver, lapis lazuli, seashell, agate, coral, amber, and other wonderful and precious gems, as well as elephants, horses, carriages, and palaces and towers made of the seven treasures, enough to fill a whole Jambudvipa. This great dispenser of charity, having handed out gifts in this manner for a full eighty years, then thinks to himself: I have already doled out objects of amusement and playthings to these living beings, responding to various desires. But these living beings are now old and decrepit, their years over eighty, their hair white, their faces wrinkled, before long they will die. I now should employ the law of the Buddha to instruct and guide them.

"Immediately he gathers all the living beings together and propagates the Law among them, teaching, benefiting and delighting them. In one moment all are able to attain the way of the srota-apanna, the way of the sakridagamin, the way of the anagamin, and the way of arhat, to exhaust all outflows and enter deeply into meditation. All attain freedom and become endowed with eight emancipations. Now what is your opinion? Are the benefits gained by this great dispenser of charity many are not?"

Maitreya said to the Buddha: "World-Honored One, this man's benefits are very many indeed, immeasurable and boundless. Even if this dispenser of charity had merely given all those playthings to living beings, his benefits would still be immeasurable. And how much more so when he has enabled them to attain the fruits of arhatship!"

The Buddhas said to Maitreya: "I will now state the matter clearly for you. This man gave all these objects of amusement to living beings in the six paths of existence of four hundred ten thousand million asamkhya worlds and also made it possible for them to attain the fruits of arhatship. But the benefits that he gains do not match the benefits of the fiftieth person who hears just one verse of the Lotus Sutra and responds with joy. They are not equal to one hundredth, one thousandth, one part in a hundred, thousand, ten thousand, a million. Indeed it is beyond the power of calculation, simile or parable to express the comparison.

"Ajita, the benefits gained by even the fiftieth person who hears the Lotus Sutra as it is handed along to him responds with joy. His blessings are greater by an immeasurable, boundless asamkhya number, and are in fact incomparable.

"Moreover, Ajita, suppose a person for the sake of this sutra visits a monks quarters and, sitting or standing, even for a moment listens to it and accepts it. As a result of the benefits so obtained, when he is reborn in his next existence he will enjoy the finest, most superior and wonderful elephants, horses and carriages, and palanquins decked with rare treasures, and will mount up to the heavenly palaces. Or suppose there is a person who is sitting in the place where the Law is expounded, and when another person appears, the first person urges them to sit down and listen, or offers to share his seat and so persuades him to sit down. The benefits gained by this person will be such that when he is reborn he will be in a place where lord Shakra is seated, where the heavenly king Brahma is seated, or were a wheel-turning sage king is seated.

"Ajita, suppose there is a person who speaks to another person, saying, 'There is a sutra called the Lotus. Let us go together and listen to it.' And suppose, having been urged, the other person goes and even for an instant listens to the sutra. The benefits of the first person will be such that when he is reborn he will be born in the same place as dharani bodhisattvas. He will have keen faculties and wisdom. For a hundred, a thousand, ten thousand ages he will never be struck dumb. His mouth will not emit a foul odor. His tongue will never been afflicted, nor will his mouth be afflicted. His teeth will not be stained or black, nor will they be yellow or widely spaced, nor will they be missing or fall out or be at an angle or crooked. His lips will not droop down or curl back or be rough or chapped or afflicted with sores or misshapen or twisted or too thick or too big or black or discolored or unsightly in any way. His nose will not be too broad or flat or crooked or too highly arched. His face will not be swarthy, nor will it be long and narrow, or sunken and distorted. He will not have a single unsightly feature. His lips, tongue and teeth will all be handsomely proportioned. His nose will be long and high, his face round and full, his eyebrows long and set high, his forehead broad, smooth, and well shaped, and he will be endowed with all the features proper to a human being. In each existence he is born into, he will see the Buddha, hear his Law, and have faith in his teachings.

"Ajita, just observe! The benefits gained merely by encouraging one person to go and listen to the Law are such as this! How much more, then, if one single-mindedly hears, preaches, reads, and recites the sutra and before the great assembly makes distinctions of the sake of people and practices it as the sutra instructs!"

At that time the World-Honored One, wishing to state his meaning once more, spoke in verse form, saying:

If someone in the Dharma assembly
is able to hear this sutra,
even just one verse,
and responding with joy, preaches it to others,
and in this way the teachings are handed along
till they a reach the fiftieth person,
the blessings gained by this last person
are such as I will now define.
Suppose there is a great dispenser of charity
who bestows goods on immeasurable multitudes,
doing this for a full eighty years,
responding to each person's desires.
Seeing the signs of decrepitude and old age,
the white hair and wrinkled face,
the missing teeth, the withered form,
he thinks, "Their death is not far off;
I must now teach them
so they can gain the fruits of the way!"
Immediately for their sake he employs an expedient means,

preaching the true Law of nirvana:
"Nothing in this world is lasting or firm
but all are like bubbles, foam, heat shimmer.
Therefore all of you must quickly
learn to hate it and be gone!"
When the people here this Law,
all are able to become arhats
endowed with the six transcendental powers,
the three understandings and eight emancipations.
But the fiftieth person
who hears one verse [of the Lotus sutra] and responds with joy
gains blessings that are far greater,
beyond description by simile or parable.
And if one who has had the teachings passed along to him
receives blessings that are immeasurable,
how much more so one who in the Dharma assembly
first hears the sutra and responds with joy.
Suppose someone encourages another person,
urging him to go and listen to the Lotus,
saying, "This sutra is profound and wonderful,
hard to encounter in a thousand, ten thousand kalpas!"
And suppose, as urged, the person goes to listen,
even though he listens for just a moment.
The blessings that the first person gets in reward

I will now describe in detail:
Age after age, no afflictions of the mouth,
no teeth missing, yellow or blackened,
lips that are not thick, curled or defective,
no fateful features,
a tongue not dry, black or too short;
nose high, long and straight,
forehead broad, smooth and well shaped,
face and eyes ball properly aligned and impressive,
the kind people delight to look at,
breath free of foul odor,
a fragrance of utpala flowers
constantly emitted by the mouth.
Suppose one goes to the monks quarters
expressly to listen the Lotus Sutra
and listens with joy for just a moment -
I will now describe his blessings.
In existences to come among heavenly and human beings
he will acquire wonderful elephants, horses, carriages,
palanquins adorned with rare jewels,
and will mount to the palaces of heaven.
If in the place where the law is expounded
one encourages someone to sit and hear the sutra,
the blessings he acquires will enable him
to gain the seat of Shakra, Brahma and the wheel-turner.
How much more so if one listens single-mindedly,
explains and expounds the meaning,
and practices the sutra as the sutra instructs -
that person's blessings know no bounds!

Chapter Nineteen: The Benefits
of the Teacher of the Law

At that time the Buddha said to the bodhisattva and mahasattva Constant Exertion: 'If good men or good women accept and uphold this Lotus Sutra, if they read it, recite it, explain and preach it, or transcribe it, such persons will obtain eight hundred eye benefits, twelve hundred ear benefits, eight hundred nose benefits, twelve hundred tongue benefits, eight hundred body benefits, and twelve hundred mind benefits. With these benefits they will be able to adorn their six sense organs, making all of them pure.

"These good men and good women, with the pure physical eyes they received from their parents at birth, will view all that exists in the inner and our parts of thousand-million-fold world, its mountains, forests, rivers and seas, down as far as the Avichi hell and up to this Summit of Being. And in the midst they will see all the living beings, and also see and understand all the causes and conditions created by their deeds and the births that await them as result and recompense for those deeds."

At that time the World-Honored One, wishing to state his meaning once more, spoke in verse form, saying:

If in the midst of the great assembly
someone with a fearless mind
preaches this Lotus Sutra,
listen to the benefits he will receive!
Such a person gains eight hundred
benefits of superior eyes.
As a result of these adornments
his eyes become extremely pure.
With the eyes received that birth from his parents
he will view all the three thousand worlds,
their inner and outer parts, their Mount Meru,
their Sumeru, the Iron Encircling Mountains
and all the other mountains and forests,
the waters of their great seas, rivers and streams,
down as far as the Avichi hell,
up to the Summit of Being heaven.
And he will see all the living beings
in their midst.
Though he has not yet gained heavenly eyes,
the power of his physical eyes will be such as this.

"Moreover, Constant Exertion, if good men or good women accept and uphold this sutra, if they read it, recite it, explain and preach it, or transcribe it, they will gain twelve hundred ear benefits with which to purify their ears so they can hear all the different varieties of words and sounds in the thousand-million fold world, down as far as the Avichi hell, up to the Summit of Being, have been in its inner and our parts. Elephant sounds, horse sounds, ox sounds, carriage sounds, weeping sounds, lamenting sounds, conch sounds, drum sounds, bell sounds, chime sounds, sounds of laughter, sounds of speaking, men's voices, women's voices, boys' voices, girls' voices, the voice that is not the Law, bitter voices, merry voices, voices of common mortals, voices of sages, happy voices, unhappy voices, voices of heavenly beings, dragon voices, yaksha voices, gandharva voices, asura voices, garuda voices, kimnara voices, mahoraga voices, the sound of fire, the sound of water, the sound of wind, voices of hell dwellers, voices of beasts, voices of hungry spirits, monks' voices, nuns' voices, voices of voice hearers, voices of pratyekabuddhas, voices of bodhisattvas and voices of Buddhas. In a word, although the person has not yet gained heavenly ears, with the pure and ordinary ears that he received at birth from his parents he will be able to hear and understand all the voices that exist in the inner and outer parts of thousand-million fold world. And though in this manner he can distinguish all the various kinds of sounds and voices, this will not impair his hearing faculty."

At that time the World-Honored One, wishing to state his meaning once more, spoke in verse form, saying:

With the ears received at birth from one's parents,
pure and without stain or defilement,
with these ordinary ears one can hear
the sounds of the three thousand worlds,
elephant, horse, carriage, ox sounds,
bell, chime, conch, drum sounds,
lute and harp sounds,
pipe and flute sounds;
the sound of pure and beautiful singing
one can hear without becoming attached to it.
The countless varieties of human voices -
one can hear and understand all these.
Again one can hear the voices of heavenly beings,
subtle and wonderful song sounds,
and one can hear men and women's voices,
the voices of young boys and young girls.
In the midst of hills, rivers and steep valleys
the voice of the kalavinka,
the jivakajivaka and other birds-
all these sounds he will hear.
From the tormented multitudes of hell
the sounds of various kinds of suffering and distress,
sounds of hungry spirits driven by famine and thirst
as they search for food and drink,
of the asuras
who live on the shores of the great sea
when they talk among themselves
or emit loud cries.
Thus he who preaches the Law
can dwell safely among all these,
hearing these many voices from afar
without ever impairing his faculties of hearing.
In the worlds of the ten directions
when beasts and birds call to another
this person who preaches the Law
hears them all from where he is.
In the Brahma heaven and above,
the Light Sound Heaven, All Pure heaven,
and up to the Summit of Being heaven,
the sounds of the voices talking there -
the teacher of the Law, dwelling here,
can hear them all.
All the multitude of monks
and all the nuns,
whether they are reading or reciting the scriptures
or preaching them for the sake of others -
the teacher of the Law dwells here,
can hear them all.
And when there are bodhisattvas
who read and recite the sutra teachings
or preach them for the sake of others
or select passage and explain their meaning,
the sounds of their voices -
he can hear them all.

When the Buddhas, great sages and venerable ones,
teach and convert living beings,
in the midst of the great assembly
expounding and preaching the subtle and wonderful Law,
one who upholds the Lotus Sutra
can hear them all.
All the sounds in the inner and outer parts
of the thousand-million-fold world,
down to the Avichi hell,
up to the Summit of Being heaven -
he can hear all these sounds
and never impair his faculties of hearing.
Because the faculties of his ears or so keen
he can distinguish and understand all the sounds.
One who upholds the Lotus Sutra,
though he has not yet gained heavenly ears,
can do this simply through the ears he was born with -
such are the benefits he gains.

"Moreover, Constant Exertion, if good men or good women accept and uphold this sutra, if they read it, recite it, explain and preach it, or transcribe it, they will succeed in gaining eight hundred nose benefits with which to purify their faculty of smell so they can detect all the different fragrances from top to bottom and in the inner and our parts of a thousand-million-fold world, the fragrance of sumana flowers, jatika flowers, mallika flowers, champaka flowers, patala flowers, red lotus flowers, blue lotus flowers, white lotus flowers, the fragrance of flowering trees, fruit trees, sandalwood, aloes, tamalapatra and tagara, as well as incense blended from thousand, ten thousand ingredients, powdered incense, pellet incense or paste incense. One who upholds this sutra while dwelling here, will be able to distinguish all these.

"Moreover he will be able to distinguish and identify the odors of living beings, of elephants, horses, oxen, sheep and so forth, the odor of a man, a woman, a boy child, a girl child, and odors of plants, trees, thickets and forests. Whether they are near or far off, he will be able to detect all these odors and distinguish one from the other without error.

"One who upholds this sutra, though he dwells right here, will also be able to detect orders of the various heavens in the sky above. The scent of a parijataka and kovidara trees, of mandarava flowers, great mandarava flowers, great manjushaka flowers, sandalwood, aloes, various kinds of powdered incense, and incense made of an assortment of flowers - of heavenly scents from which they are derived or blended, there are non that he cannot detect and identify.

"He will also be able to detect the scent of the bodies of heavenly beings. The scent when Shakra Devanam Indra is in his superb palace amusing himself and satisfying the five desires, or the scent when he is in the Hall of the Wonderful Law preaching the Law for the heavenly beings of Trayastrimsha, or the scent when he is wondering at leisure in his gardens, as well as the scent of the bodies of the other male and female heavenly beings - all these he will be able to detect from a far.

"He will thus be able to extend his awareness up to the Brahma heaven and even higher to the Summit of Being heaven, detecting the scent of all bodies of the heavenly beings, who also detect the incense burned by the heavenly beings. Moreover the scent of the voice-hearer's, of pratyekabuddhas, of bodhisattvas and of the bodies of the Buddhas - all these he will detect from afar and will know where these beings are. And although he can detect all these scents, his faculty of smell will not be impaired or disordered. If he should wish to distinguish one scent from another and describe it for someone else, he will be able to recall it without error."

At that time the World-Honored One, wishing to state his meaning once more, spoke in verse form, saying:

The purity of such person's nose will be such
that throughout this world
he will be able to detect and identify
all manner of odors, fragrant or foul,
sumana and jatika flowers,
tamalapatra and sandalwood,
the scent of aloes and cassia,
the scent of various flowers and fruits.
And he will know the scent of living beings,
the scent of men and women.
Though this preacher of the Law dwells far off,
he will detect the scents and know where the persons are.
Wheel-turning kings of great authority,
Lesser wheel turners and their sons,
their ministers and palace attendants -
he will detect their scent and know where they are.
Precious treasures adorning the body,
treasure storehouses in the earth,
jewel ladies of wheel-turning kings -
he will detect their scent where they are.
Ornaments to adorn the bodies of persons,
clothing and necklaces,
all kinds of paste incense -
by detecting these he will know who the wearers are.
When heavenly beings walk or sit,
amuse themselves or carry out magical transformations,"
the upholder of the Lotus
by detecting their scent can know all this.
Blossoms and fruits of various trees,
and aroma of butter oil -
the upholder of the sutra, dwelling here,
knows where all these are.
Deep in the mountains, in steep places
where blossoms of the sandalwood tree unfold,
living beings are in their midst -
by detecting the scent he can know all this.
Living beings in the Iron Encircling Mountains,
in the great seas or in the ground -
the upholder of this sutra detects their scent
and knows were all of them are.
When male and female asuras
and their retinues of followers
fight with one another or amuse themselves,
he detects the scent and knows all this.
On the broad plains, in narrow places,
lions, elephants, tigers, wolves,
buffaloes and water buffaloes -
by detecting their scent he knows were they are.
When a woman is pregnant
and no one can determine if the child is male or female,
if it will lack normal faculties or be inhuman,
by detecting the scent he can know all this.
And through this power to detect scents
he knows when a woman will be successful or not,
if the pregnancy will be successful or not,
if she will be delivered safely of a healthy child.

Through his power of detect scents
he knows the thoughts of men and women,
if their minds are stained by desire, stupidity or anger,
and he knows if they are practicing good.
Hoards of goods that are stored in the earth,
gold, silver and precious treasures,
things heaped in bronze vessels -
by detecting the scent he can tell where they all are.
Various kinds of necklaces
whose value cannot be appraised -
by the scent he knows if they are precious or worthless,
where they came from and where they are now.
Flowers in the heavens above,
mandaravas, manjushakas,
parijataka trees -
detecting their scent, he knows all these.
The palaces in the heavens above
in their separate grades of upper, intermediate, and lower,
adorned with numerous jeweled flowers -
detecting their scent, he knows them all.
The heavenly gardens and groves, the superb mansions,
the observatories, the Hall of the Wonderful Law,
and those taking pleasure in their midst -
detecting their scent, he knows them all.
When heavenly beings listen to the Law
or indulge the five desires,
coming and going, walking, sitting, lying down -
detecting their scent, he knows them all.
The robes worn by heavenly women
when, adorned with lovely flowers and perfumes,
they whirl and circle in enjoyment -
detecting their scent, he knows them all.
Thus extending his awareness
upward to the Brahma heaven,
by detecting their scent, he knows all those
who enter meditation or emerge from meditation.
In the Light Sound and All Pure heavens
and up to the Summit of Being,
those born for the first time, those who have departed -
detecting their scent, he knows them all.
The multitude of monks
diligent at all times with regard to the Law,
whether sitting or walking around
or reading a reciting the sutra teachings,
sometimes under the forest trees
concentrating their energies, sitting in meditation -
the upholder of the sutra detects their scent
and knows were all of them are.
Bodhisattvas firm and unbending in will,
sitting in meditation or reading the sutras
or preaching the Law for others -
by detecting their scent he knows them all.
The World-Honored Ones, present in all quarters,
revered and respected by all,
pitying the multitude, preaching the Law -
by detecting their scent he knows them all.

Living beings who in the Buddhas presence
hear the sutra and all rejoice,
who practice as the Law prescribes -
by detecting their scent he knows them all.
Though he has not yet acquired the nose possessed
by a bodhisattva of the Law of no outflows,
the upholder of the sutra before then
will acquire a nose with the marks described here.

"Moreover, Constant Exertion, if good men or good women except and uphold this sutra, if they read it, recite it, explain and preach it, or transcribe it, they will gain twelve hundred tongue benefits. Whether something is good tasting or vile, whether it is flavorful or not, and even things that are bitter or astringent, when encountered by the faculties of this person's tongue will be a changed into superb flavors as fine as the sweet dew of heaven, and there will be none that are not pleasing.

"If with these faculties of the tongue he undertakes to expound and preaching in the midst of the great assembly, he will produce a deep and wonderful voice capable of penetrating the mind and causing all who hear it to rejoice and delight. When the men and women of heaven, Shakra, Brahma and other heavenly beings, hear the sound of this deep and wonderful voice expounding and preaching, advancing and argument point by point, they will all gather to listen. Dragons and dragon daughters, yakshas and yaksha daughters, gandharvas and gandharva daughters, asuras and asura daughters, garudas and garuda daughters, kimnaras and kimnara daughters, mahoragas and mahoraga daughters will all gather close around its possessor in order to listen the Law, and will revere him and offer alms. Monks, nuns, laymen, laywomen, monarchs, princes, ministers and their retinues, petty wheel-turning kings and great wheel-turning kings with their seven treasures and thousand sons and inner and outer retinues will ascend their palaces and all come to listen to the Law.

"Because this bodhisattva is so skilled of preaching the Law, the Brahmans, householders and people throughout the country will for the remainder of their lives follow and wait on him and offer him alms. Voice-hearers, pratyekabuddhas, bodhisattvas and Buddhas will constantly delight to see him. Wherever this person is, the Buddhas will all face in that direction when they preach the Law, and he will be able to accept and uphold all the doctrines of the Buddha. And in addition he will be able to emit the deep and wonderful sound of the Law."

At that time the World-Honored One, wishing to state his meaning once more, spoke in verse form, saying:

The faculties of this person's tongue will be so pure
that he will never experience any bad tastes,
but all that he eats
will become like sweet dew.
With his deep, pure and wonderful voice
he will preach the Law in the great assembly,
employing causes, conditions and similes
to lead and guide the minds of living beings.

All who hear him will rejoice
and offer him their finest alms.
Heavenly beings, dragons, yakshas,
as well as asuras and others
will all approach him with reverent minds
and together come to hear the Law.
If this preacher of the Law
wishes to use his wonderful voice
to fill the three thousand worlds
he can do so at will.
Wheel-turning kings great and small

and their thousand sons and retinues
will press their palms together with reverent minds
and constantly come to hear and accept the Law.
Heavenly beings, dragons, yakshas,
rakshasas and pishachas
likewise with rejoicing minds
will constantly delight in coming to bring alms.
The heavenly king Brahma, the devil king,
the deities Freedom and Great Freedom,
all the multitude of heavenly beings
will constantly come to where he is.
The Buddhas and their disciples,
hearing the sound of him teaching the Law,
will keep him constantly in their thoughts and guard him
and at times show themselves for his sake.

"Moreover, Constant Exertion, if good men or good women except and uphold this sutra, if they read it, recite it, explain and preach it, or transcribe it, they will gain eight hundred body benefits. They will acquire pure bodies, like pure lapis lazuli, such as living beings delight to see. Because of the purity of their bodies, when the living beings of the thousand-million fold world are born or die, when they are born in upper or lower regions, in fair or ugly circumstances, in good places or bad, they will all be reflected [in these bodies]. The mountain kings of Iron Encircling Mountains, the Great Iron Encircling Mountains, Mount Meru and Mahameru, as well as living beings in their midst, will all be reflected therein. Down to the Avichi hell, upward to the Summit of Being, all the regions and their living beings will be reflected therein. Voice-hearers, pratyekabuddhas, bodhisattvas, Buddhas preaching the Law - the forms and shapes of these will be reflected in their bodies."

At that time the World-Honored One, wishing to state his meaning once more, spoke in verse form, saying:

If one upholds the Lotus Sutra
his body will be very pure,
like pure lapis lazuli -
living beings will all delight to see it.
And it will be like a pure bright mirror
in which forms and shapes are all reflected.
The bodhisattva in his pure body
will see all that is in the world;
he alone will see brightly
what is not visible to others.
Within the three thousand worlds
all the mass of burgeoning creatures,
heavenly and human beings, asuras,
hell dwellers, spirits, beasts -
their forms and shapes in this way
will all be reflected in his body.
The palaces of the various heavens
upward to the Summit of Being,
the Iron Encircling Mountains,
the mountains Meru and Mahameru,
the great seas and other waters -
all will be reflected in his body.
The Buddhas and voice-hearers,
Buddha sons and bodhisattvas,
whether alone or in the assembly
preaching the Law - all will be reflected.
Though this person has not yet acquired

the wonderful body of Dharma nature, free of outflows,
because the purity of his ordinary body
all things we reflected in it.

"Moreover, Constant Exertion, if good men or good women except and uphold this sutra after the Thus Come One has entered extinction, if they read it, recite it, explain and preach it, or transcribe it, they will acquire twelve hundred mind benefits. Because of purity of their mental faculties, when they hear no more than one verse or one phrase [of the sutra], they will master immeasurable and boundless numbers of principles. And once having understood these principles, they will be able to expound and preach on the single phrase or a single verse for a month, for four months, or for a whole year, and the doctrines that they preach during that time will conform to the gist of the principles and will never be contrary to true reality.

"If they should expound some text of the secular world or speak on matters of government or those relating to wealth and livelihood, they will in all cases conform to the correct Law. With regard to the living beings in the six realms of existence of a thousand-million-fold world, they will understand how the minds of those living beings work, how they move, what idle theories they entertain.

"Thus although they have not yet acquired the wisdom of no outflows, the purity of their minds will be a such that the thought of these persons, their calculations and surmises and the words they speak, will in all cases represent the Law of the Buddha, never departing from the truth, and also conform with what was preached in the sutras of former Buddhas."

At that time the World-Honored One, wishing to the state his meaning once more, spoke in verse form, saying:

The minds of these persons will be pure,
bright, keen, without stain or defilement.
And with these wonderful mental faculties
they will understand the superior, intermediate and
inferior Law.
Hearing no more than one verse,
they will master immeasurable principles
and able to preach them step by step in accordance with the Law
for a month, four months, or a year.
All the living beings
in the inner and our parts of this world,
heavenly beings, Dragons, humans,
yakshas, spirits,
those in the six realms of existence
and all the various thoughts they have -
upholders of Lotus Sutra as their reward
will know all these in an instant!
The countless Buddhas of the ten directions,
adorned with the marks of a hundred blessings,
for the sake of living beings preach the Law,
and such persons, hearing it, will be able to accept and uphold it.
They will ponder immeasurable principles,
preach the Law in an immeasurable number of ways,
yet from start to finish never forget or make a mistake,
because they are upholders of the Lotus Sutra.
They will understand the characteristics of all phenomena,
accord with principles, recognizing their proper order,
be masters of names and words,
and expound and preach things as they understand them.
What these persons preach
is in all cases the Law of former Buddhas,

and because they expound this Law
they have no fear before the assembly.
Such as a purity of the mental faculties
of these upholders of the Lotus Sutra.
Though they have not yet obtained freedom from outflows
before that they will manifest the marks described here.
While these persons uphold this sutra
they will dwell safely on rare ground,
by all living beings
delighted in, loved and respected,
able to employ a thousand, ten thousand varieties
of apt and skillful words
to make distinctions, expound and preach -
because they uphold the Lotus Sutra.

Chapter Twenty: Bodhisattva Never Disparaging

At that time the Buddha said to the bodhisattva and mahasattva Gainer of Great Authority: 'You should understand this. When monks, nuns, laymen or laywomen uphold the Lotus Sutra, if anyone should speak ill of them, curse or slander them, he will suffer severe recompense for his crime, as I have explained earlier. And I have also explained earlier the benefits gained by those who uphold the sutra, namely, purification of their eyes, ears, nose, tongue, body, and mind.

"Gainer of Great Authority, long ago, an immeasurable, boundless, inconceivable number of asamkhya kalpas in the past, there was a Buddha named Awesome Sound King Thus Come One, worthy of offerings, of right and universal knowledge, perfect clarity and conduct, well gone, understanding the world, unexcelled trainer of people, teacher of heavenly and human beings, Buddha, World-Honored One. His kalpa was called Exempt from Decay and his land was called Great Achievement.

"This Buddha Awesome Sound King during the age when he lived preached the Law for heavenly and human beings and asuras. For those who were seeking to become voice-hearers he responded by preaching the Law of the four noble truths so that they could transcend birth, old age, sickness and death and eventually attain nirvana. For those seeking to become pratyekabuddhas he responded by preaching the Law of the twelve-linked chain of causation. For the bodhisattvas, as a means to lead them to anuttara-samyak-sambodhi, he responded by preaching the Law of the six paramitas so they could eventually gain the Buddha wisdom.

"Gainer of Great Authority, this Buddha Awesome Sound King had a life span of kalpas equal to four-hundred thousand million nayutas of Ganges sands. His correct Law endured in the world for as many kalpas as there are dust particles in one Jambudvipa. His counterfeit Law endured in the world for as many kalpas as there are dust particles in the four continents. After this Buddha had finished bringing great benefits to living beings, he passed into extinction.

"After his Correct Law and Counterfeit Law had come to an end, another Buddha appeared in the same land. He too was named Awesome Sound King Thus Come One, worthy of offerings, of right and universal knowledge, perfect clarity and conduct, well gone, understanding the world, unexcelled worthy, trainer of people, teacher of heavenly and human beings, Buddha, World-Honored One. This process continue until twenty-thousand million Buddhas had appeared one after another, all bearing the same name.

"After the original Awesome sound King Thus Come One had passed into extinction, and after his Correct Law had also passed away, in the period of his Counterfeit Law, monks of overbearing arrogance exercised great authority and power. At this time there was a bodhisattva monk named Never Disparaging. Now, Gainer of Great Authority, for what reason was he named Never Disparaging? This monk, whatever persons he happened to meet, whether monks, nuns, Laymen or laywomen, would bow in obeisance to all of them and speak words of praise, saying, 'I have profound reverence for you, I would never dare treat you with disparaging and arrogance. Why? Because you are all practicing the bodhisattva way and are certain to attain Buddhahood.'

"This monk did not devote his time to reading or reciting the scriptures, but simply want about bowing to people. And if he happened to see any of the four kinds of believers far off in the distance, he would purposely go to where they were, bow to them and speak words of praise, saying, 'I would never dare disparage you, because you are all certain to attain Buddhahood!'

"Among the four kinds of believers there were the those who gave way to anger, their minds lacking in purity, and they spoke ill of him and cursed him, saying, 'This ignorant monk - were does he come from, presuming to declare that he does not disparage us and bestowing on us a prediction that we will attain Buddhahood? We have no use for such vain and irresponsible predictions!'

"Many years passed in this way, during which this monk was constantly subjected to curses and abuse. He did not give way to anger, however, but each time spoke the same words, 'You are certain to attain Buddhahood.' When he spoke in this manner, some among the group would take sticks of wood or tiles and stones and beat and pelt him. But even as he ran away and took up his stance at a distance, he continued to call out in a loud voice, ' I would never dare disparage you, for you are all certain to attain Buddhahood!' And because he always spoke these words, the overbearing arrogant monks, nuns, laymen and laywomen gave him the name Never Disparaging.

"When this monk was on the point of death, he heard up in the sky fully twenty thousand, ten thousand, a million verses of the Lotus Sutra that had been previously preached by the Buddha Awesome Sound King, and he was able to accept and uphold them all. Immediately he gained the kind of purity of vision and purity of the faculties of the ear, nose, tongue, body and mind that have been described above. Having gained this purity of the six faculties, his life span was increased by two hundred ten million nayutas of years, and he went about widely preaching the Lotus Sutra for people.

"At that time, when the four kinds of believers who were overbearingly arrogant, the monks, nuns, laymen and laywomen who had looked with contempt on this monk and given him the name Never Disparaging - when they saw that he had gained great transcendental powers, the power to preach pleasingly and eloquently, the power of great goodness and tranquility, and when they heard his preaching, they all took faith in him and willingly became his followers.

"This bodhisattva converted a multitude of a thousand, ten thousand, a million, causing them to abide in the state of anuttara-samyak-sambodhi. After his life came to an end, he was able to encounter two thousand million Buddhas, all bearing the name Sun Moon Bright, and in the midst of their Law he preached this Lotus Sutra. Through the causes and conditions created thereby, he was also able to encounter two thousand million Buddhas, all with the identical name Cloud Freedom Lamp King. In the midst of the Law of these Buddhas, he excepted, upheld, read, recited and preached this sutra for the four kinds of believers. For that reason he was able to gain perfection of his ordinary eyes, and the faculties of his ears, nose, tongue, body and mind were likewise purified. Among the four kinds of believers he preached Law with no fear in his mind.

"Gainer of Great Authority, this bodhisattva and mahasattvas Never Disparaging in this manner offered alms to a vast number of Buddhas, treating them with reverence and honor and praising them. Having planted these good roots, he was later able to encounter a thousand, ten thousand, a million Buddhas, and in the midst of the Law of these Buddhas, he preached this sutra, gaining benefits about him to attain Buddhahood.

"Gainer of Great Authority, what do you think? The bodhisattva Never Disparaging who lived at that time - could he be unknown to you? In fact he was none other than I myself! If in my previous existences I had not accepted, upheld, read and recited this sutra and preached it for others, I would never have been able boat to attain anuttara-samyak-sambodhi so quickly. Because in the presence of those earlier Buddhas I accepted, upheld, read and recited this sutra and preached it for others, I was able quickly to attain anuttara-samyak-sambodhi.

"Gainer of Great Authority, at that time before the four kinds of believers, the monks, nuns, laymen and many women, because anger arose in their minds and they threatened me with disparagement and contempt, were for two hundred million kalpas never able to encounter a Buddha, to hear the Law, or to see the community of monks. For a thousand kalpas they underwent great suffering and Avichi hell. After they had finished paying for their offenses, they once more encountered the bodhisattva Never Disparaging, who instructed them in anuttara-samyak-sambodhi.

"Gainer of Great Authority, what do you think? The four kinds of believers who at that time constantly disparaged this bodhisattva - could they be unknown to you? They are in this assembly now, Bhadrapala and his group, five hundred bodhisattvas; Lion Moon and her group, five hundred laymen, all having reached the state where they will never regress in their search for anuttara-samyak-sambodhi!

"Gainer of Great Authority, you should understand that this Lotus Sutra richly benefits the bodhisattvas and mahasattvas, for it can cause them to obtain anuttara-samyak-sambodhi. For this reason, after the Thus Come One has passed into extinction, the bodhisattvas and mahasattvas should at all times accept, uphold, read, recite, explain, preach and transcribe this sutra."

At that time the World-Honored One, wishing to state his meaning once more, spoke in verse form, saying:

In the past there was a Buddha
named Awesome Sound King,
of immeasurable supernatural powers and wisdom,
leading and guiding one and all.
Heavenly and human beings, dragons, spirits
joined in offering him alms.
After this Buddha had entered extinction,
when his Law was about to expire,
there was a bodhisattva
named Never Disparaging.
The four kinds of believers at that time
scrutinized and adhered to the Law.
The bodhisattva Never Disparaging
would go to where they were
and speak to them, saying,
"I would never disparage you,
for you are practicing the way
and all of you will become Buddhas!"
When the people heard this,
they gibed at him, cursed and reviled him,
but the bodhisattva Never Disparaging
bore all this with patience.
When his offenses had been wiped out
and his life was drawing to a close,
he was able to hear this sutra
and his six faculties were purified.
Because of his transcendental powers
his life span was extended,
and for the sake of others
he preached this sutra far and wide.
The many persons who adhered to the Law
all received teaching and conversion
from this bodhisattva,
who caused them to dwell in the Buddha way.
When Never Disparaging's life ended,
he encountered numerous Buddhas,
and because he preached this sutra
he gained measurable blessings.
Bit by bit he acquired benefits
and quickly completed the Buddha way.
Never Disparaging who lived at that time
was none other than myself.
And the four kinds of believers
who adhered to the Law then,
who heard Never Disparaging say,
"You will become Buddhas!"
and through the causes thus created
encounter numerous Buddhas -
they are here in this assembly,
a group of five hundred bodhisattvas,
and the four kinds of believers,
men and women of pure faith
who now in my presence

listen to the Law.
In previous existences
I encouraged these persons
to listen to and accept this sutra,
the foremost in the Law,
unfolding it, teaching people,
and causing them to dwell in nirvana.
So in age after age they accepted and upheld
scriptures of this kind.
A million million ten thousand kalpas,
an inconceivable time will pass
before at least one can hear
this Lotus Sutra.
A million million ten thousand kalpas,
an inconceivable time will pass
before the Buddhas, World-Honored Ones,
preach this sutra.
Therefore its practitioners
after the Buddha has entered extinction,
when they hear a sutra like this
should entertain no doubts or perplexities
but should with a single mind
preach this sutra far and wide,
age after age encountering Buddhas
and quickly completing the Buddha way.

Chapter Twenty-one: The Mystic Powers
of the Tathagata

At that time the bodhisattvas and mahasattvas who had emerged from the earth, numerous as the dust particles of a thousand worlds, all in the presence of the Buddha single-mindedly pressed their palms together, gazed up in reverence at the face of the Honored One, and said to the Buddha: "World-Honored One, after the Buddha has entered extinction, in the lands where the emanations of the World-Honored One are present, and in the place where the Buddha has passed into extinction, we will preach this sutra far and wide. Why? Because we ourselves wish to gain this great Law, true and pure, to accept, uphold, read, recite, explain, preach, transcribe and offer alms to it."

At that time the World-Honored One, in the presence of Manjushri and the other immeasurable hundreds, thousands, ten thousands, millions of bodhisattvas and mahasattvas who from of old had dwelled in the saha world, as well as the monks, nuns, laymen, laywomen, heavenly beings, dragons, yakshas, gandharvas, asuras, garudas, kimnaras, mahoragas, human and nonhuman beings-before all these he displayed his great supernatural powers. He extended his long broad tongue upward till it reached the Brahma heaven, and from all his pores he emitted immeasurable, countless beams of light that illuminated all the worlds in the ten directions.

The other Buddhas, seated on lion thrones underneath the numerous jeweled trees, did likewise, extending their long broad tongues and emitting immeasurable beams of light. When Shakyamuni Buddha and other Buddhas beneath the jeweled trees thus displayed their supernatural powers, they did so for fully a hundred thousand years. After that they drew in their long tongues again, coughed in unison, and altogether snapped her fingers. The sounds made by these two actions filled all the Buddha worlds in the ten directions, and the earth in all of them quaked and trembled in six different ways.

The living beings in their midst, the heavenly beings, dragons, yakshas, gandharvas, asuras, garudas, kimnaras, mahoragas, human and nonhuman beings, thanks to the Buddha's supernatural powers, all saw in this saha world immeasurable, boundless hundreds, thousands, ten thousands, millions of Buddhas seated on lion seats under the numerous jeweled trees, and also saw Shakyamuni Buddha and Many Treasures Thus Come One seated together on a lion seat in the treasure tower. Moreover, they saw immeasurable, boundless hundreds, thousands, ten thousands, millions of bodhisattvas and mahasattvas and the four kinds of believers who reverently surrounded Shakyamuni Buddha.

When they had seen these things, they were all filled with great joy, having gained what they had never had before. At the time the heavenly beings in the midst of the sky cried out with loud voices, saying: "Beyond these immeasurable, boundless hundreds, thousands, ten thousands, millions of asamkhya worlds there is a land named saha, and in it a Buddha named Shakyamuni. Now for the sake of the bodhisattvas and mahasattvas he is preaching in his sutra of the Great Vehicle called the Lotus of the Wonderful Law., a Law to instruct the bodhisattvas, one that is guarded and kept in mind by the Buddhas. You must respond with joy from the depths of your heart, and also offer obeisance and alms to Shakyamuni Buddha!"

When the various living beings heard the voices in the sky, they pressed their palms together, faced the saha world, and spoke these words: "Hail, Shakyamuni Buddha! Hail, Shakyamuni Buddha!"

Then they took different kinds of flowers, incense, necklaces, banners and canopies, as well as the ornaments, rare jewels and other wonderful articles that adorned their persons, and all together scattered them far off in the direction of the saha world. The objects thus scattered poured in from the ten directions like clouds gathering together. Then they changed into a jeweled curtain that completely covered the area where the Buddhas were. At that time the worlds in the ten directions were opened up so that there was unobstructed passage from one to the other and they were like a single Buddha land.

At that time the Buddha spoke to Superior Practices and the others in the great assembly of bodhisattvas, saying: "The supernatural powers of the Buddhas, as you have seen, are immeasurable, boundless, inconceivable. If in the process of entrusting this sutra to others I were to employ these supernatural powers for a measurable, boundless hundreds, thousands, ten thousands, millions of asamkhya kalpas to describe the benefits of the sutra, I could never finish doing so. To put it briefly, all the doctrines possessed by the Thus Come One, the storehouse of all the secret essentials of the Thus Come One - all these are proclaimed, revealed, and clearly expounded in this sutra.

For this reason, after the Thus Come One has entered extinction, you must single-mindedly accept, uphold, read, recite, explain, preach and transcribe it, and practice it as directed. In any of the various lands, wherever there are those who accept, uphold, read, recite, explain, preach, transcribe, or practice it as directed, or wherever the sutra rolls are preserved, whether in a garden, a forest, beneath a tree, in monks quarters, in the lodgings of white-robed laymen, in palaces, or in mountain valleys or the wide wilderness, in all these places one should erect towers and offer alms. Why? Because you should understand that such spots are places of religious practice. In such places have the Buddhas gained anuttara-samyak-sambodhi, in such places have the Buddhas turn the wheel of the Law, in such places have the Buddhas entered parinirvana."

At that time the World-Honored One, wishing to state his meaning once more, spoke in verse form, saying:

The Buddhas, saviors of the world,
abide in their great transcendental powers,
and in order to please living being
they display immeasurable supernatural powers.
Their tongues reach to the Brahma heaven,
their bodies emit countless beams of light.
For the sake of those who seek the Buddha way
they manifest these things that are rarely seen.
The sound of the Buddhas coughing,
the sound of them snapping their fingers,
is heard throughout the lands in the ten directions
and the earth in all those lands moves in six ways.
Because after the Buddha has passed into extinction
there will be those who can uphold this sutra,
the Buddhas are delighted
and manifest immeasurable supernatural powers.
Because they wish to entrust this sutra,
they praise and extol the person who accepts and upholds it,
and though they should do so for immeasurable kalpas
they could never exhaust their praises.
The benefits gained by such a person
are boundless and inexhaustible,
like the vast sky in the ten directions
that no one can set a limit to.
One who can uphold this sutra
has in effect already seen me,
and likewise has seen Many Treasures Buddha
and the Buddhas that are emanations of my body.
And he also sees me today
as I teach and convert the bodhisattvas.
One who can uphold this sutra
causes me and my emanations,
and Many Treasures Buddha who has already
entered extension,
all to be filled with joy.
The Buddhas who are present in the ten directions
and those of past and future ages -
he will see them too, offer alms to them
and cause them to be filled with joy.

The secret essentials of the Law
gained by the Buddhas who sat in the place of practice -
one who can uphold this sutra
will gain them too before long.
One who can uphold this sutra
will delight in endlessly expounding
the principles of the various doctrines
and their names and phrases
like a wind in the open sky
moving everywhere without hindrance or block.
After the Thus Come One has passed into extinction,
this person will know the sutras preached by the Buddha,
their causes and conditions and their proper sequence,
and will preach them truthfully in accordance with principle.
As the light of the sun and moon
can vanish all obscurity and gloom,
so this person as he passes through the world
can wipe out the darkness of living beings,
causing immeasurable numbers of bodhisattvas
in the end to dwell in the single vehicle.
Therefore a person of wisdom,
hearing how keen are the benefits to be gained,
after I have passed into extinction
should accept and uphold this sutra.
Such a person assuredly and without doubt
will attain the Buddha way.

Chapter Twenty-two: Entrustment

At that time Shakyamuni Buddha rose from his Dharma seat and, manifesting his great supernatural powers, with his right hand patted the heads of the immeasurable bodhisattvas and mahasattvas and spoke these words: "For immeasurable hundreds, thousands, ten thousands, millions of asamkhya kalpas I have practiced this hard-to-attain Law of anuttara-samyak-sambodhi. Now I entrust it to you. You must single-mindedly propagate this Law abroad, causing its benefits to spread far and wide."

Three times he patted the bodhisattvas and mahasattvas on the head and spoke these words: "For immeasurable hundreds, thousands, ten thousands, millions of asamkhya kalpas I have practiced this hard-to-attain Law of anuttara-samyak-sambodhi. Now I entrust it to you. You must accept, uphold, recite, and broadly propagate this Law, causing all living beings everywhere to hear and understand it. Why? Because the Thus Come One has great pity and compassion. He is in no way stingy or begrudging, nor has he any fear. He is able to bestow on living beings the wisdom of the Buddha, the wisdom of the Thus Come One, the wisdom that comes of itself. The Thus Come One is a great giver of gifts to all living beings. You for your part should respond by studying this Law of the Thus Come One. You must not be stingy or begrudging.

"In future ages if there are good man and good women who have faith in the wisdom of the Thus Come One, you should preach and expound the Lotus Sutra for them., so that others may hear and understand it. For in this way you can cause them to gain the Buddha wisdom. If there are living beings who do not believe or accept it, you should use some of the other profound doctrines of the Thus Come One to teach, benefit and bring joy to them. If you do all this, then you will have repaid the debt of gratitude that you owe to the Buddha."

When the bodhisattvas and mahasattvas heard the Buddhas speak these words, they all experienced a great joy that filled their bodies. With even greater reverence than before, they bent their bodies, bowed their heads, pressed their palms together and, facing the Buddha, raised their voices in unison, saying: "We will respectfully carry out all these things just as the World-Honored One has commanded. We beg the World-Honored One to have no concern on this account!"

The multitude of bodhisattvas and mahasattvas repeated these words three times, raising their voices in unison and saying: "We will respectfully carry out all these things just as the World-Honored One has commanded. Therefore we beg the World-Honored One to have no concern on this account!"

At that time Shakyamuni Buddha caused the Buddhas who were emanations of his body and had come from the ten directions to return each one to his original land, saying: "Each of these Buddhas may proceed at his own pleasure. The tower of Many Treasures Buddha may also return to its former position."

When he spoke these words, the immeasurable emanation Buddhas from the ten directions who were seated on lion seats under the jeweled trees, as well as Many Treasures Buddha, Superior Practices, and the others of the greater multitude of boundless asamkhya of bodhisattvas, Shariputra and the other voice-hearers and four kinds of believers, and the heavenly and human beings, asuras and others in all the worlds, hearing what the Buddha had said, were all filled with great joy.

Chapter Twenty-three: The Former Deeds
of Bodhisattva Medicine King

At that time bodhisattva Constellation King Flower spoke to the Buddha, saying: "World-Honored One, how does the bodhisattva Medicine King come and go in the saha world? World-Honored One, this bodhisattva Medicine King has carried out some hundreds, thousands, ten thousands, millions of nayutas of difficult practices, arduous practices.. Very well, World-Honored One, could I ask you to explain a little? The heavenly beings, dragons, gods, yakshas, gandharvas, asuras, garudas, kimnaras, mahrogas, human and nonhuman beings, and the bodhisattvas who have come from other lands and the multitude of voice-hearers, will all be delighted to hear you."

At that time the Buddha addressed the bodhisattva Constellation King Flower, saying: "Many kalpas in the past, immeasurable as Ganges sands, there was a Buddha named Sun Moon Pure Bright Virtue Thus Come One , worthy of offerings, of right and universal knowledge, perfect clarity and conduct, well gone, understanding the world, unexcelled worthy, trainer of people, trainer of heavenly and human beings, Buddha, World-Honored One. This Buddha had eighty million great bodhisattvas and mahasattvas and a multitude of great voice-hearers equal to the sands of seventy-two Ganges. This Buddha's life span was forty-two thousand kalpas, and the life span of the bodhisattva's was the same. In his land there were no women, hell dwellers, hungry spirits, beasts or asuras, and no kind of tribulation. The ground was as level as the palm of a hand, made of lapis lazuli and adorned with jeweled trees. Jeweled curtains covered it over, banners of jeweled flowers hung down, and jeweled urns an incense burners filled the land everywhere. There were daises made of the seven treasures, with a tree by each dais, the tree situated an arrow-shot length from the dais. These jeweled trees all had bodhisattvas and voice-hearers sitting under them, and each of the jeweled daises had hundreds of millions of heavenly beings playing on heavenly instruments and singing the praises of the Buddha as an offering.

"At the time, for the sake of the bodhisattva Gladly Seen by All Living Beings and the other numerous bodhisattvas and multitude of voice-hearers, the Buddha preached the Lotus Sutra. This bodhisattva Gladly Seen by All Living Beings delighted in carrying out arduous practices. In the midst of the Law preached by the Buddha Sun Moon Pure Bright Virtue he applied himself diligently and traveled about here and there, single-mindedly seeking Buddhahood for a period of fully twelve thousand years. After that he was able to gain the samadhi in which one can manifest all physical forms. Having gained this samadhi, his heart was filled with great joy and he thought to himself: My gaining the samadhi in which I can manifest al physical forms is due entirely to the fact that I heard the Lotus Sutra. I must now make an offering to the Buddha Sun Moon Pure Bright Virtue and to the Lotus Sutra!

"Immediately he entered the samadhi and in the midst of the sky rained down mandarava flowers, great mandarava flowers, and finely ground, hard black particles of sandalwood; they filled the whole sky like clouds as they came raining down. He also rained down the incense of the sandalwood that grows by the southern seashore. Six taels of this incense is worth as much as the saha world. All these he used as an offering to the Buddha.

"When he had finished making this offering, he rose from this samadhi and thought to himself: Though I have employed my supernatural powers to make this offering to the Buddha, it is not as good as making an offering of my own body.

"Thereupon he swallowed various perfumes, sandalwood, kunduruka, turushka, prikka, aloes, and liquidambar gum, and he also drank the fragrant oil of champaka and other kinds of flowers, doing this for a period of fully twelve hundred years. Anointing his body with the fragrant oil, he appeared before the Buddha Sun Moon Pure Bright Virtue, wrapped his body in heavenly jeweled robes, poured fragrant oil over his head and, calling on his transcendental powers, set fire to his body. The glow shown forth, illuminating worlds equal in number to the sands of eighty million Ganges. The Buddhas in these worlds simultaneously spoke out in praise, saying: 'Excellent, excellent, good man! This is true diligence. This is what is called a true Dharma offering to the Thus Come One. Though one may use flowers, incense, necklaces, incense for burning, powdered incensed, paste incense, heavenly silken banners and canopies, along with the incense of the sandalwood that grows by the southern seashore, presenting offerings of all such things as these, he can never match this! Though one may make donations of his realm and cities, his wife and children, he is no match for this! Good men, this is called the foremost donation of all. Among all donations, this is most highly prized, for one is offering the Dharma to the Thus Come One'

"After they had spoken these words, they each fell silent. The body of the bodhisattva burned for twelve hundred years, and when that period of time had passed, it at last burned itself out.

"After the bodhisattva Gladly Seen By All Living Beings had made this Dharma offering and his life had come to an end, he was reborn in the land of the Buddha Sun Moon Pure Bright Virtue, in the household of the King Pure Virtue. Sitting in cross-legged position, he was suddenly born by transformation, and at once for the benefit of his father he spoke in verse form, saying:

Great king, you should now understand this.
Having walked about in a certain place,
I immediately gained the samadhi
that allows me to manifest all physical forms.
I have carried out my endeavors with great diligence
and cast aside the body that I loved.

"When he had recited this verse, he said to his father: 'The Buddha Sun Moon Pure Bright Virtue is still present at this time. Previously I made an offering to this Buddha and gained a dharani that allows me to understand the words of all living beings. Moreover I have heard this Lotus Sutra with its eight hundred, thousand, ten thousand, millions of nayutas, kankaras, vivaras, akshobhyas of verses6 Great king, I must now once more make on offering to this Buddha.

"Having said this, he seated himself on a dais made of the seven treasures, rose up into the air to the height of seven tala trees and, proceeding to the place where the Buddha was, bowed his head to the ground in observance to the Buddha's feet, put the nails of his ten fingers together and spoken this verse in praise of the Buddha:

The countenance so rare and wonderful,
its bright beams illuminating the ten directions!
At a previous time I made an offering.
And now once more I draw near.

"At the time, after the bodhisattva Gladly Seen by All Living Beings had spoken this verse, he said to the Buddha: 'World-Honored One, is the World-Honored One still present in the world?'

"At that time the Buddha Sun Moon Pure Bright Virtue said to the bodhisattva Gladly Seen by All Living Beings: 'Good man, the time has come for my nirvana. The time has come for extinction. You may provide me with a comfortable couch, for tonight will be my parinirvana.'

"He also commanded the bodhisattva Gladly Seen by All Living Beings, saying: 'Good man, I take this Law of the Buddha and entrust it to you. In addition, the bodhisattvas and great disciples, along with the Law of anuttara-samyak-sambodhi, and the thousand-million fold seven-jeweled world, with its jeweled trees and jeweled daises and heavenly beings who wait on and attend them - all these I hand over to you. I also entrust you the relics of my body that remain after I have passed into extinction. You must distribute them abroad and arrange for offerings to them far and wide. You should erect many thousands of towers [to house them].'

"The Buddha Sun Moon Pure Bright Virtue, having given these commands to the bodhisattva Gladly Seen by Living Beings, that night, in the last watch of the night, entered Nirvana.

"At that time the bodhisattva Gladly Seen by All Living Beings, seeing the Buddha pass into extinction, was deeply grieved and distressed. Out of his great love and longing for the Buddha he at once prepared a pyre made of sandalwood from the seashore, and with this as an offering to the Buddha's body, he cremated the body. After the fire had burned out, he gathered up the relics, fashioned eighty-four thousand jeweled urns, and built eighty-four thousand towers, high as the three worlds, adorned with central poles, draped with banners and canopies and hung with a multitude of jeweled bells.

"At that time the bodhisattva Gladly Seen by All Living Beings once more thought to himself: 'Though I have made these offerings, my mind is not yet satisfied. I must make some further offering to the relics.

"Then he spoke to the other bodhisattvas and great disciples, and to the heavenly beings, dragons, yakshas, and all the members of the great assembly, saying, 'You must give your undivided attention. I will now make an offering to the relics of the Buddha Sun Moon Pure Bright Virtue.'

"Having spoken these words, immediately in the presence of the eighty-four thousand towers he burned his arms, which were adorned with a hundred blessings, for a period of seventy-two thousand years as his offering. This caused the numberless multitudes who were seeking to become voice-hearers, along with an immeasurable asamkhya of persons, to conceive the desire for anuttara-samyak-sambodhi, and all of them were able to dwell in the samadhi where one can manifest all physical forms.

"At that time the bodhisattvas, heavenly and human beings, asuras and others, seeing that the bodhisattva had destroyed his arms, were alarmed and saddened and they said: 'This bodhisattva Gladly Seen by All Living Beings is our teacher, instructing and converting us. Now he has burned his arms and his body is no longer whole!'

"At that time, in the midst of the great assembly, the bodhisattva Gladly Seen by All Living Beings made this vow, saying: 'I have cast away both my arms. I'm certain to attain the golden body of a Buddha. If this is true and not false, then may my two arms become as they were before!'

"When he had finished pronouncing this vow, his arms reappeared of themselves as they had been before. This came about because the merits and wisdom of this bodhisattva were many-fold and profound. At that time the thousand-million-fold world shook and trembled in six different ways, heaven rained down jeweled flowers, and all the heavenly and human beings gained what they had never had before."

The Buddha said to the bodhisattva Constellation King Flower: "What do you think? Is this bodhisattva Gladly Seen by All Living Beings someone unknown to you? He is in fact none other than the present bodhisattva Medicine King! He cast aside his body as an offering in this fashion immeasurable hundreds, thousands, ten thousands, millions of nayutas of times.

"Constellation King Flower, if there are those have made up their minds and wish to gain anuttara-samyak-sambodhi, they would do well to burn a finger or one toe of their foot as an offering to the Buddha towers. It is better than offering one's realm and cities, wife and children, or the mountains, forests, Rivers, and lakes in the 'lands of thousand-million-fold world, or all their precious treasures. even if a person were to fill the whole thousand-million-fold world with the seven treasures as an offering to the Buddha and the great bodhisattvas, pratyekabuddhas and arhats, the benefits gained by such a person cannot match those gained by accepting and upholding this Lotus Sutra, even just one four-line verse of it! The latter brings the most numerous blessings of all.

"Constellation King Flower, among all the rivers, streams, and other bodies of water, for example, the ocean is foremost. And this Lotus Sutra is likewise, being the most profound and greatest of the sutras preached by the Thus Come Ones. Again just as among the Dirt Mountains, Black Mountains, Small Iron Encircling Mountains, Great Iron Encircling mountains, Ten Treasure Mountains and all the other mountains, Mount Sumeru is foremost, so this Lotus Sutra is likewise. Among all the sutras, it holds the highest place. And just as among all the stars and their like, the moon, a god's son, is foremost, so this Lotus Sutra is likewise. For among all the thousands, ten thousands, millions of types a sutra teachings, it shines the brightest. And just as the sun, a god's son, con banish all darkness, so too this sutra is capable of destroying the darkness of all that is not good.

"As among the petty kings the wheel-turning sage king is foremost, so this sutra is the most honored among all the many sutras. As the lord Shakra is king among the thirty-three heavenly beings, so this sutra likewise is king among all the sutras. And as the heavenly king, great Brahma, is the father of all living beings, so this sutra likewise is father of all sages, worthies, those still learning, those who have completed their learning, and those who set their minds on becoming bodhisattvas. And as among all the ordinary mortals, the srotaapanna, sakridagamin, anagamin, arhats and pratyekabuddhas are foremost, so this sutra likewise is foremost among all the sutra teachings preached by all the Thus Come Ones, preached by all the bodhisattvas, or preached by all the voice-hearers and pratyekabuddhas, and in the same way this sutra is foremost among all the sutra teachings. As the Buddha is king of the doctrines, so likewise this sutra is king of the sutras.

"Constellation King Flower, this sutra can save all living beings. The sutra can cause all living beings to free themselves from suffering and anguish. The sutra can bring great benefits to living beings and fulfill their desires, as a clear pond can satisfy all those who are thirsty. It is like a fire to one who is cold, a robe to one who is naked, like a band of merchants finding a leader, the child finding its mother, someone finding a ship in which to cross the water, a sick man finding a doctor, someone in darkness finding a lamp, the poor finding riches, the people finding a ruler, a traveling merchant finding his way to the sea. It is like a torch that banishes darkness, Such is this Lotus Sutra. It can cause living beings to cast off all distress, all sickness and pain. It can unloose all the bonds of birth and death.

"If a person is able to hear this Lotus Sutra, if he copies it himself or causes others to copy it, the benefits he gains thereby will be such that even the Buddha wisdom could never finish calculating their extent. If one copies these sutra scrolls and uses flowers, incense, necklaces, incense for burning, powdered incense, paste incense, banners, canopies, robes, various kinds of lamps such as lamps of butter oil, oil lamps, lamps with various fragrant oils, lamps of champaka oil, or lamps of navamalika oil to make offerings to them, the benefits that he acquires will likewise be immeasurable.

"Constellation King Flower, if there is a person who hears this chapter on the Former Affairs of the Bodhisattva Medicine King, he too will gain immeasurable and boundless benefits. If there is a woman hears this chapter of the Former Affairs of the Bodhisattva Medicine King and is able to accept and hold it, that will be her last appearance in a woman's body and she will never be born in that form again.

"If in the last five hundred year period after the Thus Come One has entered extinction there a woman who hears this sutra and carries out its practices as this sutra directs, when her life here on earth comes to an end she will immediately go to the world of Peace and Delight where the Buddha Amitayus dwells surrounded by the assembly of great bodhisattvas and there will be born seated on a jeweled seat in the center of a lotus blossom. He 7 will no longer know the torments of greed, desire, anger, rage, stupidity or ignorance, or the torments brought about by arrogance, envy or other defilements. He will gain the bodhisattva's transcendental powers and the truth of the birthlessness of all phenomena. Having gained this truth, his faculty of sight will be clear and pure, and with this clear pure faculty of sight he will see Buddhas and Thus Come Ones equal in number to the sands of Åven hundred twelve thousand million nayutas of Ganges.

"At that time Buddhas will join him praising them from afar, saying: 'Excellent, excellent, good man! In the midst of the Law of Shakyamuni Buddha you have been able to accept, uphold, read, recite and ponder this sutra and to preach it for others. The good fortune you gain thereby is immeasurable and boundless. It cannot be burned by fire or washed away by water. Your benefits are such that a thousand Buddhas speaking altogether could never finish describing them. Now you have been able to destroy all devils and thieves, to annihilate the army of birth and death, and all others who bore you enmity or malice have likewise been wiped out.

"Good man, a hundred, a thousand Buddhas will employ their transcendental powers to join in guarding and protecting you. Among the heavenly and human beings of all the worlds, there will been no one like you. With the sole exception of the Thus Come One, there will be none among the voice-hearer, pratyekabuddhas or bodhisattvas whose wisdom and ability in meditation can equal yours!'

"Constellation King Flower, such will be the benefits and the power of wisdom successfully acquired by this bodhisattva.

"If there is a person who, hearing this chapter on the Former Affairs of the Bodhisattva Medicine King, is able to welcome it with joy and praise its excellence, then in this present existence this person's mouth will constantly emit the fragrance of the blue lotus flower, and the pores of his body will constantly emit the fragrance of ox-head sandalwood. His benefits will be such as have been described above.

"For this reason, Constellation King Flower, I entrust this chapter on the Former Affairs of the Bodhisattva Medicine King to you. After I pass into extinction, in the last five hundred period you must spread it abroad widely throughout Jambudvipa and never allowed to be cut off, nor must you allow evil devils, the devils' people, heavenly beings, dragons, yakshas or kumbhanda demons to seize the advantage!

"Constellation King Flower, you must use your transcendental powers to guard and protect this sutra. Why? Because this sutra provides good medicine for the ills of the people of Jambudvipa. If a person who has an illness is able to hear this sutra, then his illness will be wiped out and he will know neither old age or death.

"Constellation King Flower, if you see someone who accepts an upholds this sutra, you must take blue lotus blossoms, heap them with powdered incense, and scatter them over him as an offering. And when you have scattered them, you should think to yourself: Before long this person will pick grasses, spread them as a seat in the place of practice, and conquer the armies of the devil. Then he will sound the conch of the Law, beat the drum of the great Law, and free all living beings from the sea of old age, sickness and death!

"For this reason when those who seek the Buddha way see so someone who accepts and upholds this sutra, they should approach him with this kind of respect and reference."

When [the Buddha] preached this chapter on the Former Affairs of the Bodhisattva Medicine King, eighty-four thousand bodhisattvas gained the dharani that allows them to understand the words of all living beings. Many Treasures Thus Come One in the midst of his treasure tower praised the bodhisattva Constellation King Flower, saying: "Excellent, excellent, Constellation King Flower. You succeeded in acquiring inconceivable benefits and thus were able to question Shakyamuni Buddha about this matter, profiting immeasurable numbers of living beings."

Chapter Twenty-four: Bodhisattva Myozon

At that time Shakyamuni Buddha emitted a beam of bright light from the knob of flesh [on top of his head], one of the features of a great man, and also emitted a beam of light from the tuft of white hair between his eyebrows, illuminating the Buddha worlds in the eastern direction equal in number to the sands of one hundred eighty thousand million nayutas of Ganges. Beyond these numerous worlds was a world called Adorned with Pure Light. In this realm there was a Buddha named Pure Flower Constellation King Wisdom Thus Come One, worthy of offerings, of right and universal knowledge, perfect clarity and conduct, well gone, understanding the world, unexcelled worthy, trainer of people, teacher of heavenly and human beings, Buddha, World-Honored One. An immeasurably and boundlessly great multitude of bodhisattvas surrounded him and paid reverence, and for these he preached the Law. The beam of bright light from the white tuft of Shakyamuni Buddha illuminated the whole land.

At that time in the land Adorned with Pure Light there was a bodhisattva named Wonderful Sound, who long ago had planted numerous roots of virtue, offering alms to and waiting upon immeasurable hundreds, thousands, ten thousands, millions of Buddhas. He had succeeded in acquiring all kinds of profound wisdom, gaining the samadhi of the wonderful banner mark, the Dharma flower samadhi, the pure virtue samadhi, the samadhi of the Constellation King's sport, the condition-less samadhi, the seal of wisdom samadhi, the samadhi that allows one to understand the words of all living beings, the samadhi that gathers together all benefits, the pure samadhi, with the samadhi of the sport of transcendental powers, the wisdom torch samadhi, the adorned king samadhi, the pure light glow samadhi, the pure storehouse samadhi, the unshared samadhi, and the samadhi of the suns revolving. He has gained all these great samadhis equal in number to the sands of a hundred, a thousand, ten thousand, a million Ganges.

When the light emitted by Shakyamuni Buddha illuminated his body, he immediately spoke to the Buddha Pure Flower Constellation King Wisdom, saying: "World-Honored One, I must journey to the saha world to do obeisance, wait on, and offer alms to Shakyamuni Buddha, and to see Bodhisattva Manjushri, Prince of the Dharma, Bodhisattva Medicine King, Bodhisattva Brave donor, Bodhisattva Constellation King Flower, Bodhisattva Superior Practices Intent, Bodhisattva Adorned King, and Bodhisattva Medicine Superior."

At that time the Buddha Pure Flower Constellation King Wisdom said to Bodhisattva Wonderful Sound: "You must not look with contempt on the land or come to think of it as a means and inferior. Good man, that saha world is uneven, high in places, low in others, and full of dirt, stones, mountains, foulness, and impurity. The Buddha is puny in stature and the numerous bodhisattvas are likewise small in form, whereas your body is forty-two thousand yojanas in height and mine is six million eight hundred thousand yojanas. Your body is foremost in shapeliness, with hundreds, thousands, ten thousands of blessings and a radiance that is particularly wonderful. Therefore when you journey there, you must not look with contempt on that land or come to think of the Buddha and bodhisattvas or the land itself as mean and inferior!"

Bodhisattva Wonderful Sound said to the Buddha: "World-Honored One, my journey now to the saha world is in all respects due to the power of the Thus Come One, a sport carried out by the Thus Come One's transcendental powers, an adornment to the Thus Come One's blessings and wisdom."

Thereupon the Bodhisattva Wonderful Sound, without raising from his seat or swaying his body, entered into the samadhi, and through the power of the samadhi, in a place not far removed from the Dharma seat on Mount Gridhrakuta, created a jeweled mass of eighty-four thousand lotus blossoms. Their stems were made of Jambunada gold, their leaves were of silver, their stamens of diamond, and their calyxes of kimshuka jewels.

At that time the Dharma Prince Manjushri, spying the lotus flowers, spoke to the Buddha, saying: "World-Honored One, what causes have brought about the appearance of this auspicious sign? Here are many ten thousands of lotus blossoms, their stems made of Jambunada gold, their stamens of diamond and their calyxes of kimshuka jewels!"

At that time Shakyamuni Buddha said to Manjushri: "This bodhisattva and mahasattva Wonderful Sound wishes to leave the land of the Buddha Pure Flower Constellation King Wisdom and, surrounded by eighty-four thousand bodhisattvas, to come to this saha world to offer alms, wait on, and pay obeisance to me. He also wishes to offer alms to and hear the Lotus Sutra."

Manjushri said to the Buddha: "World-Honored One, what good roots has this bodhisattva planted, what benefits has he cultivated, that he can exercise such great transcendental powers as this? What samadhi does he carry out? I beg you to explain for us the name of this samadhi, for we too would look like to apply ourselves diligently to its practice. If we carry out this samadhi, then we will be able to observe the aspect and size of this bodhisattva and his bearing and conduct. We beg the World-Honored One to employ his transcendental powers to bring this bodhisattva here and enable us to see him!"

At that time Shakyamuni Buddha said to Manjushri, "Many Treasures Thus Come One, who entered extinction so long ago, will manifest his form for you.

Then the Buddha Many Treasures said to the bodhisattva [Wonderful Sound], "Come, good man. The Dharma Prince Manjushri wishes to see your body."

With that, Bodhisattva Wonderful Sound vanished from his own land and, accompanied by eight-four thousand bodhisattvas, appeared here [in this saha world]. The lands that he passed through on his way quaked and trembled in six different ways, and in all of them seven jeweled lotus flowers rained down and instruments of hundreds and thousands of the musicians sounded of themselves without having been struck.

This bodhisattva's eyes were as big and broad an the leaves of the blue Lotus, and a hundred, thousand, ten thousand moons put together could not surpass the perfection of this face. His body was pure gold in color, adorned with immeasurable hundreds and thousands of blessings. His dignity and virtue were splendid, his light shone brightly, he was endowed with many special marks and as stalwart in body as Narayana.

Taking his place on the dais made of seven treasures, he had risen up into the air until he was raised above the earth the height of seven tala trees. Then with a host of bodhisattvas surrounding him and paying reverence, he had journeyed to Mount Gridhrakuta in this saha world. When he arrived there he descended from the dais of seven of seven pressures. Bearing a necklace worth hundreds and thousands, he proceeded to the place where Shakyamuni Buddha was, bowed his head to the ground, made obeisance to the Buddha's feet, and presented the necklace, addressing the Buddha in these words: "World-Honored One, the Buddha Pure Flower Constellation King Wisdom wishes to inquire about the World-Honored One. Are your illnesses few, are your worries few? Can you come and go easily and conveniently, can you move about in comfort? Are the four elements properly harmonized in you? Can you endure the worlds affairs? Are the living beings easy to the rescue? Are they not excessive in their greed, anger, stupidity, jealousy, stinginess, and arrogance? Are they not lacking in filial conduct toward their parents? Are they not disrespectful toward shramanas and given to heterodox views and other evil? Do they not fail to control their five emotions? World-Honored One, are the living beings able to conquer and overcome the enmity of the devils? Has Many Treasures Thus Come One, who entered extinction so long ago, come in his tower of seven treasures to listen to the Law? The Buddha also wishes to inquire about Many Treasures Thus Come One, whether he is tranquil and at ease, with few worries, patient and long abiding. World-Honored One, I would like to see the body of the Buddha Many Treasures. I beg the World-Honored One to allow me to see him!"

At the time Shakyamuni Buddha said to Many Treasures Buddha, "This bodhisattva Wonderful Sound wishes to see you."

Then Many Treasures Buddha addressed Wonderful Sound, saying, "Excellent, excellent! You have come here in order to be able to offer alms to a Shakyamuni Buddha and to listen to the Lotus Sutra and see Manjushri and the others."

At that time the Bodhisattva Flower Virtue said to the Buddha, "World-Honored One, this bodhisattva Wonderful Sound - what good roots has he planted, what benefits has he cultivated, that he possesses these supernatural powers?"

The Buddha replied to Bodhisattva flower Virtual: "In ages past there was a Buddha named cloud Thunder Sound King, tathagata, arhats, samyak-sambuddha. His land was called Manifesting All Worlds and his kalpa was called Gladly Seen. For twelve thousand years the Bodhisattva Wonderful Sound employed a hundred thousand types of musical instruments to provide an offering to the Buddha Cloud Thunder Sound King, and e also presented to him eighty-four thousand alms bowls made of the seven treasures. In recompense for these actions he has now been born in the land of the Buddha Pure Flower Constellation King Wisdom and possesses these supernatural powers.

"Flower Virtue, what is your opinion? The bodhisattva Wonderful Sound who at that time made musical offerings to the Buddha Cloud Thunder Sound King and presented him with jeweled vessels - was he someone unknown to you? In fact is none other than the bodhisattva and mahasattva Wonderful Sound who is here now!

"Flower Virtue, this bodhisattva Wonderful Sound has already made offerings to and waited on an immeasurable number of Buddhas. Long ago he planted the roots of virtue and encountered hundreds, thousands, ten thousands, millions of nayutas of Buddhist equal in number to the sands of the Ganges.

Flower Virtue, you see only the body of Bodhisattva Wonderful Sound which is here. But this bodhisattva manifests himself in various different bodies and preaches this sutra for the sake of living beings in various different places. At times he appears as King Brahma, at times as Lord Shakra, at times as the heavenly Being Freedom, at times as a great general of heaven, at times as the heavenly King Vaishravana, at times as a wheel-turning sage king, at times as one of the petty kings, at times as rich man, at times as a householder, to times the chief minister, at times as a Brahman, at times as a monk, a nun, a layman believer, or laywomen believer, at times as the wife of a rich man or a householder, at times as a wife of a chief minister, a times as a wife of a Brahman, at times as a young boy or a young girl, at times as a heavenly being, a dragon, a yaksha, a gandharva, an asura, a garuda, a kimnara, a mahoraga, a human or a nonhuman being, so preaches this sutra. The hell dwellers, hungry spirits, beasts, and the numerous others who are in difficult circumstances are thus are able to be saved. And for the sake of those who are in women's quarters of the royal palace, he changes himself into a woman's form and preaches this sutra.

"Flower Virtue, this bodhisattva Wonderful Sound can save and protect the various living beings of the saha world. This bodhisattva Wonderful Sound performs various transformations, manifesting himself in different forms in this saha land and preaches this sutra for the sake of living beings, and yet his transcendental powers, his transformations, and his Wisdom suffer no injury or diminution thereby. This bodhisattva employs various types of wisdom to illuminate the saha world, causing each one among all the living beings to acquire the appropriate understanding, and does the same in all the other worlds of the ten directions which are numerous as Ganges sands.

"If the form of a voice-hearer is what is needed to bring salvation, he manifests himself in the form of a voice-hearer and proceeds to preach the Law. If the form of a pratyekabuddha will bring salvation, he manifests himself in the form of a pratyekabuddha and preaches the Law. If the form of a bodhisattva will bring salvation, he manifests a bodhisattva form and preaches the Law. If the form of a Buddha will bring salvation, he immediately manifests a Buddha form and preaches the Law. Thus he manifests himself in various different forms, depending upon what is appropriate for salvation. And if it is appropriate to enter extinction in order to bring salvation, he manifests himself as entering extinction.

"Flower virtue, the bodhisattva mahasattvas Wonderful Sound has acquired great transcendental powers and the power of wisdom that enable him to do all this!"

At that time the bodhisattva Flower Virtue said to the Buddha, "World-Honored One, this bodhisattva Wonderful Sound as planted the roots of goodness very deeply. World-Honored One, samadhi does this bodhisattva dwell in, that he is able to carry out all these transformations and manifestations to save living beings?"

The Buddha said to Bodhisattva Flower Virtue, "Good man, this samadhi is called Manifesting All Kinds of bodies. The bodhisattva Wonderful Sound, dwelling in this samadhi, is able in this manner to enrich and benefit immeasurable living beings."

When [the Buddha] preached this chapter on Bodhisattva Wonderful Sound, the eighty-four thousand persons who had come with bodhisattva Wonderful Sound all acquired the samadhi enabling them to manifest all kinds of bodies, and the immeasurable bodhisattvas in this saha world also acquired this samadhi and dharani.

At that time the bodhisattva and mahasattva Wonderful Sound, having finished offering alms to Shakyamuni Buddha and to the tower of Many Treasures Buddha, returned to his original land. The lands that he passed through on his way quaked and trembled in six different ways, jeweled lotus flowers rained down, and hundreds, thousands, ten thousands, millions of different kinds of music played.

After he had arrived in his original land and was surrounded by his eighty-four thousand bodhisattvas, he proceeded to the place of the Buddha Pure Flower Constellation King Wisdom and addressed the Buddha saying, "World-Honored One, I have visited the saha world, enriched and benefited the living beings, saw Shakyamuni Buddha and the tower of Many Treasures Buddha, and offered obeisance and alms to them. I also saw bodhisattva Manjushri, prince of the Dharma, as well as Bodhisattva Medicine King, Bodhisattva Gaining Diligent Exertion Power, Bodhisattva Brave Donor, and others. And I made it possible for these eighty-four thousand bodhisattvas to gain the samadhi enabling them to manifest all kinds of bodies."

When [the Buddha] preached this chapter on the comings and goings of Bodhisattva Wonderful Sound, forty-two thousand sons of gods gained the truth of the birthless-ness of all phenomena, and Bodhisattva Flower Virtue gained the Dharma flower samadhi.

Chapter Twenty-five: The Universal Gate
of Bodhisattva Kanzeon

At that time the bodhisattva Inexhaustible Intent immediately rose from his seat, bared his right shoulder, pressed his palms together and, facing the Buddha, spoke these words: "World Honored One, this Bodhisattva Perceiver of the World's Sounds-- why is he called Perceiver of the World's Sounds?"

The Buddha said to Bodhisattva Inexhaustible Intent: "Good man, suppose there are immeasurable hundreds, thousands, ten thousands, millions of living beings who are undergoing various trials and suffering. If they hear of this Bodhisattva Perceiver of the Word's Sounds and single-mindedly call his name, then at once he will perceive the sound of their voices and they will all gain deliverance from their trials.

If someone, holding fast to the name of bodhisattva perceiver of the world's sounds, should enter a great fire, the fire could not burn him. This would come about because of this bodhisattva's authority and supernatural power. If one were washed away by a great flood and call upon his name, one would immediately find himself in a shallow place.

"Suppose there were a hundred, a thousand, ten thousand, a million living beings who, seeking for gold, silver, lapis lazuli, seashell, agate, coral, amber, pearls, and other treasures, set out on the great sea. and suppose a fierce wind should blow their ship off course and it drifted to the land of rakshasas demons. If among those people there is even just one who calls the name of Bodhisattva Perceiver of the World's sounds, then all those people will be delivered from their troubles with the rakshasas. This is why he is called Perceiver of the World's Sounds.

"If a person who faces imminent threat of attack should call the name of Bodhisattva Perceiver of the World's sounds, then the swords and staves wielded by his attackers would instantly shatter into so many pieces and he would be delivered.

Thought enough yakshas and rakshasas to fill all the thousand-million-fold world should try to come and torment a person, if they hear him calling the name of Bodhisattva Perceiver of the World's Sounds, then these evil demons will not even be able to look at him with their evil eyes, much less do him harm.

"Suppose, in a place filled with all the evil-hearted bandits of the thousand-million-fold world, there is a merchant leader who is guiding a band of merchants carrying valuable treasures over a steep and dangerous road, and that one man shouts out these words: 'Good men, do not be afraid! You must single-mindedly call on the name of Bodhisattva Perceiver of the World's Sounds. This bodhisattva can grant fearlessness to living beings. If you call his name, you will be delivered from these evil-hearted bandits!' When the band if merchants hear this, they all together raise their voices, saying, 'Hail to the Bodhisattva Perceiver of the World's Sounds!' And because they call his name, they are at once able to gain deliverance. Inexhaustible Intent, the authority and supernatural power of the Bodhisattva and mahasattva Perceiver of the World's Sounds are as mighty as this!

"If there should be living beings beset by numerous lusts and cravings, let them think with constant reverence of Bodhisattva Perceiver of the World's Sounds and then they can shed their desires. If they have great wrath and ire, let them think with constant reverence of Bodhisattva Perceiver of the World's Sounds and then they can shed their ire. If they have great ignorance and stupidity, let them think with constant reverence of Bodhisattva Perceiver of the World's Sounds and they can rid themselves of stupidity.

"Inexhaustible Intent, the Bodhisattva Perceiver of the World's Sounds possesses great authority and supernatural powers, as I have described, and can confer many benefits. For this reason, living beings should constantly keep the thought of him in mind.

"If a woman wishes to give birth to a male child, she should offer obeisance and alms to Bodhisattva Perceiver of the World's Sounds and then she will bear a son blessed with merit, virtue, and wisdom. And if she wishes to bear a daughter, she will bear one with al the marks of comeliness, one who in the past planted the roots of virtue and is loved and respected by many persons.

"Inexhaustible Intent, the Bodhisattva Perceiver of the World's Sounds has power to do all this. If there are living beings who pay respect and obeisance to Bodhisattva Perceiver of the World's Sounds, their good fortune will not be fleeting or vain. Therefore living beings should all accept and uphold the name of Bodhisattva Perceiver of the World's Sounds.

"Inexhaustible Intent, suppose there is a person who accepts and upholds the names of as many bodhisattvas as there are sands in sixty-two million Ganges, and for as long as his present body lasts, he offers them alms in the form of food and drink, clothing, bedding and medicines. What is your opinion? Would this good man or good woman gain many benefits or would he not?"

Inexhaustible Intent replied, "They would be very many, World-Honored One."

The Buddha said: "Suppose also that there is a person who accepts and upholds the name of Bodhisattva Perceiver of the World's Sounds and even just once offers him obeisance and alms. The good fortune pained by these two persons would be exactly equal and without difference. For a hundred, a thousand, ten thousand, a million kalpas it would never be exhausted or run out. Inexhaustible Intent, if one accepts and upholds the name of Bodhisattva Perceiver of the World's Sounds, he will gain the benefit of merit and virtue that is as immeasurable and boundless as this!"

Bodhisattva Inexhaustible Intent said to the Buddha, "World-Honored One, Bodhisattva Perceiver of the World's Sounds-- how does he come and go in this saha world? How does he preach the Law for the sake of living beings? How does the power of expedient means apply in this case?"

The Buddha said to Bodhisattva Inexhaustible Intent: "Good man, if there are living beings in the land who need someone in the body of a Buddha in order to be saved, Bodhisattva Perceiver of the World's Sounds immediately manifests himself in a Buddha body and preaches the Law for them. If they need someone in a pratyekabuddha's body in order to be saved, immediately he manifests a pratyekabuddha's body and preaches the Law to them. If the need a voice-hearer to be saved, immediately he becomes a voice-hearer and preaches the Law for them. If they need King Brahma to be saved, immediately he becomes King Brahma and preaches the Law for them. If they need the lord Shakra to be saved, immediately he becomes the lord Shakra and preaches the Law for them. If they need the heavenly being Freedom to be saved, immediately he becomes the heavenly being Freedom and preaches the Law for them. If they need a great general of heaven to be saved, immediately he becomes a great general of heaven and preaches the Law for them. If they need Vaishravana to be saved, immediately he becomes Vaishravana and preaches the Law for them. If they need a petty king to be saved, immediately he becomes a petty king and preaches the law for them.

If they need a rich man to be saved, immediately he becomes a rich man and preaches the Law for them. If they need a householder to be saved, immediately he becomes a householder and preaches the Law for them. If they need a chief minister to be saved, immediately he becomes a chief minister and preaches the Law for them. If they need a Brahman to be saved, immediately he becomes a Brahman and preaches the Law for them. If they need a monk, a nun, a layman believer, or a laywoman believer and preaches the Law for them. If they need the wife of a rich man, of a householder, a chief minister, or a Brahman to be saved, immediately he becomes those wives and preaches the Law for them. If they need a young boy or a young girl and preaches the Law for them. If they need a heavenly being, a dragon, a yaksha, a gandharva, an asura, a garuda, a kimnara, a mahoraga, a human or a nonhuman being to be saved, immediately he becomes all of these and preaches the Law for them. If they need a vajra-bearing god and preaches the Law for them.

"Inexhaustible Intent, this Bodhisattva Perceiver of the World's Sounds has succeeded in acquiring benefits such as these and. Taking on a variety of different forms, goes about among the lands saving living beings. For this reason you and the others should single-mindedly offer alms to Bodhisattva Perceiver of the World's Sounds can bestow fearlessness on those who are in fearful, pressing or difficult circumstances. That is why in this saha world everyone calls him Bestower of Fearlessness."

"Bodhisattva Inexhaustible Intent said to the Buddha, "World-Honored One, now I must offer alms to Bodhisattva Perceiver of the World's Sounds."

Then he took from his neck a necklace adorned with numerous precious gems, worth a hundred or a thousand taels of gold, and presented it to [the bodhisattva], saying, "Sir, please accept this necklace of precious gems as a gift in the Dharma."

At that time Bodhisattva Perceiver of the World's Sounds was unwilling to accept the gift.

Inexhaustible Intent spoke once more to Bodhisattva Perceiver of the World's Sounds, saying, "Sir, out of compassion for us, please accept this necklace."

Then the Buddha said to Bodhisattva Perceiver of the World's Sounds, "Out of compassion for this Bodhisattva Inexhaustible Intent and for the four kinds of believers, the heavenly kings, dragons, yakshas, gandharvas, asuras, garudas, kimnaras, mahoragas, human and nonhuman beings, you should accept this necklace."

Thereupon Bodhisattva Perceiver of the World's Sounds, having compassion for the four kinds of believers and the heavenly beings, dragons, human and nonhuman beings and the others, accepted the necklace and, dividing it into two parts, presented one part to Shakyamuni Buddha and presented the other to the tower of the Buddha Many Treasures.

[The Buddha said,] "Inexhaustible Intent, these are the kinds of freely exercised supernatural powers that Bodhisattva Perceiver of the World's Sounds displays in his comings and goings in the saha world."

At that time Bodhisattva Inexhaustible Intent posed this question in verse form:

World-Honored One replete with wonderful features,
I now ask you once again
for what reason that Buddha's son
is named Bodhisattva Perceiver of the World's Sounds?
The honored One endowed with wonderful features
replied to Inexhaustible Intent in verse:
Listen to the actions of the Perceiver of Sounds,
how aptly he responds in various quarters.
His vast oath is deep as the ocean;
kalpas pass but it remains unfathomable.
He has attended many thousands and millions of Buddhas,
setting forth his great pure vow.
I will describe him in outline for you-
listen to his name, observe his body,
bear him in mind, not passing the time vainly,
for he can wipe out the pains of existence.
Suppose someone should conceive a wish to harm you,
should push you into a great pit of fire.
Think on the power of that Perceiver of Sounds
and the pit of fire will change into a pond!
If you should be cast adrift on the vast ocean,
menaced by dragons, fish and various demons,
think on the power of that Perceiver of Sounds
and the billows and waves cannot drown you!
Suppose you are on the peak of Mount Sumeru
and someone pushes you off.
Think on the power of that Perceiver of Sounds
and you will hang in midair like the sun!
Suppose you are pursued by evil men

who wish to throw you down from a diamond mountain.
Think on the power of that Perceiver of Sounds
and they cannot harm a hair of you!
Suppose you are surrounded by evil-hearted bandits,
each brandishing a knife to wound you.
Think on the power of that Perceiver of Sounds
and at once all will be swayed by compassion!
Suppose you encounter trouble with the king's law,
face punishment, about to forfeit your life.
Think on the power of that Perceiver of Sounds
and the executioner's sword will be broken to bits!
Suppose you are imprisoned in cangue and lock,
hands and feet bound by fetters and chains.
Think on the power of that Perceiver of Sounds
and they will fall off, leaving you free!
Suppose with curses and various poisonous herbs
someone should try to injure you.
Think on the power of that Perceiver of Sounds
and the injury will rebound upon the originator.
Suppose you encounter evil rakshasas,
poison dragons and various demons.
Think on the power of that Perceiver of Sounds
and then none of them will dare to harm you.
If evil beasts should encircle you,
their sharp fangs and claws inspiring terror,
think on the power of that Perceiver of sounds
and they will scamper away in boundless retreat.
If lizards, snakes, vipers, scorpions
threaten you with poison breath that sears like flame,
think on the power of that Perceiver of Sounds
and, hearing your voice, they will flee of themselves.
If clouds should bring thunder, and lightning strike,
if hail pelts or drenching rain comes down,
think on the power of that Perceiver of Sounds
and at that moment they will vanish away.
If living beings encounter weariness or peril,
immeasurable suffering pressing them down,
the power of the Perceiver of Sounds' wonderful wisdom
can save them from the sufferings of the world.
He is endowed with transcendental powers
and widely practices the expedient means of wisdom.
Throughout the lands in the ten directions
there is no region where he does not manifest himself.
In many different kinds of evil circumstances,
in the realms of hell, hungry spirits or beasts,
the sufferings of birth, old age, sickness and death--
all these he bit by bit wipes out.
He of the true gaze, the pure gaze,
the gaze of great and encompassing wisdom,
the gaze of pity, the gaze of compassion--
constantly we implore him, constantly look up in reverence.
His pure light, free of blemish,
is a sun of wisdom dispelling all darknesses.
He can quell the wind and fire of misfortune
and everywhere bring light to the world.
The precepts from his compassionate body shake us

like thunder,
the wonder of his pitying mind is like a great cloud.
He sends down the sweet dew, the Dharma rain,
to quench the flames of earthly desires.
When law suits bring you before the officials,
when terrified in the midst of an army,
think on the power of that Perceiver of Sounds
and hatred in all its forms will be dispelled.
Wonderful sound, Perceiver of the World's Sounds,
Brahma's sound, the sea tide sound--
they surpass those sounds of the world;
therefore you should constantly think on them
from thought to thought never entertaining doubt!
Perceiver of the World's Sounds, pure sage--
to those in suffering, in danger of death,
he can offer aid and support.
Endowed with all benefits,
he views living beings with compassionate eyes.
The sea of his accumulated blessings is immeasurable;
therefore you should bow your head to him!

At that time the Bodhisattva Earth Holder immediately rose from his seat, advanced, and said to the Buddha, "World-Honored One, if there are living beings who hear this chapter on Bodhisattva Perceiver of the World's Sounds, on the freedom of his actions, his manifestation of a universal gateway, and his transcendental powers, it should be known that the benefits these persons gain are not few!"

When the Buddha preached this chapter on the Universal Gateway, a multitude of eighty-four thousand persons in the assembly all conceived a determination to attain the unparalleled state of anuttara-samyak-sambodhi.

Chapter Twenty-six: Dharani

At that time the Bodhisattva Medicine king rose from his seat, bared his right shoulder, pressed his palms together and, facing the Buddha, spoke to him, saying, "World-Honored One, if there are good men or good women who can accept and uphold the Lotus Sutra, if they read and recite it, penetrate its meaning, or copy the sutra scrolls, how much merit will they gain?"

The Buddha said to Medicine King, "If there are good men or good women who offer alms to Buddhas equal in number to the sands of eight hundred ten thousand million nayutas of Ganges, what is your opinion? The merit they gain will surely be great, will it not?"

"Very great, World-Honored One."

The Buddha said, "If there are good men or good women who, with regard to this sutra, can accept and uphold even one four-line verse, if they read and recite it, understand the principle and practice it as the sutra directs, the benefits will be very many."

At that time Bodhisattva Medicine King said to the Buddha, "World-Honored One, I will now give to those who preach the Law dharani spells, which will guard and protect them." Then he pronounced these spells:

anye manye mane mamane chitte harite shame shamitavi
shante mukte muktatame same avashame sama same kshaye
akshaye akshine shante shame dharani alokabhashe-
pratyavekshani nivshte abhyantaranivishte atyantaparishuddhi
ukkule mukkule arade parade shukakashi asamasame
buddhavilokite dharmaparikshite samghanirghoshani
bhayabhayashodhani mantre mantrakshayate rute
rutakaushalye akshaye akshayavanataya abalo amanyanataya.

"World-Honored One, these dharanis, these supernatural spells, are pronounced by Buddhas equal in number to the sands of sixty-two million Ganges. If anyone should assault or injure these teachers of the Law, then he will have assaulted and injured these Buddhas!"

At that time Shakyamuni Buddha praised Bodhisattva Medicine King, saying, "Excellent, excellent, Medicine King! You keep these teachers of the Law in your compassionate thoughts, shield and guard them, and for that reason you pronounce these dharanis. They will bring great benefit to living beings."

At that time Bodhisattva Brave Donor said to the Buddha, "World-Honored One, I too will pronounce dharanis to shield and guard those who read, recite, accept, and uphold the Lotus Sutra. If a teacher of the Law acquires these dharanis, then although yakshas, rakshasas, putanas, krityas, kumbhandas or hungry spirits should spy out his shortcomings and try to take advantage of them, they will be unable to do so." Then in the presence of the Buddha he pronounced these spells:

jvale mahajvale ukke mukke ade adavati nritye nrityavati ittini
vittini chittini nrityani nrityakati

"World-Honored One, these dharanis, these supernatural spells, are pronounced by Buddhas equal in number to the sands of the Ganges, and all of them respond with joy. If anyone should assault or injure these teachers of the Law, then he will have assaulted and injured these Buddhas!"

At that time the heavenly king Vaishravana, protector of the world, said to the Buddha, "World-Honored One, I too think compassionately of living beings and shield and guard these teachers of the Law, and therefore I pronounce these dharanis." Then he pronounced these spells:

atte natte nunatte anada nade kunadi

"World-Honored One, with these supernatural spells I shield and guard the teachers of the Law. And I will also shield and guard those who uphold this sutra, making certain that they suffer no decline or harm within the area of a hundred yojanas."

At that time heavenly king Upholder of the Nation, who was in the assembly along with a host of thousands, ten thousands, millions of nayutas of gandharvas who surrounded him and paid him reverence, advanced to the place where the Buddha was, pressed his palms together and said to the Buddha, "World-Honored One, I too will employ dharanis, supernatural spells, to shield and guard those who uphold the Lotus Sutra." Then he pronounced these spells:

agane gane gauri gandhari chandali matangi janguly vrusani
agashti

"World-Honored One, these dharanis, these supernatural spells, are pronounced by forty-two million Buddhas. If anyone should assault or injure these teachers of the Law, then he will have assaulted and injured these Buddhas!"

At that time there were daughters of rakshasa demons, the first named Lamba, the second named Vilamba, the third named Crooked Teeth, the fourth named Flowery Teeth, the fifth named Black Teeth, the sixth named Much Hair, the seventh named Insatiable, the eighth named Necklace Bearer, the ninth named Kunti, and the tenth named Stealer of the Vital Spirit of All Living Beings. These ten rakshasa daughters, along with the Mother of Devil Children, her offspring, and her attendants, all proceeded to the place where the Buddha was and spoke to the Buddha in unison, saying, "World-Honored One, we too wish to shield and guard those who read, recite, accept, and uphold the Lotus Sutra and spare them from decline or harm. If anyone should spy out the shortcomings of these teachers of the Law and try to take advantage of them, we will make it impossible for him to do so." Then in the presence of the Buddha they pronounce these spells:

itime itime itime atime itime nime nime nime nime nime ruhe
ruhe ruhe ruhe stahe stahe stahe stuhe shuhe

"Though they climb upon our very heads, they will never trouble the teachers of the Law! Whether it be a yaksha, or a pakshasa, or a hungry spirit, or a putana, or a kritya, or a vetada, or a skanda 8, or an umaraka, or an apasmaraka, or a yaksha kritya, or a human kritya, or a fever, a one day, a two day, a three day, or a four day, or up to a seven day or a constant fever, whether it be in a man's form, in a woman's form, in young boy's form, in young girl's form, though it be only in a dream, it will never trouble them!"

Then in the presence of the Buddha they spoke in verse form, saying:

If there are those who fail to heed our spells
and trouble and disrupt the preachers of the Law,
their heads will split into seven pieces
like the branches of the arjaka tree.
Their crime will be like that of one who kills father and mother,
or one who presses out oil,
or cheats others with measures and scales,
or, like Devadatta, disrupts the Order of monks.
Anyone who commits a crime against these teachers of the Law
will bring on himself guilt such as this!"

After the rakshasa daughters had spoken these verses, they said to the Buddha, "World-Honored One, we will use our own bodies to shield and guard those who accept, uphold, read, recite, and practice this sutra. We will see that they gain peace and tranquility, freeing them from decline and harm and nulling the effect of all poison herbs."

The Buddha said to the rakshasa daughters, "Excellent, excellent! If you can shield and guard those who accept and uphold the mere name of the Lotus Sutra, your merit will be immeasurable. How much more so if you shield and guard those who accept and uphold it in its entirety, who offer alms to the sutra scrolls, flowers, incense, necklaces, powdered incense, paste incense, incense for burning, banners, canopies, music, who burn various kinds of lamps, lamps of butter oil, oil lamps, lamps of various fragrant oils, lamps of sumana flower oil, and lamps of utpala flower oil, and who in this manner offer hundreds and thousands of varieties of alms? Kunti, you and your attendants should shield and guard the teachers of the Law such as these!"

When [the Buddha] preached this Dharani chapter, sixty-eight thousand persons gained the truth of birthlessness.

Chapter Twenty-seven: The Former Deeds
of King Wondrous Splendor

At that time the Buddha addressed the great assembly, saying: "In an age long ago, an immeasurable, boundless, inconceivable number of asamkhya kalpas in the past, there was a Buddha named Cloud Thunder Sound Constellation King Flower Wisdom, tathagata, arhat, samyak-sambuddha. His land was named Light Bright Adornment and his kalpa was named Gladly Seen. In the midst of this Buddha's Law there was a king named Wonderful Adornment. This king's consort was named Pure Virtue, and he had two sons, one named Pure Storehouse and the other named Pure Eye. These two sons possessed great supernatural powers, merit, virtue, wisdom, and for a long time they had been practicing the way appropriate to a bodhisattva, carrying out the dana-paramita, shila-paramita, kshanti-paramita, virya-paramita, dhyana-paramita, pragna-paramita, the paramita of expedient means, pity, compassion, joy and indifference, as well as the thirty-seven aids to the way 9. All of these they had thoroughly understood and mastered. In addition, they had gained the samadhis of the bodhisattva, namely, the pure samadhi; sun, star, and constellation samadhi; pure light samadhi; pure color samadhi; pure illumination samadhi; long adornment samadhi; and great dignity and virtue storehouse samadhi, and had thoroughly mastered all these samadhis.

"At that time that Buddha, wishing to attract and guide King Wonderful Adornment, and because he thought with compassion of living beings, preached the Lotus Sutra. The king's two sons, Pure Storehouse and Pure Eye, went to where their mother was, pressed their palms and the nails of their ten fingers together, and said to her, 'We beg our mother to go and visit the place where the Buddha Cloud Thunder Sound Constellation King Flower Wisdom is. We too will attend him, drawing near to the Buddha and offering alms and obeisance. Why? Because this Buddha is preaching the Lotus Sutra in the midst of all the multitude of heavenly and human beings and it is right that we should listen and accept it.'

"The mother announced to her sons, 'Your father puts his faith in non-Buddhist doctrines and is deeply attached to the Brahmanical Law. You should go to your father, tell him about this, and persuade him to go with you.'

"Pure Storehouse and Pure Eye pressed their palms and ten fingernails together and said to their mother, 'We are sons of the Dharma King, and yet we have been born into this family of heretical views!'

"The mother said to her sons, 'You are right to think with concern about your father. You should manifest some supernatural wonder for him. When he sees that, his mind will surely be cleansed and purified and he will permit us to go to where the Buddha is.'

The two sons, being concerned about their father, leaped up into the air to the height of seven tala trees and there performed various types of supernatural wonders, walking, standing, sitting, and lying down in midair; making water come out of the upper part of their bodies; making fire come out of the lower part of their bodies, making water come out of the lower part of their bodies; making fire come at of the upper part of their bodies; manifesting huge bodies that filled the sky and then making themselves small again; after becoming small, making themselves big again; disappearing in the midst of the sky and then suddenly appearing on the ground; sinking into the ground as though it were water; walking on the water as though it were land. They manifested these various types of supernatural wonders in order to cause the mind of their royal father to become pure and to make him believe and understand.

"At that time when the father saw his sons displaying supernatural powers of this kind, his mind was filled with great delight, as he had never known before, and he pressed his palms together, faced his sons and said, "Who is your teacher? Whose disciples are you?'

"The two sons replied, "Great king, the Buddha Cloud Thunder Sound Constellation King Flower Wisdom is at present sitting in the Dharma seat under the seven-jeweled bodhi tree and, amid the multitudes of heavenly and human beings of all the world, is broadly expounding the Lotus Sutra. This is our teacher and we are his disciples.'

"The father said to his sons, 'I would like to go now and see your teacher, You can go with me.'

"With this the two sons descended from the air, proceeded to where their mother was, pressed their palms together and said to their mother, 'Our royal father has now come to believe and understand, he is fully capable of conceiving a desire for anuttara-samyak-sambodhi. We have finished doing the Buddha's work for the sake of our father. We beg that our mother will permit us to go to the place where the Buddha is, to leave the household life and to practice the way.'

"At that time the two sons, wishing to state their meaning once more, spoke in verse form, saying to their mother:

We beg our mother to permit us
to leave the household and become shramanas.
The Buddhas are very hard to encounter;
we will follow this Buddha and learn from him.
Rare as is the udumbara flower,
rarer is it to encounter a Buddha,
and escaping from difficulties is also difficult--
we beg you to allow us to leave the household.

"Their mother then said to them, 'I will permit you to leave the household life. Why? Because the Buddha is difficult to encounter.'

"The two sons then addressed their father and mother, saying: 'Excellent, father and mother! And we beg you in due time to go to the place where the Buddha Cloud Thunder Sound Constellation King Flower Wisdom is, attend him in person and offer alms. Why? Because encountering the Buddha is as difficult as encountering the udumbara flower. Or as difficult as it is for a one-eyed turtle to encounter a floating log with a hole in it. We have been blessed with great good fortune from past existences and so have been born in an age where we can encounter the Buddha's Law. For this reason our father and mother should permit us to leave household life. Why? Because the Buddhas are difficult to encounter, and the proper time is also hard to come upon.'

"At that time the eighty-four thousand persons in the women's quarters of King Wonderful Adornment were all capable of accepting and upholding the Lotus Sutra. Bodhisattva Pure Eye had long ago mastered the Dharma flower samadhi, and Bodhisattva Pure Storehouse had already, some hundreds, thousands, ten thousands, millions of kalpas in the past, mastered the samadhi of the escape from the evil realms of existence. This was because he wished to make it possible for all living beings to escape the evil realms. The king's consort had gained the samadhi of the Buddhas' assembly and was capable of understanding the secret storehouse of the Buddhas. Her two sons, as already described, had employed the power of expedient means to improve and transform their father so that he could acquire a mind of faith and understanding and love and delight in the Buddha's Law.

"Thereupon King Wonderful Adornment, accompanied by his ranks of ministers and his attendants; his queen Pure Virtue and all the ladies-in-waiting and attendants of the women's quarters; and the king's two sons and their forty-two thousand attendants, all at the same time went to where the Buddha was. Arriving there, they bowed their heads to the ground in obeisance to his feet, circled around the Buddha three times, and then withdrew and stood to one side.

"At that time that Buddha preached the Law for the sake of the king, instructing him and bringing him benefit and joy. The king was exceedingly delighted.

"At that time King Wonderful Adornment and his queen removed from their necks necklaces of pearls worth hundreds and thousands and scattered them over the Buddha. In midair the necklaces changed into a jeweled dais with four pillars. On the dais was a large jeweled couch spread with hundreds, thousands, ten thousands of heavenly robes. Seated cross-legged on them was a Buddha who emitted a brilliant light.

"At that time King Wonderful Adornment thought to himself: The Buddha's body is rare indeed, extraordinary in dignity and adornment, constituting a form of utmost subtlety and wonder! Then the Buddha Cloud Thunder Sound Constellation King Flower Wisdom spoke to the four kinds of believers, saying, 'Do you see this King Wonderful Adornment who stands before me with his palms pressed together? In the midst of my Law this king will become a monk, diligently practicing the Law that aids the Buddha way. He will be able to become a Buddha. His name will be Sal Tree King, his land will be called Great Light, and his kalpa will be called Great Lofty King. This Buddha Sal Tree King will have an immeasurable multitude of bodhisattvas, as well as immeasurable voice-hearers. His land will be level and smooth. Such will be his benefits.'

"The king immediately turned his kingdom to his younger brother and he himself, along with his queen, his two sons, and all their attendants, in the midst of the Buddha's Law renounced the household life to practice the way.

"After the king had left the household life, for the space of eighty-four thousand yours he constantly applied himself with diligence, practicing the Lotus Sutra of the Wonderful Law. When his period had passed, he gained the samadhi of the adornment of all pure benefits. Rising into the air to the height of seven tala trees, he addressed the Buddha saying: 'World-Honored One, these two sons of mine have carried out the Buddha's work, employing transcendental powers and transformations to turn my mind away from heresies, enabling me to abide safely in the Buddha's Law, and permitting me to see the World-Honored One. These two sons have been good friends to me. They wished to awaken the good roots from my past existences and to enrich and benefit me, and for that reason they were born into my household.'

"At that time the Buddha Cloud Thunder Sound Constellation King Flower Wisdom said to King Wonderful Adornment, 'Just so, just so. It is as you have said. If good men and good women have planted good roots, and as a result in existence after existence have been able to gain good friends, then these good friends can do the Buddha's work, teaching, benefiting, delighting, and enabling them to enter anuttara-samyak-sambodhi. Great king, you should understand that a good friend is the great cause and condition by which one is guided and led, and which enables one to see the Buddha and to conceive the desire for anuttara-samyak-sambodhi. Great king, do you see these two sons? These two sons have already offered alms to Buddhas equal in number to the sands of sixty-five hundred, thousand, ten thousand, million nayutas of Ganges, have drawn near to them with reverence, and in the presence of those Buddhas have accepted and upheld the Lotus Sutra, thinking with compassion of living beings who embrace heretical views and causing them to abide in correct views.'

"King Wonderful Adornment then descended from midair and said to the Buddha, 'World-Honored One, the Thus Come One is a very rare being! Because of his benefits and wisdom, the knob of flesh on the top of his head illuminates all with bright light. His eyes are long, broad, and dark blue in color. The tuft of hair in between his eyebrows, one of his features, is white as a crystal moon. His teeth are white, even, closely spaced, and constantly have a bright gleam. His lips are red and beautiful as the bimba fruit.'

"At that time King Wonderful Adornment, having praised the Buddha's immeasurable hundreds, thousands, ten thousands, millions of benefits in this manner, in the presence of the Thus Come One single-mindedly pressed his palms together and addressed the Buddha once more, saying 'World-Honored One, such a thing as this has never been known before! The law of the Thus Come One is fully endowed with inconceivably subtle and wonderful benefits. Where his teachings and precepts are observed there will be tranquility and good feeling. From this day on I will give way to heretical views or to arrogance, anger, or other evil states of mind.'

"When he had spoken these words, he bowed to the Buddha and departed."

The Buddha said to the great assembly: "What is your opinion? Is this King Wonderful Adornment someone unknown to you? In fact he is none other than the present Bodhisattva Flower Virtue. And his queen Pure Virtue is Bodhisattva Light Shining Adornment Marks who is now in the Buddha's presence. Out of pity and compassion for King Wonderful Adornment and his attendants, he was born in their midst. The king's sons are the present bodhisattvas Medicine King and Medicine Superior.

"These bodhisattvas Medicine King and Medicine Superior have already succeeded in acquiring great benefits such as these, and in the presence of immeasurable hundreds, thousands, ten thousands, millions of Buddhas have planted numerous roots of virtue and acquired inconceivably good benefits. If there are persons who are acquainted with the names of these two bodhisattvas, the heavenly and human beings of all the world will surely do obeisance to them."

When the Buddha preached this chapter on the Former Affairs of King Wonderful Adornment, eighty-four thousand persons removed themselves from dust and defilement and with respect to the various phenomena attained the pure Dharma eye.

Chapter Twenty-eight: The Encouragement
of Bodhisattva Universally Worthy

At that time Bodhisattva Universal worthy, famed for his freely exercised transcendental powers, dignity and virtue, in company with great bodhisattvas in immeasurable, boundless, indescribable numbers, arrived from the east. The lands that he passed through one and all quaked and trembled, jeweled lotus flowers rained down, and immeasurable hundreds, thousands, ten thousands, millions of different kinds of music played. In addition, numberless heavenly beings, dragons yakshas, gandharvas, asuras, garudas, kimnaras, mahoragas, human and nonhuman beings surrounded him in a great assembly, each displaying his dignity, virtue, and transcendental powers.

When [Bodhisattva Universal Worthy] arrived in the midst of Mount Gridhrakuta in the saha world, he bowed his head to the ground in obeisance to Shakyamuni Buddha, circled around him to the right seven times, and said to the Buddha: 'World-Honored One, when I was in the land of the Buddha King Above Jeweled Dignity and Virtue, from far away I heard the Lotus Sutra being preached in this saha world. In company with this multitude of immeasurable, boundless hundreds, thousands, ten thousands, millions of bodhisattvas I have come to listen to and accept it. I beg that the World-Honored One will preach it for us. And good men and good women in the time after the Thus Come One has entered extinction--how will they be able to acquire this Lotus Sutra?"

The Buddha said to Bodhisattva Universal Worthy: "If good men and good women will fulfill four conditions in the time after the Thus Come One has entered extinction, then they will be able to acquire this Lotus Sutra. First, they must be protected and kept in mind by the Buddhas. Second, they must plant the roots of virtue. Third, they must enter the stage where they are sure of reaching enlightenment. Fourth, they must conceive a determination to save all living beings. If good men and good women fulfill these four conditions, then after the Thus Come One has entered extinction they will be certain to acquire this sutra."

At that time Bodhisattva Universal Worthy said to the Buddha: "World-Honored One , in the evil and corrupt age of the last five-hundred-year period, if there is someone who accepts and upholds this sutra, I will guard and protect him, free him from decline and harm, see that he attains peace and tranquility, and make certain that no one can spy out and take advantage of his shortcomings, no devil, devil's son, devil's daughter, devil's minion, or one possessed by the devil, no yaksha, rakshasa, kumdhanda, pishacha, krithya, putana, vetada, or other being that torments humans will be able to take advantage of him.

"Whether that person is walking or standing, if he reads and recites this sutra, then at that time I will mount my six-tusked kingly white elephant and with my multitude of great bodhisattvas will proceed to where he is. I will manifest myself, offer alms, guard and protect him, and bring comfort to his mind. I will do this because I too want to offer alms to the Lotus Sutra. If when that person is seated he ponders this sutra, at that time too I will mount my kingly white elephant and manifest myself in his presence. If that person should forget a single phrase or verse of the Lotus Sutra, I will prompt him and join him in reading and reciting so that he will gain understanding. At that time the person who accepts, upholds, reads and recites the Lotus Sutra will be able to see my body, will be filled with great joy, and will apply himself with greater diligence than ever. Because he has seen me, he will immediately acquire samadhis and dharanis. These are called the repetition dharani, the hundred, thousand, ten thousand, million repetition dharani, and the Dharma sound expedient dharani. He will acquire dharanis such as these.

"World-Honored One, in that later time, in the evil and corrupt age of the last five-hundred-year period, if monks, nuns, laymen believers or laywomen believers who seek out, accept, uphold, read, recite, and transcribe this Lotus Sutra should wish to practice it, they should do so diligently and with a single mind for a period of twenty-one days. When the twenty-one days have been fulfilled, I will mount my six-tusked white elephant and, with immeasurable numbers of bodhisattvas surrounding me and with this body that all living beings delight to see, I will manifest myself in the presence of the person and preach the Law for him, bringing him instruction, benefit, and joy. I will also give him dharani spells. And because he has acquired these spells, no nonhuman being will be able to injure him and he cannot be confused or lead astray by women. I too will personally guard him at all times. Therefore, World-Honored One, I hope you will permit me to pronounce these dharanis." Then in the presence of the Buddha he pronounced these spells:

adande dandapati dandavarte dandakushale dandasudhare
sudhare sudharapati buddhapashyane sarvadharani-avartani
sarvandhashyavartani su-avartani samghaparikshani
samghanarghatani asamge samgapagate tri-adhvasamgatulya-
arate-prapty savasamgasamatikrante sarvadharmasuparikshite
sarvasattvarutakaushalyanugate simhavikridite

"World-Honored One, if any bodhisattva is able to hear these dharanis, he should understand that it is due to the transcendental powers of Universal Worthy. If when the Lotus Sutra is propagated throughout Jambudvipa there are those who accept and uphold it, they should think to themselves: This is all due to the authority and supernatural power of Universal Worthy! If there are those who accept this sutra, memorize it correctly, understand its principles, and practice it as the sutra prescribes, these persons should know that they are carrying out the practices of Universal Worthy himself. In the presence of immeasurable, boundless members of Buddhas they will have planted good roots deep in the ground, and the hands of the Thus Come Ones will pat them on the head.

"If they do no more than copy the sutra, when their lives come to an end they will be reborn in the Trayastrimsha heaven. At that time eighty-four thousand heavenly women, performing all kinds of music, will come to greet them. Such persons will put on crowns made of seven treasures amidst the ladies-in-waiting will amuse and enjoy themselves. How much more so, then, if they accept, uphold, read and recite the sutra, memorize it correctly, understand its principles, when the lives of these persons come to an end, they will be received into the hands of a thousand Buddhas, who will free them from all fear and keep them from falling into the evil paths of existence. Immediately they will proceed to the Tushita heaven, to the place of Bodhisattva Maitreya. Bodhisattva Maitreya possesses the thirty-two features and is surrounded by a multitude of great bodhisattvas. He has hundreds, thousands, ten thousands, millions of heavenly women attendants, and these persons will be reborn in their midst. Such will be the benefits and advantages they enjoy.

"Therefore persons of wisdom should single-mindedly copy the sutra themselves, or cause others to copy it, should accept, uphold, read, and recite it, memorize it correctly and practice it as the sutra prescribes. "World-Honored One, I now therefore employ my transcendental powers to guard and protect this sutra. And after the Thus Come One had entered extinction, I will cause it to be widely propagated throughout Jambudvipa and will see that it never comes to an end."

At that time Shakyamuni Buddha spoke these words of praise: "Excellent, excellent, Universal Worthy! You are able to guard and assist this sutra and cause many living beings to gain peace and happiness and advantages. You have already acquired inconceivable benefits and profound great pity and compassion. Since long ages in the past you have shown a desire for anuttara-samyak-sambodhi, and have taken a vow to use your transcendental powers to guard and protect this sutra. And I will employ my transcendental powers to guard and protect those who can accept and uphold the name of Bodhisattva Universal Worthy.

"Universal Worthy, if there are those who accept, uphold, read and recite this Lotus Sutra, memorize it correctly, practice and transcribe it, you should know that such persons have seen Shakyamuni Buddha. It is as though they heard his sutra from the Buddha's mouth. You should know that such persons have offered alms to Shakyamuni Buddha you should know that such persons have been patted on the head by Shakyamuni Buddha. You should know that such persons have been covered in the robes of Shakyamuni Buddha.

"They will no longer be greedy for or attached to worldly pleasures, they will have no taste for the scriptures or jottings of the non-Buddhists. They will take no pleasure in associating this such people, or with those engaged in evil occupations such as butchers, raisers of pigs sheep, chickens or dogs, hunters, or those who offer women's charms for sale. These persons will be honest and upright in mind and intent, correct in memory, and will possess the power of merit and virtue. They will not be troubled by the three poisons, nor will they be troubled by jealousy, self-importance, ill-founded conceit, or arrogance. These persons will have few desires, will be easily satisfied, and will know how to carry out the practices of Universal Worthy.

"Universal Worthy, after the Thus Come One has entered extinction, in the last five-hundred-year period, if you see someone who accepts, upholds reads, and recites the Lotus Sutra, you should think to yourself: Before long this person will proceed to the place of practice, conquer the devil hosts, and attain anuttara-samyak-sambodhi. He will turn the wheel of the Dharma, beat the Dharma drum, and sound the Dharma conch, and rain down the Dharma rain. He is worthy to sit in the lion seat of the Dharma, amid the great assembly of heavenly and human beings.

"Universal Worthy, in later ages if there are those who accept, uphold, read, and recite this sutra, such persons will no longer be greedy for or attached to clothing, bedding, food and drink, or other necessities of daily life. Their wishes will not be in vain, and in this present existence they will gain the reward of good fortune. If there is anyone who disparages or makes light of them, saying, 'You are mere idiots! It is useless to carry out these practices--in the end they will gain you nothing!, then as punishment for his offense that person will be born eyeless in existence after existence. But if there is anyone who offers alms to them and praises them, then in this present existence he will have manifest reward for it.

"If anyone sees a person who accepts and upholds this sutra and tries to expose the faults or evils of that person, whether what he speaks is true or not, he will in his present existence be afflicted with white leprosy. If anyone disparages or laughs at that person, then in existence after existence he will have teeth that are missing or spaced far apart, ugly lips, a flat nose, hands and feet that are gnarled or deformed, and eyes that are squinty. His body will have a foul odor, with evil sores that run pus and blood, and he will suffer from water in the belly, shortness of breath, and other severe and malignant illnesses. Therefore, Universal Worthy, if you see a person who accepts and upholds this sutra, you should rise and greet him from afar, showing him the same respect you would a Buddha."

When this chapter on the Encouragements of the Bodhisattva Universal Worthy was preached, bodhisattvas immeasurable and boundless as Ganges sands acquired dharanis allowing them to memorize a hundred, a thousand, ten thousand, a million repetitions of the teachings, and bodhisattvas equal to the dust particles of the thousand-million-fold world perfected the way of Universal Worthy.

When the Buddha preached this sutra, Universal Worthy and the other bodhisattvas, Shariputra and the other voice-hearers, along with the heavenly beings, dragons, humans and nonhuman beings--the entire membership of the great assembly were all filled with great joy. Accepting and upholding the words of the Buddha, they bowed in obeisance and departed.

The Sutra of meditation on The Bodhisattva Universal Virtue

THUS HAVE I HEARD. Once the Buddha was staying at the two storied assembly hall in the great forest monastery, Vaisali; then he addressed all the bhikshus, saying, "after three months I shall surely enter parinirvana." Thereupon the honored Ananda rose from his seat, straightened his garment, and with joined palms and folded hands, he made procession around the Buddha three times, and saluted him, kneeling with folded hands, and attentively gazed at the Tathagata without turning away his eyes for even a moment. The elder Mahakashyapa and the Bodhisattva-Mahasattva Maitreya also rose from their seats, and with folded arms gazed up at the honored face. Then the three great leaders with one voice spoke the Buddha saying, "World Honored One! After the extinction of the Tathagata, how can living beings raise the mind of the Bodhisattva, practice the sutras of Great Extent, The Great Vehicle, and ponder the world of one reality with right thought? How can they keep from losing the mind of supreme Buddha hood? How, without cutting off their earthly care and the five desires, can they also purify their organs and destroy their sins? How, with the natural pure eyes received from their birth by their parents and without forsaking the five desires can, they see things without all impediment?

The Buddha said to Ananda, "Do you listen to me attentively! Do you listen to me attentively, ponder and remember it! Of yore on Mount Grdhrakuta (Eagle Peak) and in other places the Tathagata had already extensively explained the way of one reality. But now in this place, to all living beings and others in the world to come who desire to practice the great law of the supreme law of the Great Vehicle, and to those who desire to learn the works of Universal Virtue and to follow the works of Universal Virtue, I will now preach the law that I have entertained. I will now widely make clear to you the matter of eliminating numerous sins for any one who may happen to see or not see Universal Virtue. Ananda! The Bodhisattva Universal Virtue was born in the eastern pure wonderland, whose form I have already clearly and extensively explained in the sutra of miscellaneous flowers. Now I, in this sutra will briefly explain it.

"Ananda, if there be Bhikshus, Bhiksunis, Upasakas, Upasikas, the eight groups of gods and dragons, and all living beings who recite the great vehicle, practice it, aspire to it, delight to see the form and body of The Bodhisattva Universal Virtue, have pleasure in seeing the stupa of the Buddha Abundant Treasures, take joy in seeing Shakyamuni Buddha, and the Buddhas who emanated from him, and rejoice to obtain the purify of the six organs, they must learn this meditation. The merits of this mediation will make them free from all hindrances and make them see the excellent forms. Even though they have not yet entered into contemplation just because they recite and keep the great vehicle they will devote themselves to practicing it, and after having kept their minds continuously on the great vehicle for a day, or three times seven days, they will be able to see Universal Virtue; Those who have heavier impediments will see him after seven times seven; again those who have a heavier one will see him after one birth, those who have a much heavier one will see him after two births; again those who have a still heavier one will see him after three births. Thus the retribution for this karma is various and is not equal. For this reason I preach the teaching variously.

The Bodhisattva Universal Virtue is boundless in the size of his body, boundless in the sound of his voice, and boundless in the form of his image. Desiring to come to this world, he makes use of his free transcendent powers and shrinks his stature to the small size of a human being. Because the people in Jambudvipa have the three heavy hindrances, by his wisdom-power he appears transformed as mounted on a white elephant. The elephant has six tusks and, with its seven legs, it supports its body on the ground. Under it's seven legs seven lotus flowers grow. The elephant is white as snow, the most brilliant of all shades of white, so pure that even crystal and the Himalayan Mountains cannot be compared with it. The body of the elephant is four hundred and fifty yojanas in length and four hundred yojanas in height. At the end of the six tusks there are six bathing pools. In each bathing pool grow fourteen lotus flowers exactly the size of the pools. The flowers are in full bloom as the king of celestial trees. On each of these flowers is a precious daughter whose continence is red as crimson and whose radiance surpasses that of nymphs. In the hand of that daughter there appear, transformed of themselves, five harps, and each of them has five hundred musical instruments as accompaniment. There are five hundred birds, including ducks, wild geese, and mandarin ducks, all having the color of precious things, arising among flowers and leaves. On the trunk of the elephant there is a flower, and its stalk is the color of a red pearl. That golden flower is still a bud and has not yet blossomed. Having finished beholding this matter, if one further repents one's sins, meditates on the Great Vehicle attentively with entire devotion, and ponders it in his mind incessantly, he will be able to see the flower instantly bloom and light up with a golden color. The cup of the lotus flower is a cup of kimshuka gems with wonderful Brahma jewels, and the stamens are of diamond. A transformed Buddha is seen sitting on the petals of the lotus flower with a host of Bodhisattvas sitting on the stamens of the lotus flower. From the eyebrows of the transformed Buddha a ray of light is sent forth and enters the elephant's trunk. This ray, having the color of a red lotus flower, emanates from the elephants trunk and enters it's eyes; the ray then emanates from the elephants eyes and enters it's ears; it then emanates from the elephant's ears, illuminates its head, and changes into a golden cup. On the head of the elephant there are three transformed men: one holds a golden wheel, another a jewel, and yet another with a diamond-pounder. When he raises the pounder and points it at the elephant, the latter walks a few steps immediately. The Elephant does not tread on the ground but hovers seven feet above the earth, yet the elephant leaves on the ground it's footprints, which are altogether perfect, making the wheels hub with a thousand spokes. From each mark the wheels hub, there grows a great lotus flower, on which a transformed elephant appears. This elephant also has seven legs and walks after the great Elephant, Every time the transformed elephant raises and brings down it's legs, seven thousand elephants appear, all following the great elephant and it's retinue. On the elephant's trunk, having the color of a red lotus, there is a transformed Buddha, who emits a ray of light from his eyebrow. This ray of light, as mentioned before, enters the elephant's trunk. The ray emanates from the elephants trunk and enters its eyes; the ray then emanates from the elephants eyes and enters its ears; it then emanates from the elephant's ears, and reaches its head. Gradually rising to the elephants back, this ray is transformed into a golden saddle, which is adorned with he precious seven, which are decorated with precious things, forming a jewel pedestal. On this pedestal there is a lotus flower stamen bearing the precious seven, and that that stamen is also composed of a hundred jewels. The cup of that lotus flower is also made of a great jewel.

On the cup there is a Bodhisattva called Universal Virtue who sits cross-legged. His body, pure as a white jewel, radiates fifty rays of fifty different colors, forming a brightness around his head. From the pores of his body he emits rays of light, and innumerable transformed Buddhas are at the end of the rays, accompanied by the transformed Bodhisattvas as their retinue.

The elephant walks quietly and slowly, and goes before the follower of the great vehicle, raining large jeweled lotus flowers. When this elephant opens it's mouth, the precious daughters, dwelling in the bathing pools on the elephants tusks, play music whose sound is mystic and extols the way of one reality in the great vehicle. Having seen this wonder, the follower rejoices and reveres, again further reads and recites the profound sutras, salutes universally, the innumerable Buddhas in all directions, makes obedience to the stupa of the of the Buddha Abundant Treasures, and Shakyamuni Buddha, and salutes Universal Virtue and all the other the other great Bodhisattvas. Then the follower makes this vow, "Had I received some blessing through my former destinies, I could surely see The Bodhisattva Universal Virtue. Be pleased, honored Universal Fortune, to show me your form and body!"

Having thus made this vow, the follower must salute the Buddhas in all directions six times day and night, and must practice the law of repentance; he must read the Great Vehicle sutras and recite them, think of the meaning of the great vehicle. And reflect over it's practice, revere and serve those who keep it, see all people as if he were thinking of the Buddha, and treat living beings as if he were thinking of his mother and father. When he finishes reflecting thus, The Bodhisattva Universal Virtue will at once send forth a ray of light from the white hair circle, the sign of a great man, between his eyebrows. When this ray is displayed the body of The Bodhisattva Universal Virtue will be dignified as a mountain of deep gold, so well ordered and refined that it possesses all the thirty-two signs. From the pores of his body he will emit great rays of light, which will illuminate the great elephant and turn it to the color gold. All transformed elephants will also be colored gold, and all transformed Bodhisattvas will be colored gold. When these rays of light shine on the innumerable worlds in the eastern quarter, they will turn them all to the color gold. So, too, will it be in the southern, western, and northern quarters, in the four intermediate directions, and in the zenith and nadir.

Then in each quarter of all directions there is Bodhisattva who, mounting the six tusked white elephant king, is exactly equal to The Bodhisattva Universal Virtue. Like this, by his transcendental powers The Bodhisattva Universal Virtue will enable all the keepers of the great vehicle sutras to see transformed elephants filling the infinite and boundless worlds in all directions. At this time the follower will rejoice in body and mind, seeing all the Bodhisattvas, and will salute them and speak to them, saying, "Great merciful and great compassionate ones! Out of compassion for me, be pleased to explain the law to me!" When he speaks thus, all the Bodhisattvas and others with one voice will each explain the pure law of the great vehicle sutras and will praise him in various verses. This is called the first stage of mind, in which the follower first meditates on The Bodhisattva Universal Virtue.

Thereupon, when the follower, having beheld this matter, keeps the great vehicle in mind without forsaking it, day and night, even while sleeping, he will be able to see The Bodhisattva Universal Virtue preach the law to him in a dream. Exactly as if the follower were awake, The Bodhisattva will console and pacify the follower's mind, speaking thus, "In the sutras you have recited and kept, you have forgotten this word, or lost this verse." Then the follower, hearing The Bodhisattva Universal Virtue preach the profound law, will comprehend it's meaning, and keep it in his memory without forgetting it. As he does like this day by day, his mind will gradually acquire spiritual profit. The Bodhisattva Universal Virtue will cause the follower to remember the Buddhas in all directions. According to the teaching of Universal Virtue, the follower will rightly think and remember everything, and with spiritual eyes he will gradually see the eastward Buddhas, whose bodies are gold colored and very wonderful in their majesty. Having seen one Buddha, he will again see another Buddha. In this manner he will gradually see all the Buddhas in the eastern quarter, and because of his profitable reflection, he will universally see all the Buddhas in all directions.

Having seen the Buddhas, he conceives joy in his heart and utters these words, "By means of the great vehicle, I have been able to see the great leaders. By means of their powers, I have also been able to see the Buddhas. Though I have seen these Buddhas, I have yet failed to make them plain. Closing my eyes, I see the Buddhas, but when I open my eyes I lose sight of them." After speaking thus, the follower should universally make obeisance, prostrating himself down to the ground toward the Buddhas in all directions. Having made obeisance to them, he should kneel with folded hands and speak thus, "The Buddhas, The World Honored Ones, posses the ten powers, the fearlessnesses, the eighteen unique characteristics, the great mercy, the great compassion, the three kinds of stability, in contemplation. These Buddhas, forever remaining in this world, have the finest appearance of all forms. By what sin do I fail to see these Buddhas?" Having spoken thus, the follower should again practice further repentance. When he has achieved the purity of his repentance, The Bodhisattva Universal Virtue will again appear before him and will not leave his side, in his walking, standing, sitting, lying, and even his dreams, ceaselessly preach the law to him. After awaking from his dreams, this person will take delight in the law. In this manner, after three times seven days and nights have passed, he will thereupon attain the dharani of revolution. Through acquiring the dharani, he will keep in his memory without losing it the wonderful, which the Buddhas and bodhisattvas have taught. In his dreams, he will constantly see the Seven Buddhas of the past, among whom only Shakyamuni Buddha will preach the law to him. These World Honored Ones will each praise the great vehicle sutras. At that time the follower will again further rejoice and universally salute the Buddha's in all directions, The Bodhisattva Universal Virtue, abiding before him will teach and explain to him all karmas and environments of his former lives, and will cause him to confess his black and evil sins. Turning to the World Honored Ones he should confess his sins with his own mouth.

After he finishes confessing his sins, he will then attain the contemplation of the revelation of Buddhas to men. Having attained this contemplation he will plainly and clearly see the Buddha Akshobhya and the kingdom of wonderful joy in the eastern quarter. In like manner he will plainly and clearly see the mystic lands of the Buddhas in all directions. After he has seen the Buddhas in all directions, he will have a dream: On the elephants head is diamond man pointing his diamond pounder at the six organs; after pointing it at the six organs, The Bodhisattva Universal Virtue will preach to the follower the law of repentance to obtain the purity of the six organs. In this way the follower will do repentance for a day or three times seven days. Then by the power of the contemplation of the revelation of Buddhas to men and by the adornment of the preaching of The Bodhisattva Universal Virtue, the followers ears will gradually hear sounds without impediment, his eyes will gradually see things without impediment, and his nose will gradually smell odors without impediment. This is as preached extensively in the Wonderful Law Flower Sutra. Having obtained the purity of the six organs, he will have joy of body and mind and freedom from evil ideas, and will devote himself to this law so that he can conform to it. He will then further acquire a hundred thousand myriad kotis of the dharani of revolution and will again see extensively a hundred thousand myriad kotis of innumerable Buddhas. These World Honored Ones will all stretch out their right hands, laying them on the head of the follower, and will speak thus "Good! Good! You are a follower of the great vehicle, an aspirant to the spirit of great adornment, and one who keeps the great vehicle in his mind. When of old we aspired to Buddhahood, we were also like you. Do you be zealous and do not lose the great Vehicle! Because we practiced it in our former lives, we have now become the pure body of the All Wise. Do you now be diligent and not lazy! These great vehicle sutras are the law treasury of the Buddhas, The eyes of the Buddhas from all directions in the past, present, and future. He who keeps these sutras has the body of a Buddha, and does the work of a Buddha; Know that such is the apostle sent by the Buddhas; such is covered by the robes of the Buddhas; The world Honored Ones; such is a true law heir of the Buddhas; the Tathagatas. Do you practice the great vehicle and do not cut off the law seeds! Do you now attentively behold the Buddhas in the eastern quarter!

When these words are spoken the follower sees all the innumerable worlds in the eastern quarter, whose lands are as even as one's palm, with no mounds or hills or thorns, but with the ground of lapis lazuli and with gold to bound the ways. So, too, is it in the worlds of all directions. Having finished beholding this matter, the follower will see a jewel tree, which is lofty, wonderful, and five thousand yojanas high. This tree will always produce deep gold and white silver, and will be adorned with the precious seven; under this tree there will be jeweled lion throne of itself; the lion throne will be two thousand yojanas high. And from the throne will radiate the light of a hundred jewels. In like manner, from all of the trees, the other jewel thrones, and each jewel throne will radiate the light of a hundred jewels. In like manner, from all the trees, the other jewel thrones, and each jewel throne will emerge of themselves five hundred white elephants on which all of The Bodhisattva Universal Virtues mount. Thereupon the follower, making obeisance to all of the Universal Virtues will speak thus; "By what sin have I only seen the jewel grounds, jewel thrones, and jewel trees, but have been unable to see the Buddhas?"

When the follower finishes speaking thus, he will see that on each of the jewel thrones there is a World Honored One sitting on a jewel throne and very wonderful in his majesty. Having seen the Buddhas, the follower will be greatly pleased, and will again further recite and study the great vehicle sutras. By the power of the great vehicle, from the sky there will come a voice, praising and saying; "Good! Good! Good Son! By the cause of the merit you have acquired practicing the great vehicle you have seen the Buddhas. Though you have now seen the Buddhas, the World Honored Ones, you cannot yet see Shakyamuni Buddha, the Buddhas who emanated from him, and the stupa of the Buddha Abundant Treasures."

After hearing the voice in the sky, the follower will again zealously recite and study the great vehicle sutras. Because he recites and studies the sutras of great extent, the great vehicle, even in his dreams he will see Shakyamuni Buddha staying on mount Grdhrakuta with the great assembly, preaching the law flower sutra and expounding the meaning of the one reality. After the teaching is preached, with repentance and a thirsting heart of hope, he will wish to see the Buddha. Then he must fold his hands, and kneeling in the direction of Mount Grdhrakuta, he must speak thus; "Tathagata, the world's hero forever remains in this world. Out of compassion for me, please reveal yourself to me."

After he has spoken thus, he will see Mount Grdhrakuta adorned with the precious seven and filled with countless Bhikshus, Sravakas, and a great assembly; this place is lined with jeweled trees, and it's jewel ground is even and smooth; There a wonderfully Jeweled Lion Throne is spread. On it sits Shakyamuni Buddha, who sends forth from his eyebrows a ray of light, which shines everywhere throughout all directions of the universe and passes through innumerable worlds in all directions. The Buddhas emanated from Shakyamuni Buddha in all directions where this ray reaches assemble like a cloud at one time, and preach extensively the Wonderful Law—as it is said in the Wonderful Law Flower Sutra. Each of these emanated Buddhas, having a body of deep gold, is boundless in the size of his body and sits on his lion throne, accompanied by countless hundreds of kotis of great bodhisattvas as his retinue. The practice of each Bodhisattva is equal to that of The Bodhisattva Universal Virtue. So, too, is it in the retinue of the countless Buddhas and Bodhisattvas in all directions. When the great assembly have gathered together like a cloud they will see Shakyamuni Buddha, who from the pores of his whole body emits rays of light in each of which a hundred kotis of transformed Buddhas dwell. The emanated Buddhas will also emit rays of light from the white hair circles, the sign of a great man, between their eyebrows, streaming on the head of Shakyamuni Buddha.

Beholding this aspect, the emanated Buddhas will also emit from the pores of their bodies rays of light in each of which transformed Buddhas, as numerous as the atoms of the sands of the Ganges, abide.

Thereupon The Bodhisattva Universal Virtue Will again emit the ray of light, the sign of a great man, between his eyebrows, and put it into the heart of the follower. After this ray has entered into his heart, the follower himself will remember that under the countless hundreds and thousands of Buddhas in the past he received and kept, read and recited the great vehicle sutras, and he will himself plainly and clearly see his former lives. He will possess the very faculty of transcendent remembrance of former states of existence. Immediately attaining a great enlightenment he will acquire the dharani of revolution and a hundred thousand myriad kotis of dharanis. Rising from his contemplation, he will see before himself all the emanated Buddhas sitting on lion thrones under all the jewel trees. He will also see the ground of Lapis Lazuli springing up from the lower sky like heaps of Lotus Flowers; between each flower there will be Bodhisattvas, numerous as the atoms of the sands of the Ganges and sitting cross legged. He will also see the Bodhisattvas that emanated from The Bodhisattva Universal Virtue, extolling and expounding the great vehicle among their assembly. Then the Bodhisattvas with one voice will cause the follower to purify his six organs.

One Bodhisattvas preaching will say: "Do you reflect on the Buddha"; another's preaching will say "Do you reflect on the law"; Yet another preaching will say "Do you reflect on the Sangha"; Still another preaching will say "Do you reflect on the precepts"; Still another one's preaching will say "Do you reflect on gift giving"; Yet another's preaching will say "Do you reflect on the heavens". And the preaching will further say, "Such six laws are the aspiration to Buddhahood and are the ones that begat the Bodhisattvas. Before the Buddhas, do you now confess you previous sins and repent of them sincerely."

In your innumerable former lives, by reason of your organ of the eye, you have attached to all forms. Because of your attachment to forms, you hanker after all dust. Because of your hankering for dust, you receive a woman's body and you are pleasurably absorbed in all forms everywhere and you are born age after age. Forms harm your eyes and you become a slave to human affections. Therefore forms cause you to wander in the triple world. Such fatigue of your wandering there makes you so blind that you can see nothing at all. You have now recited the sutras of great extent, the great vehicle. In these sutras, the Buddhas of all directions preach that their forms and bodies are not extinct. You have now been able to see them—is this not true? The evil of your eye organ often does much harm to you. Obediently following my words, you must take refuge in the Buddhas and Shakyamuni Buddha, and confess the sins due to your organ of the eye, saying "Law water of wisdom eye possessed by the Buddhas and Bodhisattvas! Be pleased, by means of it, to wash me and to let me become pure!"

Having finished speaking thus, the follower should universally salute the Buddhas in the ten directions, and turning to Shakyamuni Buddha and the great vehicle sutras, he should again speak thus "The heavy sins of my eye-organ of which now I repent are such an impediment and are so tainted that I am blind and can see nothing at all. May the Buddha be pleased to pity and protect me by his great mercy! The Bodhisattva Universal Virtue on board the ship of the law ferries the company of the countless Bodhisattvas everywhere in all directions. Out of compassion for me, be pleased to permit me to hear the law of repenting the evil of my eye organ and the impediment of my bad karma!"

Speaking thus three times the follower must prostrate himself down to the ground and rightly reflect on the great vehicle without forgetting it. This is called the law of repenting the sin of the organ of the eye. If there be anyone who calls upon the names of the Buddhas, burns incense, strews flowers, aspires to the great vehicle, hangs silks, flags, and canopies, speaks of the errors of his eyes, and repents his sins, such a one in the present world will see Shakyamuni Buddha, the Buddhas who emanated from him, and the countless other Buddhas, and will not fall in the evil paths for asamkhyeya kalpas. Thanks to the power and to the vow of the great vehicle, such a one will become an attendant of the Buddhas, together with all the Bodhisattvas of dharani. Anyone who reflects thus is one who thinks rightly. If anyone reflects otherwise, such is called one who thinks falsely. This is called the sign of the first stage of the purification of the eye organ.

Having finished purifying the organ of the eye, the follower should again further read and recite the great vehicle sutras, kneel and repent six times day and night, and should speak thus, "Why can I see only Shakyamuni Buddha and the Buddhas who emitted from him, but cannot see the Buddhas relics of his whole body in the stupa of abundant treasures? The stupa of the Buddha Abundant Treasure exists forever and is not extinct. I have defiled and evil eyes. For this reason I cannot see the stupa." After speaking thus the follower should again practice further repentance.

After seven days have passed, the stupa of the Buddha Abundant Treasures will spring out of the earth. Shakyamuni Buddha with his right hand opens the door of the stupa, where the Buddha abundant treasures is seen deep in the contemplation of the universal revelation of forms. From each pore of his body he emits rays of light as numerous as the Atoms of the sands of the Ganges. In each ray there dwells one of a hundred transformed Buddhas. When such signs appear, the follower will rejoice and make procession around it seven times, the tathagata Abundant treasures with a great voice praises him, saying, "Heir of the law! You have truly practiced the great vehicle and have obediently followed The Bodhisattva Universal Virtue, repenting the sins of your eye organ. For this reason, I will go to you and bear testimony to you." Having spoken thus the tathagata extols the Buddha saying, "Excellent! Excellent! Shakyamuni Buddha! Thou art able to preach the great law, to pour the rain of the great law, and to cause all the defiled living to obtain Buddhahood." Thereupon the follower, having beheld the stupa of the stupa of Abundant Treasures, again goes to The Bodhisattva Universal Virtue, and folding his hands and saluting him, speaks to him saying, "Great Teacher! Please teach me the repentance of my errors."

The Bodhisattva Universal Virtue again speaks to the follower saying, "through many kalpas, because of your ear organ, you dangle after external sounds; your hearing of mystics sounds begets attachment to them; your hearing evil sounds causes the harm of one hundred and eight illusions. Such retribution of your hearing evils brings about evil things and your incessant hearing of evil sounds produces various entanglements. Because of your perverted hearing, you will fall into evil paths, faraway places of false views, where the law cannot be heard. At present you have recited and kept the great vehicle, the ocean store of your merits. For this reason, you have come to see, the Buddhas in all directions, and the stupa of the Buddha Abundant Treasures has appeared to bear testimony to you. You must yourself confess your own errors and evils and must repent all of your sins.

Then the follower, having heard this, must again further fold his hands, and prostrating himself down to the ground, he must speak thus, saying, "All Wise, World Honored One! Be pleased to reveal yourself and bear testimony to me! The sutras of great extent are masters of compassion. Be pleased to look upon me and hear my words! Until my present life, for many kalpas, because of my ear organ, I have been attached to hearing evil sounds, like glue sticking to grass; my hearing of evil sounds causes the poison of illusions, which are attached to every condition and I am not able to rest for even a little while; my raising evil sounds fatigues my nerves and makes me fall into the three evil ways. Now having for the first time understood this, I confess and repent it, turning to the World Honored Ones." Having finished repenting thus, the follower will see the Buddha Abundant Treasures emitting a great ray of light which is golden colored and universally illuminates the eastern quarter as well as the worlds in all directions, where the countless Buddhas appear with their bodies of pure gold color. In the sky of the eastern quarter there comes a voice uttering thus, "Here is a Buddha, the World Honored One named Excellent Virtue, who also possesses innumerable emanated Buddhas, sitting cross legged on lion thrones under jewel trees. All of these World Honored Ones who enter in to the contemplation of the universal revelation of forms speak to the follower, praising him and saying, "Good! Good! Good Son! You have now read and recited the great vehicle sutras. That which you have recited is the mental stage of the Buddha."

After these words have been spoken, The Bodhisattva Universal Virtue will again further preach to the follower the law of repentance, saying, "in the innumerable kalpas of your former lives because of your attachment to odors, your discrimination and your perception are attached to every condition and you fall into birth and death. Do you now meditate on the cause of the Great Vehicle! The cause of the great vehicle is the reality of all existence.

Having heard these words the follower should again further repent, prostrating himself down on the ground. When he has repented, he should exclaim thus, "Namah Shakyamuni Buddha! Namah stupa of the Buddha Abundant Treasures! Namah all the Buddhas emanated from Shakyamuni Buddha!" Having spoken thus he should universally salute the Buddhas in all directions, Exclaim" Namah the Buddha of Excellent Virtue in the eastern quarter and the Buddhas who emanate from him!" The follower should also make obeisance to each of these Buddhas as wholeheartedly as if he saw them with his naked eyes, and should pay homage to them with incense and flowers. After paying homage to the Buddhas, he should kneel with folded hands and extol them with various verses. After extolling them, he should speak of the ten evil karmas and repent all his sins. Having repented, he should speak thus, saying, "During the innumerable kalpas of my former lives, I yearned after odors, flavors, and contacts and produced all manner of evils. For this reason, for innumerable lives I have continuously received states of evil existence, including hells, hungry spirits, animals, and faraway places of false views. Now I confess such evil karmas, and take refuge in the Buddhas, the kings of the righteous law, I confess and repent my sins."

Having repented thus, the follower must again read and recite the Great vehicle sutras without negligence of body and mind. By the power of the great vehicle, from the sky there comes a voice saying, "Heir of the law! Do you now praise and explain the law of the great vehicle, turning to the Buddhas in all directions, and before them do you yourself speak of your errors! The Buddhas, the Tathagatas, are your merciful fathers. Do you yourself speak of the evils and bad karmas produced by your organ of the tongue, saying, "This organ of the tongue, moved by the thought of evil karmas, causes me to praise false speaking, improper language, ill speaking, a double tongue, slandering, lying, and words of false views, and also causes me to utter useless words. Because of such many and various evil karmas I provoke fights and dissentions and speak of the law as if it were not the law. I now confess all such sins of mine."

Having spoken thus before the before the worlds heroes, the follower must universally revere the Buddhas in all directions, prostrating himself down to the ground, and folding his hands and kneeling salute them, and he must speak thus saying, "The errors of this tongue are numberless and boundless. All the thorns of evil karma come from the organ of the tongue. This tongue causes the cutting off of the wheel of the righteous law. Such an evil tongue cuts off the seeds of merits. Preaching of meaningless things is frequently forced upon others. Praising false views is like adding wood to a fire and further wounding living beings who already suffer in raging flames. It is like one who dies drinking poison, without showing sores or pustules. Such reward of sins is evil, false and bad, and causes me to fall into the evil paths during a hundred or a thousand kalpas. Lying causes me to fall into a great hell. I now take refuge in the Buddhas of the southern quarter and confess my errors and sins.

When the follower reflects thus, there will come a voice from the sky saying: "In the southern quarter there is a Buddha named Sandalwood virtue who also possesses countless emanated Buddhas. All these Buddhas preach the great vehicle and extinguish sins and evils. Turning to the innumerable Buddhas and the great merciful world honored ones in all directions, you must confess such sins, false evils, and repent them with a sincere heart." When these words have been spoken, the follower should again salute the Buddhas, prostrating himself down to the ground.

Thereupon the Buddhas will send forth rays of light, which illuminate the follower's body and cause him naturally to feel joy of body and mind, to raise a great mercy, and to reflect on all things extensively. At that time the Buddhas will widely preach to the follower the law of great kindness, compassion, joy and indifference, and also teach him kind words to make him practice the six ways of harmony and reverence. Then the follower, having heard this royal teaching, will greatly rejoice in his heart and will again further recite and study it without laziness.

From the sky there again comes a mystic voice, speaking thus; "Do you now practice the repentance of body and mind! The sins of the body are killing, stealing, and committing adultery, while the sins of the mind are entertaining thoughts of various evils. Producing the ten evil karmas and the five deadly sins, is just like living as a monkey, like birdlime and glue, and the attachment to all sorts of conditions leads universally to the passions of the six organs of all living beings. The karmas of these six organs with their boughs, twigs, flowers, and leaves entirely fill the triple world, the twenty-five abodes of living beings, and all the places where creatures are born. Such karmas also increase ignorance, old age, death and the twelve sufferings, and infallibly reach through the eight falsenesses and the eight circumstances. Do you now repent such evil and bad karmas!" Then the follower, having heard thus, asks the voice in the sky, saying, "At what place may I practice the law of repentance?"

Thereupon the voice in the sky will speak thus saying, "Shakyamuni Buddha is called Vairocana Who Pervades All Places, and his dwelling place is called Eternally Tranquil Light, the place which is composed of Permanency Paramita, and is stabilized by self paramita, the place where the purity paramita extinguishes the aspect of existence, where the bliss paramita does not abide in the aspect of one's body and mind, where the aspects of all laws cannot be seen as either existing, nor non existing, the place of tranquil emancipation, or prajna paramita. Because these forms are based on permanent law, thus you must now meditate on the Buddhas in all directions"

Then the Buddhas in all directions will stretch out there right hands, laying them on the head of the follower, and speak thus, "Good! Good! Good Son! Because you have now read and recited the great vehicle sutras, the Buddhas in all directions will preach the law of repentance. The Bodhisattva practice is not to be cut off binding or driving, nor to abide in the ocean of driving. In meditating on ones mind, there is no mind one can seize, except the mind that comes from one's perverted thought. The mind, present in such a form rises from one's false imagination. Like the wind in the sky, which has no foothold. Such a form of the law neither appears, nor disappears. What is sin? What is blessedness? As one's own mind is void of itself, sin and blessedness have no existence. In like manner all the laws are neither fixed nor going towards destruction. If one repents like this, meditating on his mind, there is no mind he can seize the law also does not dwell in the law. All the laws are emancipation, the truth of extinction, and quiescence. Such an aspect is called the great repentance, the greatly adorned repentance, the repentance of the non-sin aspect, and the destruction of discrimination. He who practices this repentance has the purity of body and mind in the law but free as the flowing water. Through each reflection, he will be the see The Bodhisattva Universal Virtue and the Buddhas in all directions"

Thereupon the world honored ones, sending forth the ray of great mercy, preach the law of non-aspect to the follower. He hears the world honored ones preaching the void of the first principle. When he has heard it, his mind becomes imperturbable. In due time, he will enter into the real Bodhisattva Standing". The Buddha addressed Ananda, "to practice in this manner is called repentance. This is the law of repentance. This is the law of repentance which the Buddhas and the great Bodhisattvas in all directions practice."

The Buddha addressed Ananda, "After the extinction of the Buddha, if all disciples should repent their evil and bad karmas, they must only read and recite the great vehicle sutras. These sutras of great extent are the eyes of the Buddhas. By means of the sutras the Buddhas have perfected the five kinds of eyes. The three of the Buddhas bodies grow out of the sutras of Great Extent. This is the seal of the great law with which the ocean of nirvana is sealed. From such an ocean are born the three kinds of pure bodies of the Buddha. These three kinds of Buddha bodies are the blessing field for gods and men, and the supreme object of worship. If there be any who recite and read the sutras of great extent, the great vehicle, know that such are endowed with the Buddhas merits and, having extinguished their longstanding evils, are born of the Buddhas wisdom." At that time the world honored one spoke thus in verse:

If one has evil in eye organ
And his eyes are impure with the impediments of Karmas,
He must only recite the great vehicle
And reflect on the great principle.
This is called the repentance of the eye,
Ending all bad karmas.
His ear organ hears disordered sounds
And disturbs the principle of harmony.
This produces in him a demented mind,
Like that of a foolish monkey.
He must only recite the great vehicle
And meditate on the void nonaspect of the law,
Ending all the longstanding evils,
So that with the heavenly ears he may hear Sounds from all directions.
His organ of smell is attached to all odors,
Causing all contacts according to lusts.
His nose thus deluded

Gives birth to all dust of illusions according to his lusts.
If one recites the great vehicle sutras
And meditates on the fundamental truth of the law,
He will become free from his longstanding evil karmas
And will not again produce them in future lives.
His organ of the tongue causes five kinds
Of bad karmas of evil speech.
Should one wish to control them by himself,
He must zealously practice mercy,
And considering the true principle of the quiescence of the Law,
He should not conceive discrimination.
His organ of thought is like that of a monkey,
Never resting for even a little while.
Should one desire to subdue this organ,
He must zealously recite the great vehicle,
Reflecting on the Buddha's greatly enlightened body,
The completion of his power, and his fearlessness.
The body is the master of its organs,
Freely without obstacles.
If one desires to destroy these evils,
To be removed from the longstanding illusion of dust,
Ever dwelling in the city of nirvana,
And to be at ease with mind tranquil,
He should recite the great vehicle sutras
And reflect on the mother of Bodhisattvas.
Innumerable surpassing means of tactfulness
Will be obtained on one's reflection of reality.
Such six laws
Are called the purification of the six sense organs.
The ocean of impediment of all karmas
Is produced from one's false imagination.
Should one wish to repent of it
Let him sit upright and meditate on the true aspect of reality.
All sins are just as frost and dew,
So wisdom's sun can disperse them.
Therefore with entire devotion
Let him repent of his six organs.

Having spoken these verses, the Buddha addressed Ananda: "Do you now repent of these six organs, keep the law of meditating on The Bodhisattva Universal Virtue, and discriminate and explain it widely to all the gods of the universe and men. After the extinction of the Buddha, if all his disciples keep, read and recite, and expound the sutras of great extent, whether in a quiet place or in a graveyard, or under a tree, or in a place of the aranya, they must read and recite the sutras of great extent, and must think of the meaning of the great vehicle. By virtue of their strong power of their reflecting on the sutras they will be able to see myself, the stupa of the Buddha Abundant Treasures, the countless emanated Buddhas from all directions, The Bodhisattva Universal Virtue, The Bodhisattva Manjurshi, The Bodhisattva Medicine King, And the Bodhisattva Medicine Lord. By virtue in their revering the law, these Buddhas and Bodhisattvas, abiding in the sky with various wonderfulflowers, will extol and revere those who practice and keep the law. by virtue of their only reciting the sutras of great extent, the great vehicle, the Buddhas and Bodhisattvas will day and night pay homage to those who keep the law."

The Buddha addressed Ananda: "I as well as The Bodhisattvas in the Virtuous Kalpa and the Buddhas in all directions, by means of our thinking of the true meaning of the great vehicle, have now rid ourselves of the sins of birth and death during hundreds of myriad kotis of asamkhya kalpas. By means of this supreme and wonderful law of repentance, we have each become the Buddhas in all directions. If one desires to accomplish perfect enlightenment rapidly an wishes in his present life to see the Buddhas in all directions and The Bodhisattva Universal Virtue, he must take a bath to purify himself, wear clean robes, and burn rare incense, and must dwell in a secluded place, where he should read and recite the great vehicle sutras and think of the meaning of the great vehicle."

The Buddha addressed Ananda: "if there are living beings who desire to meditate on The Bodhisattva Universal Virtue, they must meditate thus. If anyone meditates thus, such is called one who meditates rightly. If anyone meditates otherwise, such is called one who meditates falsely. After the extinction of the Buddha, if all his disciples obediently follow the Buddhas words and practice repentance, let it be known that these are doing the work of The Bodhisattva Universal Virtue. Those who do not work of universal virtue see neither evil aspects nor the retributions of evil karmas. If there be any living beings who salute Buddhas in all directions six times day and night, recite the great vehicle sutras, and consider the profound law of the void of the first principle, they will rid themselves of the sins of birth and death produced during hundreds of myriad kotis of asamkhya kalpas in the short time it takes one to snap his fingers. Anyone doing this work is a real Buddha son who is born from the Buddhas. The Buddhas in all directions and the Bodhisattvas will become his preceptors. This is called one who is perfect in the precepts of the Bodhisattvas. Without going through the ceremony of confession, he will of himself accomplish Bodhisattva-hood and he will be revered by all the gods and men.

At that time if the follower desires to be perfect in the precepts of the Bodhisattva, he must fold his hands, dwell in the seclusion of the wilds, universally salute the Buddhas in all directions, and repent his sins, and must himself confess his errors. After this, in a calm place, he should speak to the Buddhas in all directions, saying thus, "the Buddhas, the world honored ones, remain forever in this world. Because of the impediments of my karmas, though I believe in the sutra great extent, I cannot clearly see the Buddhas. I have now taken refuge in the Buddhas. Be pleased, Shakyamuni Buddhas, all wise and world honored one, to be my preceptor! Manjurshi, possessor of great compassion! With your wisdom, be pleased to bestow on me the laws of pure Bodhisattvas! Bodhisattva Maitreya, supreme and great merciful sun! Out of your compassion for me, be pleased to permit me to receive the laws of the Bodhisattvas! Buddhas in all directions! Be pleased to reveal yourselves and bear testimony to me! Great Bodhisattvas! Through calling each upon your names, be pleased, supreme, great leaders, to protect all living beings and to help us! At present I have received and kept the sutras of great extent. Even if I should lose my life, fall into hell, and receive innumerable sufferings, I would never slander the righteous law of the Buddhas. For this reason and by the power of this merit, Shakyamuni Buddha! Be now pleased to be my preceptor! Manjurshi! Be pleased to be my teacher! Maitreya! in the world to come! Be pleased to bestow upon me the law! Buddhas in all directions! Be pleased to bear witness to me! Bodhisattvas of great virtues! Be pleased to be my friends! I now, by means of the profound and mysterious meaning of the great of the great vehicle sutra, take refuge in the law, and take refuge in the Sangha."

The follower must speak thus three times. Having taken refuge in the three treasures, next he must himself vow to receive the six fold laws. Having received the six fold laws, next he must zealously practice the unhindered Brahma conduct, raise the mind of universally saving all living beings, and receive the eightfold laws. Having made such vows in the seclusion of the wilds, he must burn rare incense, strew flowers, pay homage to all the Buddhas, the Bodhisattvas, and the sutras of great extent, the great vehicle, and must speak thus, saying: "I have now raised the aspiration to Buddhahood: may this merit save all the living!"

Having spoken thus the follower should again further prostrate himself before the all the Buddhas and the Bodhisattvas, and should think of the meaning of the sutras of great extent, During a day, or three times seven days, whether he be a monk or a layperson, he has no need of a preceptor, nor does he need a teacher; even without attending the ceremony of the jnapti-karman, because of the power coming from his receiving and keeping, reading, and reciting the great vehicle sutras and because of the works which The Bodhisattva Universal Virtue helps and inspires him to do—they are in fact the eyes of the righteous law of the Buddhas in all directions—he will be able, through this law, to perform by himself the five kinds of Law-Bodies: precepts, meditation, wisdom, emancipation, and knowledge of emancipation. All the Buddhas, the Tathagatas, have been born of this law and have received the prediction of their enlightenment in the great vehicle sutras. Therefore, O wise man! Suppose that a Sravaka breaks the threefold refuge, the five precepts, and the eight precepts, the precepts of the monks and nuns, of shramaneras, of shramanikas, and of sikshamanas and their dignified behavior. If he desires to rid himself of and destroy these errors, to become a monk again and to fulfill the laws of monks, he must diligently read the sutras of great extent, considering the profound law of the void of the first principle and must bring this wisdom of the void to his heart; know that in each one of his thoughts such a one will gradually end the defilement of all his longstanding sins without any remainder—this is called one who is perfect in the laws and the precepts of monks and fulfills their dignified behavior. Such a one will be served by all gods and men. Suppose any Upasaka violates his dignified behavior and does bad things. To do bad things means, namely, to proclaim the errors and sins of the Buddha laws, to discus evil things perpetrated by the four groups, and do not feel shame even in committing theft or adultery. If he desires to repent and rid himself of these sins, he must zealously read and recite the sutras of great extent and must think of the first principle. Suppose a king, a minister, a Brahman, a citizen, an elder, a state official, all of these persons seek greedily and untiringly after desires, commit the five deadly sins, slander the sutras of great extent, and perform the ten evil karmas. Their recompense for these great evils will cause them to fall into evil paths faster than the breaking of a rainstorm. They will be sure to fall into the Avichi Hell. If they desire to rid themselves of and destroy these impediments of karmas, they must raise shame and repent all their sins.

The Buddha spoke saying, "why is it called the law of repentance of Kshatriyas and citizens? The law of repentance of Kshatriyas and citizens is that they must constantly have the right mind, not slander the three treasures nor hinder the monks nor persecute anyone practicing Brahma conduct; they must not forget to practice the law of the six reflections; they must again support, pay homage to, and surely salute the keepers of the great vehicle; they must remember the profound doctrine of sutras and the void of the first principle. One who thinks of this law is called one who practices the first repentance of Kshatriyas and citizens. The second repentance is to discharge their filial duty to their fathers and mothers and to respect their teachers and seniors—this is called one who practices the law of the second repentance. Their third repentance is to rule their countries with the righteous law and not to oppress their people unjustly—this is called one who practices the third repentance. Their fourth repentance is to issue within their states the ordinance of the six days of fasting and to cause their people to abstain from killing wherever their powers reach. One who practices such a law is called one who practices the fourth repentance. Their fifth repentance is to believe deeply the causes and results of things, to have faith in the way of one reality, and to know that the Buddha is never extinct—this is called one who practices the fifth repentance."

The Buddha addressed Ananda: "If in future worlds, there be any who practices these laws of repentance, know that such a man has put on the robe of shame, is protected and helped by the Buddhas, and will attain perfect enlightenment before long". As these words were spoken, ten thousand divine sons acquired pure spiritual eyes, and also the great Bodhisattvas, the Bodhisattva Maitreya and others, and Ananda, hearing the preaching of the Buddha, all rejoiced and did as the Buddha commanded.